THE NATURE
OF COLONY
CONSTITUTIONS

TRICENTENNIAL EDITION, NUMBER 1

This volume is part of a series of
Tricentennial Editions published by the
University of South Carolina Press,
Columbia, South Carolina,
on behalf of the South Carolina Tricentennial
Commission, to commemorate the founding of
South Carolina in 1670

THE NATURE
OF COLONY
CONSTITUTIONS

Two Pamphlets on the Wilkes Fund
Controversy in South Carolina
By Sir Egerton Leigh and Arthur Lee
Edited and with an Introduction by

JACK P. GREENE

COPYRIGHT © 1970 BY THE UNIVERSITY OF SOUTH CAROLINA PRESS

PUBLISHED IN COLUMBIA, S.C., BY THE

UNIVERSITY OF SOUTH CAROLINA PRESS, 1970

INTERNATIONAL STANDARD BOOK NUMBER: 0–87249–185–4

LIBRARY OF CONGRESS CATALOG CARD NUMBER: 74–120577

Manufactured in the UNITED STATES OF AMERICA

Composition and Printing by HERITAGE PRINTERS, INC.

Binding by KINGSPORT PRESS, INC.

DESIGNED BY ROBERT L. NANCE

CONTENTS

INTRODUCTION

I

That the decade of debate preceding the American Revolution
wrought profound changes in the ways Americans conceived of
their political environment is by now a commonplace. How that
debate called into question and helped to reshape established pat-
terns of thought about many of the traditional problems of political
thought—the nature of representation, consent, law, rights, sovereignty—has recently been explained with clarity and in detail.[1]
What has been much less thoroughly studied is the extent to which
it also exposed and brought clearly and fully into focus for the first
time the ancient ambiguities in the constitutional relationship
between Great Britain and the colonies. Most importantly, it revealed a deep intellectual fissure within the British Empire over
the degree and character of colonial self-government. Although it
had been implicit in—had, in fact, been one of the primary sources
of—much of the recurrent and seemingly endemic political conflict
between Britain and the colonies since the middle of the seventeenth century,[2] the depth of the fissure was explicitly revealed
only between 1765 and 1776 as a result of the fierce exchange over
Parliament's right to tax the colonies for revenue and the bitter
debates over the Crown's several efforts to make the political sys-
tems of individual colonies conform to imperial ideals and precedents. As many Englishmen realized from the beginning, and as
Americans became aware during the Crisis of Independence in
1774–1776, the problem of sovereignty was, of course, the ultimate
issue in dispute.[3] But much of the debate over most of the decade

---

[1] Bernard Bailyn, *The Ideological Origins of the American Revolution*
(Cambridge, Mass., 1967), 160–229.

[2] On this subject, see the cursory treatment in Lawrence H. Leder, *Liberty
and Authority: Early American Political Ideology, 1689–1763* (Chicago,
1968), 95–117; and the more extended analysis in the introduction to Jack
P. Greene, *Great Britain and the American Colonies, 1607–1763* (New York,
1970).

[3] On the importance of the issue of sovereignty, see Bailyn, *Ideological
Origins*, 198–229; Gordon S. Wood, *The Creation of the American Republic,
1776–1787* (Chapel Hill, 1969), 344–54; and Jack P. Greene, "The Plunge

3

turned around a more immediate and more obvious question: the nature of the constitutions of the colonies. Often broached, but never directly confronted or thoroughly explored during the colonial period, this question involved the relationship of the colonies not only to Parliament—a subject that has been adequately canvassed by historians[4]—but also to the Crown. The disagreement over it reflected and, to a considerable degree, was a direct expression of a fundamental rift in seventeenth-century English constitutional thought, a rift that in Britain, in contrast to the colonies, had been largely patched over by the Glorious Revolution.

The continued existence and character of this rift in the colonies, as well as its place in the pre-Revolutionary debate, are perhaps nowhere more clearly discernible than in the two pamphlets here reprinted: Sir Egerton Leigh, *Considerations on Certain Political Transactions of the Province of South Carolina*, and Arthur Lee, *Answer to Considerations on Certain Political Transactions of the Province of South Carolina*, both published in London in early 1774. These pamphlets came near the end of a prolonged, bitter, and alienating dispute between the Crown and the South Carolina Commons House of Assembly that engrossed the political attention of South Carolina for over five years beginning in December, 1769, and has since come to be known as the Wilkes Fund Controversy.[5]

---

of Lemmings: A Consideration of Recent Writings on British Politics and the American Revolution," *South Atlantic Quarterly*, LXVII (Winter, 1967), 141–75.

[4] See, especially, Bailyn, *Ideological Origins*, 209–19, and C. H. McIlwain, *The American Revolution: A Constitutional Interpretation* (New York, 1923).

[5] The only more or less contemporaneous account of the Wilkes Fund Controversy is the brief section in John Drayton, *Memoirs of the American Revolution* (2 vols.; Charleston, 1821), I, 91–114. There is no satisfactory modern account, though brief summaries are scattered through most of the general studies of colonial South Carolina, including Edward McCrady, *The History of South Carolina Under the Royal Government, 1719–1776* (New York, 1899), 659–744; W. Roy Smith, *South Carolina As a Royal Province, 1719–1776* (New York, 1903), 368–87; and David D. Wallace, *South Carolina: A Short History, 1520–1948* (Chapel Hill, 1951), 243–46. Easily the best published account is Wallace's *The Life of Henry Laurens . . .* (New York, 1915), 159–76, though it necessarily focuses on Henry Laurens (hereafter in these citations identified as Laurens), who was not in the colony during much of the period of the controversy.

II

American protests against the Townshend revenue program coincided with the most intense phase of the demonstrations in London inspired by the celebrated radical John Wilkes.[6] Since his attack on George III's speech from the throne in *North Briton* No. 45 on April 23, 1763, Wilkes had been popularly associated with the cause of liberty. After his return from exile in France in 1768, "Wilkes and Liberty" became the slogan of a numerous miscellany of supporters in Middlesex, London, and elsewhere in Britain. With his trial in early 1768 for various misdemeanors including libel against the government, his conviction on June 8, and his subsequent imprisonment, he became the martyr of English liberty.[7]

Americans as well as Englishmen were infatuated with Wilkes's cause. To Americans, the ministry's harassment of Wilkes and Parliament's attempts to tax the colonies seemed to be part of the same general conspiracy of power against liberty. In the colonies no less than in the heart of London, Wilkes became the symbol of liberty and 45 the charmed number of American patriotism. Americans vied with English radicals in heaping encomium upon him. Wilkes, said one American newspaper, was the "unshaken colossus of freedom; the patriot of England, the rightful and legal representative of Middlesex; the favourite of the people; the British Hercules, that has cleaned a stable fouler than the Augean."[8] He

---

[6] This section is adapted from Jack P. Greene, "Bridge to Revolution: The Wilkes Fund Controversy in South Carolina, 1769–1775," *The Journal of Southern History*, XXIX (February, 1963), 19–52. Copyright 1963 by the Southern Historical Association; reprinted by permission of the Managing Editor.

[7] Recent studies of the Wilkite movement in London are George Rudé, *Wilkes & Liberty: A Social Study of 1763 to 1774* (Oxford, 1962) and Ian R. Christie, *Wilkes, Wyvill and Reform: The Parliamentary Reform Movement in British Politics, 1760–1785* (London, 1962).

[8] Charleston *South Carolina Gazette*, March 15, 1770. A general brief discussion of the American reaction to Wilkes is Pauline Maier, "John Wilkes

was "not merely the idol of the mob," declared an article in the *South Carolina Gazette,* "but a man whose very intrepid public conduct is thought deserving universal applause by the most candid, sensible, and prudent."[9] With such extraordinary adulation from the colonies, it is not surprising that Wilkes's English supporters turned to Americans for money when in early 1769 they formed the Society of the Gentlemen Supporters of the Bill of Rights to "defend and maintain the legal constitutional Liberty of the subject" and, more immediately, to pay Wilkes's sizable debts.[10] Relatively few Americans were willing to translate their enthusiasm for Wilkes into more tangible favors, however. The Friends of Liberty in Boston sent their wishes for his restoration to his liberty, family, friends, and country, but no money. In Maryland and Virginia two different groups of planters contributed 45 hogsheads of tobacco each.[11] The only official governmental body to respond was the South Carolina Commons House of Assembly.

Among the colonists solicited by the Bill of Rights Society was Christopher Gadsden, 45-year-old wealthy merchant and veteran politician, delegate to the Stamp Act Congress, staunch opponent of parliamentary taxation, and acknowledged leader of the Charleston radicals. The Society's request arrived in the fall of 1769, when South Carolina was in the midst of a heated political controversy over the justice of the nonimportation agreements against the Townshend Acts.[12] South Carolina patriots were particularly sensitive to the charge, made by the critics of nonimportation, that they

---

and American Disillusionment with Britain," *William and Mary Quarterly,* 3d ser., XX (July, 1963), 373–95.

   [9] *South Carolina Gazette,* December 28, 1769.

   [10] Rudé, *Wilkes & Liberty,* 61–62.

   [11] *South Carolina Gazette,* December 28, 1769; London *St. James Chronicle; or, British Evening Post,* February 10, 1770; Boston Friends of Liberty to John Wilkes, November 4, 1769, in Wilkes Papers, Additional Manuscripts (British Museum, London), 30870, ff. 222–23. The Virginia hogsheads were probably never sent; the official collector, Miles, appears to have sold them and applied the money to his own use. See George Mason to————, December 6, 1770, in Kate Mason Rowland, *The Life of George Mason, 1725–1792* (2 vols.; New York, 1892), I, 150.

   [12] Charleston *South Carolina American and General Gazette,* December 13, 1769; Robert Morris to John Wilkes, February 6, 1770, in Wilkes Papers, Add. MSS., 30871, f. 7. On the debate over the Townshend Acts in South Carolina see McCrady, *South Carolina Under Royal Government,* 644–58.

were "servilely" imitating their Northern neighbors, waiting—as young William Henry Drayton later wrote—"till in the Northern hemisphere, a *light* appeared to show the political course we were to steer."[13] To South Carolina patriots the Society's request suggested an action that would at once demonstrate their boldness and their originality. There was no more conspicuous and dramatic way to display their devotion to American liberty than to vote a sum for the support of liberty in Britain. On December 8, 1769, they made their proposal to the Commons House, which overwhelmingly accepted it. Without the consent of either the South Carolina Council or Lt. Gov. William Bull II, the House ordered Treasurer Jacob Motte to advance £1,500 sterling to a committee that was to send it to the Bill of Rights Society.[14] The committee promptly executed the Commons' order, stipulating to the Society that the money be used "for supporting such of our Fellow Subjects who by asserting the Just Rights of the People, have or shall become obnoxious to administration, and suffer from the hand of Power"— a clear indication that the Commons intended the grant to be used to support Wilkes.[15] For once South Carolina patriots had acted independently of, and more boldly than, their Northern counterparts. "In this instance," Peter Timothy proudly proclaimed in the Charleston *South Carolina Gazette*, "it cannot be said *we* have followed the Example of the Northern Colonies."[16]

Just how bold this action was will be apparent when it is recalled that since the seventeenth century the Crown had stipulated in instructions to its governors that money be issued from colonial treasuries only upon warrants signed by the governors.[17] During the early years of royal government in South Carolina, the executive as well as both houses of the legislature had complied with

---

[13] *South Carolina Gazette*, September 21, December 28, 1769.

[14] Journals of the Commons House of Assembly (South Carolina Archives Department, Columbia), XXXVIII, 215 (December 8, 1769).

[15] Committee to Robert Morris, December 9, 1769, in "Correspondence of Charles Garth," *South Carolina Historical and Genealogical Magazine*, XXXI (April, 1930), 132–33; Committee to Messrs. Hankey and Partners, December 9, 1769, in John Almon (ed.), *The Correspondence of the Late John Wilkes with His Friends* . . . (5 vols.; London, 1805) V, 42–43.

[16] *South Carolina Gazette*, December 8, 1769.

[17] Leonard W. Labaree (ed.), *Royal Instructions to British Colonial Governors, 1670–1776* (2 vols.; New York, 1935), I, 203–204.

this instruction.[18] But after 1750 the Commons increasingly resorted to the practice of borrowing money from the treasury for a particular service without the consent of either governor or Council and repaying the money later by an appropriation in the annual tax bill.[19] The Commons probably did not realize the implications of this practice at first, but it enabled the Commons by its single authority to order money from the treasury. Because the Commons had effectively denied the right of the governor and Council to amend money bills,[20] the only way the executive could hope to put a stop to the practice was to reject an entire tax bill that appropriated money to repay the treasurer for a sum advanced on the Commons' order. Such action not only would have provoked a serious political dispute but also might have put the colony in severe financial straits. Consequently, as long as the Commons limited its orders to routine services to which the executive had no serious objection, both the governor and Council let the matter pass without comment. Even when the Commons voted £600 sterling to defray the cost of sending delegates to the Stamp Act Congress in New York in 1765, both Lieutenant Governor Bull and the Council, though neither approved, allowed the matter to pass—as Bull later remarked—"sub silentio" rather than provoke a violent dispute.[21]

But neither Bull nor the Council could allow the Wilkes vote to pass *sub silentio*. Wilkes was too much the center of attention in London for the Commons' action not to come to the notice of imperial authorities. Bull could have publicly indicated his disapproval by dissolving the Commons, but he was never one to act rashly. As a former speaker for the Commons and as an experi-

---

[18] See William Bull to Earl of Hillsborough, September 8, 1770, in Transcripts of Records Relating to South Carolina in the British Public Record Office (South Carolina Archives Department), XXXII, 320–30.

[19] Committee of Correspondence to Garth, September 6, 1770, in "Correspondence of Charles Garth," *South Carolina Historical and Genealogical Magazine*, XXXI (July, 1930), 244–53.

[20] For a study of this development, see Jack P. Greene, *The Quest for Power: The Lower Houses of Assembly in the Southern Royal Colonies 1689–1776* (Chapel Hill, 1963), 52–65, 82–84, 88–96.

[21] Commons Journals, XXXVII, 97 (August 2, 1765), 194 (June 27, 1766); Bull to Hillsborough, September 8, 1770, in Transcripts of Records Relating to South Carolina, XXXII, 320–30.

enced and astute politician, he well knew that such a move might throw the colony into turmoil and seriously impair his harmonious relationship with the House. Had there been any sizable opposition to what the Commons had done, the risk might have been worth taking, but the indications are that there was no such resistance. Merchant Henry Laurens—absent from the Commons on a tour of the back country on the day of the vote—thought the measure too radical and predicted that "these Chaps will get a rap o' the knuckles for this";[22] and William Henry Drayton in the *South Carolina Gazette* congratulated the colony on its "sudden increase" in wealth and snidely complimented "those of our patriots, who were most active in promoting a measure . . . to defray the *bills* of a *certain club* of patriots, at the *London Tavern*."[23] But most South Carolina politicians appear to have favored the grant. Only seven members of a full House voted against the measure, and Timothy's newspaper reported that the "Vote would have been *unanimous*" if the order had been for only £1,000 sterling and that some were inclined to increase the sum to £2,000.[24] Moreover, the committee charged with transmitting the money to Wilkes consisted of seven of the ten most important members of the House, men with economic and social position who had, for the most part, been prominent in the Commons for over a decade and were the leading politicians in the colony. Peter Manigault, James Parsons, and John Rutledge were wealthy lawyers, Christopher Gadsden and Benjamin Dart were large merchants, and Thomas Ferguson and Thomas Lynch were successful planters.[25]

Because he could not avoid reporting the matter to authorities in London, Bull decided to leave the choice of retaliatory measures to them and immediately sent the colonial secretary, Lord Hills-

---

[22] Laurens' Petition to Ministry, June 23, 1781, in Emmet Collection (New York Public Library), as quoted in Wallace, *Henry Laurens*, 379.

[23] *South Carolina Gazette*, December 28, 1769.

[24] *Ibid.*, December 8, 1769.

[25] The importance of members was determined by an analysis of committee assignments for the entire period, 1769–1775. The other three most important leaders in this House were merchant Henry Laurens, lawyer Charles Pinckney, and planter Rawlins Lowndes, who later became speaker. In subsequent Houses, lawyers Thomas Bee, Thomas Heyward, Jr., and Charles Cotesworth Pinckney, and merchant Miles Brewton also played prominent roles. See Greene, *Quest for Power*, 475–88.

borough, an account of the affair. To excuse himself and to explain his inability to prevent the Commons' sending the money, he noted that, from "the great religious and Civil indulgences granted by the Crown to encourage Adventurers to settle in America, the Government of the Colonies has gradually inclined more to the democratical than regal side" and that "since the late unhappy discontents and the universal extension of the Claims of the American Commons" the power of the South Carolina Commons had "risen to a great Heighth." So extensive was its power, Bull reported, that the House had adopted the practice of ordering money out of the treasury by its single authority "as less liable to obstruction from the Governor or Council" to its "pursuing any favorite object."[26]

News of the grant to Wilkes got a mixed reception in London, where it received considerable attention from the press.[27] Wilkes himself was annoyed because the Commons had sent the money to the Society instead of directly to him for his private use. He wrote a peevish reply which, he contended in a marked display of his notorious dislike for Americans, "was admirably calculated for the Meridian of South-Carolina"; but the Society rejected Wilkes's letter, thanked the Commons, and pledged its support in maintaining the rights of all Britons.[28] William Henry Drayton, who had left South Carolina for London in early January, published a satirical attack on the South Carolina Commons in which he congratulated its members for having "broke loose from the shackles of their constitution, and the imperious restrictions of a royal commission and instructions."[29] But London merchant William Lee

---

[26] Bull to Hillsborough, December 12, 16, 1769, in Transcripts of Records Relating to South Carolina, XXXII, 132–36.

[27] See London *Daily Advertiser*, February 7, 1770; London *Chronicle*, February 6–8, 1770; and London *Middlesex Journal, or Chronicle of Liberty*, February 10–13, 13–15, 15–17, 1770.

[28] John Horne, "Relation," *Controversial Letters of John Wilkes, Esq., the Reverend John Horne, and Their Principle Adherents* (London, 1771), 156–59; *South Carolina Gazette*, August 23, 1770.

[29] R[obert] M[orris] to Speaker of South Carolina Commons, February 23, 1770, in London *Lloyd's Evening Post*, March 19–21, 1770. This letter, which was widely reprinted, apparently first appeared in the London *Publick Advertiser*, March 20, 1770. See *South Carolina American and General Gazette*, May 23, 1770. For the attribution of the letter to Drayton, see extract of a letter from London, March 30, 1770, in *South Carolina Gazette*, May 17, 1770. On

thought the Commons had "done nobly," and another London correspondent wrote that the vote to Wilkes had "given a greater Shock to the mini[steria]l Operations, for binding Liberty in Fetters, than any one Act of the Americans since the Stamp Act bounced out of Pandora's Box" and predicted that South Carolina would "be revered, and considered, as the first in America," though he warned South Carolina patriots that "you *must expect* every Engine will be set to work to engage you to *rescind* that Vote."[30]

The timeliness of the warning was immediately discernible in the reaction of imperial authorities. When they received Bull's letter, they were both indignant and astonished. The Commons' audacity in voting money to support the ministry's most violent and effective critic deeply offended them, and they were amazed to learn that the Commons had acquired the power to order money out of the treasury without the consent of the executive. Moving with unusual alacrity, they sought an opinion from Attorney General De Grey, who reported early in February, 1770, that the Commons could not "by the Constitution" order money from the treasury without the consent of the governor and Council. The Commons' exercise of that power, he declared, was contrary to the governor's commission and instructions and could not "be warranted by the modern practice of a few years, irregularly introduced, and improvidently acquiesced in." The assumptions were that the Commons could not alter the constitution of South Carolina or acquire new powers by usage and that both royal instructions and commissions took precedence over local practice. De Grey also questioned whether the Commons could vote money for other than purely local services and whether it could divert to different purposes money already appropriated by law. He concluded that the Commons' grant to Wilkes was illegal and suggested that "preventive measures for the future . . . to protect the subject from the Repetition of such exactions" should be

Drayton's going to England, see Charleston *South Carolina Gazette and Country Journal*, January 9, 1770.

[30] William Lee to Richard Henry Lee, February 6, 1770, in Brock Collection (Henry E. Huntington Library, San Marino, Calif.), Box 4; extract of a letter from London, March 30, 1770, in *South Carolina Gazette*, May 17, 1770.

taken either "by the Parliament here, or by Instructions to the Governor."[31]

The Privy Council agreed with De Grey, and upon its order the Board of Trade prepared in early April an instruction that embodied the substance of his report. Threatening the governor with removal if he passed any bill raising money for other than local services, the instruction stipulated that he assent to no revenue measure that did not appropriate the money arising from it to specific purposes and that did not expressly limit the use of that money to the services for which it was appropriated. The instruction also directed that all money bills contain a clause subjecting the treasurer to permanent exclusion from public office and a penalty triple the sum involved if he issued money from the treasury solely upon the Commons' order. After the Privy Council had formally approved the instruction, Hillsborough transmitted it to Bull on April 14, 1770, along with a letter expressing his hopes that it would prevent further abuses.[32] But Hillsborough's hopes were soon disappointed. Far from solving the problem, the instruction only served to aggravate an already tense political situation in South Carolina.

Indeed, while the Board of Trade was preparing the additional instruction in London, the South Carolina Council was challenging the Commons' right to order money from the treasury without the consent of the other two branches of the legislature. In early April, 1770, the Council objected to the Commons' inclusion of an item in the annual tax bill to repay the Wilkes grant to the treasury. Declaring that the grant was a tacit affront to "His Majesty's Government" and in no "sense honourable, fit, or decent," the Council denied that the Commons could legally appropriate money for uses that did not directly concern the colony.[33]

The reply of the Commons—drawn up by a committee headed by Thomas Lynch and including James Parsons, Christopher Gadsden, Henry Laurens, Thomas Ferguson, and Benjamin Dart—outlined

---

[31] Report of De Grey, February 13, 1770, in Transcripts of Records Relating to South Carolina, XXXII, 166–81.

[32] Orders in Council, April 3, 5, 1770, and Hillsborough to Bull, April 14, 1770, all *ibid.*, 233–34, 241–48, 253–55; Labaree (ed.), *Royal Instructions*, I, 208–209.

[33] Commons Journals, XXXVIII, 382, 387–88 (April 7–9, 1770).

the position it would tenaciously adhere to for the next four years. It contended that to grant money to support "the Just and Constitutional Rights and Liberties for the People of Great Britain and America" could hardly be "disrespectful or Affrontive to His Majesty, the great patron of the Liberty and Rights of all His Subjects." The Commons also pointed out that the Council's insinuation that there were limitations upon its authority to appropriate money implied that some power could raise money from the inhabitants "other than their own Representatives." That "Seditious Doctrine," the Commons declared, "must manifestly tend, to increase the Discontents and Disorder which have but too long subsisted in his Majesty's American Dominions." Upon the central point at issue—whether or not it could issue money from the treasury by its sole authority—the Commons resolved that it had always "exercised a Right of Borrowing monies out of the Treasury," that no governor had ever attempted to abridge that right, and that it had always "faithfully and punctually" repaid the money. Here the Commons was arguing that it could alter the constitution of South Carolina by its own action and that local precedents, habits, traditions, and statutes were important parts of that constitution—views directly opposite to those put forth by De Grey in London just two months earlier. From this vigorous defense the Commons took the offensive by pointing out "the inconsistency and absurdity" of the Council's acting as both an upper house of the legislature and an advisory council, and the House resolved to ask the Crown to appoint a separate upper house "composed of independent men, and men of Property." This request, in part the consequence of the Crown's recent policy of filling the Council with placemen who were not natives of the colony, was the logical culmination of the longstanding rivalry between the Commons and the Council which had seen the Council continuously decline in status and in political influence within the colony.[34]

This altercation, if anything, intensified the ardor of South Caro-

---

[34] *Ibid.*, 382, 387–92 (April 7–10, 1770); Bull to Hillsborough, April 15, 1770, in Transcripts of Records Relating to South Carolina, XXXII, 256–59. On the decline of the Council, see M. Eugene Sirmans, "The South Carolina Royal Council, 1720–1763," *William and Mary Quarterly*, 3d ser., XVIII (July, 1961), 373–92.

lina patriots for "Wilkes and Liberty." News of the activities of Wilkes and his London supporters frequently appeared in detail in Charleston newspapers, and no opportunity was lost to make a public display in support of Wilkes.[35] The numbers 45, 92 (the number of Massachusetts representatives who had voted not to rescind the Massachusetts circular letter in June, 1768), and 26 (the number of South Carolina representatives who had voted to adopt resolutions approving the refusal of the Massachusetts Assembly to withdraw the circular letter) were part of the standard ritual on all such occasions. Wednesday, April 18, 1770, the day of Wilkes's release from prison, was celebrated by ringing church bells, displaying colors, and illuminating over 150 houses in Charleston, "many of them with Forty-five Lights." "Ninety-Two Members of CLUB FORTY-FIVE," preceded by "26 Candles," met at "45 Minutes after Seven o'Clock" for "a most elegant Entertainment" at the house of Robert Dillon and, after drinking 45 "loyal and patriotic Toasts," broke up at "45 Minutes past 12." Among the toasts were: "May the Endeavours of John Wilkes, Esq. be rewarded as those of Junius were by the Romans" and "The patriotic Supporters of the Bill of Rights." This celebration, Peter Timothy's *Gazette* declared, indicated the "great . . . Regard we pay to those, who suffer in the Cause of Liberty, by a resolute and steady Opposition, to the arbitrary and tyrannical Attempts, of such wicked and corrupt Ministers as would overturn the English Constitution."[36] A similar demonstration followed the erection of a statue of William Pitt, Earl of Chatham, in Broad Street on July 5.

One of the 45 toasts on this last occasion—"Firmness and Perseverance in our Resolutions, not to flinch a single inch"—gave ample warning of the position the Commons would take on the Crown's additional instruction.[37] That instruction had reached Charleston before the Commons met again on August 14. Anticipating the storm it would raise, Lieutenant Governor Bull chose to lay it casually before the Commons rather than risk impairing his good

---

[35] See *South Carolina Gazette*, April 12, 19, July 5, 1770; *South Carolina Gazette and Country Journal*, April 10, 24, July 10, 1770; and *South Carolina American and General Gazette*, April 6, 1770.

[36] *South Carolina Gazette*, April 19, 1770; *South Carolina Gazette and Country Journal*, April 24, 1770.

[37] *South Carolina Gazette*, July 5, 1770.

relations by making too great an issue of it. He was under no illusion that the House would compliantly recede from its position even in the face of a royal mandate.[38] That he had gauged the temper of the Commons correctly was apparent early in the session.

The Commons quickly adopted a report—prepared by a committee headed by John Rutledge and Thomas Lynch and including Christopher Gadsden, Henry Laurens, John Mackenzie, Rawlins Lowndes, and Charles Cotesworth Pinckney—that defied the additional instruction. Declaring that the instruction was based upon "false, partial and insidious" information, the Commons denied that it had recently assumed the power to order the treasurer to advance money without consulting the governor or Council. It pointed out that it had for some time exercised and would continue to exercise that power, repaying the money later in the annual tax law. Far from being unconstitutional, the vote of funds to the Bill of Rights Society was, the Commons asserted, "agreeable to the usage and practice both ancient and Modern of the Commons House of Assembly"—again clearly implying that precedent and custom were important elements in the constitution of the colony and that no mandate from the Crown could supersede them. Categorically rejecting the instruction's contention that the South Carolina legislature could grant money only for local uses, the Commons affirmed its "undoubted Right" to vote funds for whatever services it thought fit and emphasized its disapproval of the instruction's requiring an insertion of specific clauses in money bills by flatly declaring that "Ministers dictating how a Money Bill shall be framed, is an Infringement of the Privileges of this House; to whom alone it belongs to Originate and prepare the same, for the concurrence and Assent of the Governor and Council without any Alteration or Amendment whatsoever." Finally, the Commons dared to suggest that its actions would not have been considered dangerous "if the Money borrowed had not been applied towards frustrating the unjust and unconstitutional measures of an Arbitrary and Oppressive Ministry" and declared its intention of endeavor-

---

[38] Bull to Hillsborough, August 23, 1770, in Transcripts of Records Relating to South Carolina, XXXII, 316–19.

ing to obtain the withdrawal of the instruction by presenting the affair in a true light to the home officials through its London agent.[39]

That the Commons did not intend to confine its actions to mere parliamentary assertions of its rights was indicated when it once again tried to pass a tax measure containing an article to repay the treasurer the controversial £1,500, only to have the Council again turn it down. Further disagreement between the two houses arose over a bill to appoint a treasurer. The death of Treasurer Jacob Motte the previous June had interjected a new element into the dispute. With the consent of the Council, Bull had appointed Assistant Treasurer Henry Perronneau to fill the office until the legislature met, when, according to law, a permanent treasurer should have been formally appointed by statute. But the insistence of the Council upon including the clauses required by the additional instruction which would penalize the treasurers for advancing money without the consent of the entire legislature prevented passage of an appointing statute.[40]

These proceedings left Bull with little hope for settling the matter without some concession from imperial authorities. To Hillsborough he ventured to suggest that the additional instruction did not specifically preclude his assenting to a tax bill containing provision to repay the grant to Wilkes. In addition, he counseled Hillsborough that the Commons would "very tenaciously adhere to" its two "grand points": the right to order money from the treasury by its single authority and the right to appropriate money to any purposes it thought proper, whether they were local or not.[41] But Hillsborough, no less adamant than the Commons, showed no disposition to yield. Replying that the instruction prohibited the passing of *any* measure that authorized repayment of the Wilkes Fund, he declared that the Commons' resolutions were

---

[39] Commons Journals, XXXVIII, 430–33 (August 29, 1770); Committee of Correspondence to Garth, September 6, 1770, in "Correspondence of Charles Garth," *South Carolina Historical and Genealogical Magazine*, XXXI (July, 1930), 244–46.

[40] Commons Journals, XXXVIII, 422–23, 440–41, 449–50, 453–56 (August 23, 30, September 6–7, 1770); Bull to Hillsborough, July 16, 1770, in Transcripts of Records Relating to South Carolina, XXXII, 297–98; *South Carolina Gazette and Country Journal*, June 19, 1770.

[41] Bull to Hillsborough, August 23, September 8, 1770, in Transcripts of Records Relating to South Carolina, XXXII, 316–30.

"ill founded" and "unbecoming," and he directed Bull to veto money bills that did not comply with the additional instruction.[42]

The Commons' attempt to secure revocation of the instruction produced the same results. Shortly before Bull prorogued the Commons in September, 1770, its committee of correspondence directed the colony's London agent, Charles Garth, to secure removal of the instruction on the grounds that it had been issued as a result of misinformation. The committee emphasized that in the Wilkes vote the Commons had not diverted money appropriated to other purposes but had only followed the long-established practice of borrowing surplus funds from the treasury with a promise to repay them in the next annual tax bill. The committee admitted that "in Britain Votes of Credit only follow a Royal Requisition" but asserted that it was "not therefore necessary or proper that it should do so in America, for the distance must make the King's immediate Requisition impracticable on emergent Occasions, and if it were left to the Governor, a weak, ignorant or Corrupt one, might suffer the Public safety to be greatly endangered, or even lost before he would take the necessary steps to avert the Dangers which threatened it." Predicating its assertion upon the premise that the South Carolina Commons' right to grant its constituents' money stood "upon the same ground as that of the House of Commons," the committee pointed out that "it was never heard that the Commons, could not give unasked."[43]

In compliance with the committee's directions, Garth petitioned the Privy Council in late November, 1770, to withdraw the instruction. Incorporating the committee's objections, he emphasized that the Commons regarded any such "Dictate or Direction" a violation of its "first and essential Privilege . . . to originate and prepare . . . all Money Bills." Early in December the Privy Council referred the agent's petition to the Board of Trade for a report.[44] Despite Garth's

---

[42] Hillsborough to Bull, October 19, November 15, 1770, *ibid.*, 339–40, 353.

[43] Committee of Correspondence to Garth, September 6, 1770, in "Correspondence of Charles Garth," *South Carolina Historical and Genealogical Magazine,* XXXI (July, 1930), 244–53.

[44] Garth to Committee of Correspondence, November 24, December 17, 1770, and Garth's Petition to Crown, November 22, 1770, all *ibid.*, XXXIII (April, 1932), 117–24; Order in Council, December 9, 1770, in Transcripts of Records Relating to South Carolina, XXXII, 420–28.

endeavors, the Board at a formal hearing on March 25 echoed Hillsborough's sentiments and steadfastly maintained that money could be ordered from the treasury only upon consent of all three branches of the legislature. The Board denied that the instruction was intended to interfere "with the Privilege of the House in originating Money Bills" and declared ambiguously that its stipulations constituted not an "Interposition in the Mode of raising or granting to His Majesty" but merely directions to the governor from which he was not to depart. On the Board's recommendation, the Privy Council rejected Garth's petition.[45]

If London authorities were unyielding, so was the South Carolina Commons. In January and February, 1771, while Garth's petition was awaiting action from the Board of Trade, the Commons tried to inveigle Bull into recognizing its right to order money from the treasury without executive consent by adopting the apparently innocent measure of ordering Treasurer Perronneau to pay Bull £7 current money for each of a number of recent poor Irish Protestant immigrants in order to help settle them. But Bull would not be ensnared; he declined to accept the money unless it was provided for by an ordinance passed by all three branches of the legislature. Nor did he change his mind when the Commons ingeniously distinguished between unappropriated surplus monies and appropriated funds and contended that the additional instruction applied only to appropriated funds, which left the Commons free to dispose of surplus funds by its sole authority.[46] This session also failed to produce a tax bill, although it avoided the disagreement that arose during the previous session over the bill to appoint a treasurer. After Bull had arranged to include in the treasurer's bonds the penalty clauses required by the additional instructions, the Council no longer insisted upon their being in the bill of appointment. An ordinance passed in late February formally appointed as joint treasurers Henry Perronneau and Benjamin Dart, the former the candidate of Bull and the Council and the latter—a "warm" patriot who

[45] Garth to Committee of Correspondence, March 27, 1771, and Board of Trade to Privy Council Committee on Plantation Affairs, March 27, 1771, both in "Correspondence of Charles Garth," *South Carolina Historical and Genealogical Magazine*, XXXIII (April, 1932), 125–29, 130–31.

[46] Commons Journals, XXXVIII, 474, 476, 481–82, 487–88, 497–500 (January 31, February 7, 9, 15, 26, 1771).

had demonstrated "violent Opposition to Acts of Parliament in 1765 and 1770"—the nominee of the Commons.[47]

A decline in enthusiasm for Wilkes both in London and in South Carolina followed the repeal of most of the Townshend duties in the early 1770's and the subsequent collapse of the nonimportation agreements,[48] but the additional instruction of April 5, 1770, continued to be the *cause célèbre* of South Carolina politics. Returning from a two-year stay in Great Britain in September, 1771, Gov. Lord Charles Greville Montagu tried every possible tack to persuade the Commons to comply with the instruction; but it steadfastly resisted, preferring, it declared, to submit to the public and private calamities that might result from not having a tax bill rather than adopt any measure that was inconsistent with "the established mode of Proceedings, and the proper Rights of the People." The moderate Henry Laurens, who, beginning in late 1771, observed the dispute from London, correctly expressed the views of the colony's leading politicians when he wrote that he would rather "have no Tax Bill for seven Years" or even "forfeit my whole Estate and be reduced to the necessity of working for my Bread" than "give up that important point." The issue, as he saw it, was "Nothing less than the very Essence of true Liberty." The "*Right* of the People to give and grant voluntarily in mode and in Quantity free from the Fetters of ministerial Instructions, restrictive, or obligatory," was "indubitable," and the instruction was no less a threat to that right than the "Stamp Act or Internal Duties." For the members of the Commons to submit would be to "sell the Birth Right and dearest Privilege of their Constituents," to "incur the Hatred and Detestation of the present Age," and to brand themselves "in all future Ages with the infamous Character of Betrayers of the Trust reposed in them by the People."[49]

---

47 *Ibid.*, 462–63, 466–67, 476–78, 494 (January 27–28, February 7, 23, 1771); Thomas Cooper and David J. McCord (eds.), *The Statutes at Large of South Carolina* (10 vols.; Columbia, 1836–1841), IV, 326–27; Laurens to John L. Gervais, December 28, 1771, in [Henry] Laurens Letter Books (Laurens Papers, South Carolina Historical Society, Charleston), 1771–1772, pp. 142–44, 146.

48 See, for examples, Laurens to Thomas Franklin and Laurens to James Laurens, both December 26, 1771, both *ibid.*, 130–31.

49 Commons Journals, XXXVIII, 522 (September 19, 1771); Laurens to James Habersham, April 10, 1770; Laurens to William Williamson, November

The cleverest politician would have found it difficult to make headway against such determined opposition; Montagu's blustering efforts failed completely. For a brief period after he met with the Commons on September 17, 1771, he was optimistic. Along with Bull he hoped that the ministry's firm stand would discourage the Commons from further opposition. Late in September he wrote Hillsborough that there were "scarcely above Two Members in the House" who did not privately condemn the Commons' earlier actions, although he added that "a certain kind of Pride" might well prevent them from receding "from Orders they have so Publickly made." By mid-October, however, Montagu had had time to appraise the situation more realistically, and he warned Hillsborough that the dispute might not be settled for some time.[50]

Subsequent events indicated that Montagu's change of opinion was well warranted. Garth's failure to secure the withdrawal of the instruction had convinced many South Carolina political leaders that it was futile for the Commons to continue demanding recognition of its power to issue money from the treasury by its sole authority. Peter Timothy reported that "all the *Patriots* and *principal Speakers*" in the House were willing for political reasons to admit that the vote to Wilkes "was irregular."[51] They were not, however, willing to comply with the instruction or to abandon the attempt to repay the £1,500. They merely devised an expedient to obtain by guile what they had not been able to get by direct action. The Commons inserted in the annual tax bill an item providing for the payment of a certain sum to the estate of Jacob Motte for money he had advanced to pay bounties to Irish immigrants, provide for a survey of the colony, encourage silk culture, and provide "for other services." When the Council examined the bill, it quickly recognized that the "other services" included the Wilkes grant and

---

28, 1771; Laurens to John Rose, December 5, 1771; Laurens to James Laurens, December 12, 1771; and Laurens to Alexander Garden, May 24, 1772, all in Laurens Letter Book, 1767–1771, p. 492; 1771–1772, pp. 74–79, 93–104, 286–93; *South Carolina Gazette*, September 19, 1771; *South Carolina Gazette and Country Journal*, October 8, 1771.

[50] Montagu to Hillsborough, September 26, October 20, 1771, in Transcripts of Records Relating to South Carolina, XXXIII, 84, 87.

[51] Peter Timothy to Benjamin Franklin, October 20, 1771, in Franklin Papers (American Philosophical Society, Philadelphia); Commons Journals, XXXVIII, 556 (October 11, 1770).

refused to pass the measure until the item was omitted and the clauses required by the instruction were included. The Commons acidly replied that it would never "regard any Ministerial Instruction in the framing of a Money Bill, nor alter any part of the Schedule upon your requisition." Neither body would yield. For the fourth consecutive session the debate over the additional instruction prevented passage of a tax bill.[52]

The Commons at this session reasserted its claim to the power to order surplus funds from the treasury on its sole authority by ordering the treasurers to advance £3,000 Carolina currency to the commissioners for silk manufacturing to purchase South Carolina silk for sale in Britain. The Commons probably expected Treasurer Dart, as a former House leader, to comply with its order, but neither he nor Perronneau would honor the commissioners' request for money. When the Commons demanded an explanation, the treasurers defended their behavior on the grounds that Montagu and the Council had ordered them not to comply with the order and that to have done so would have been to violate their bonds and to subject themselves to possible legal action. The Commons had no sympathy for the treasurers' dilemma. After the treasurers admitted that the treasury contained sufficient unappropriated funds to cover its order, the Commons declared them "guilty of a violation and Contempt of the Authority and Privileges of this House" and with "but one dissenting Voice" boldly ordered them committed to the Charleston jail. Before the commitment order could be carried out, however, Montagu dissolved the House.[53]

London authorities wholeheartedly approved Montagu's action. George III, it was reported from London, had "set his Face against that £1,500" and was determined to see "*his Instructions* obeyed"; and Hillsborough directed Montagu in January, 1772, to dissolve the House again if it continued to reject the additional instruction. Indeed, Henry Laurens heard from "a Gentleman of good Intelligence" that Hillsborough, who seemed to have "a Mist before his

---

52 *Ibid.*, 577–78 (November 4, 1771). An indication of the pressure on the Council to pass the tax bill is in *South Carolina Gazette*, October 24, 1771.

53 Commons Journals, XXXVIII, 543, 579–84 (October 2, November 4–5, 1771); *South Carolina Gazette*, November 7, 1771; *South Carolina American and General Gazette*, November 11, 1771; Laurens to Gervais, December 28, 1771, in Laurens Letter Book, 1771–1772, pp. 142–44, 146.

... Eyes" and to be "disposed to believe every evil of and to do every Evil in his Power to us," had said that he "wished for a continued Opposition to the Instruction, in order . . . to enable him to get a Law made for us."[54]

But Montagu's dissolution of the House had so stiffened the Commons' opposition that not even the threat of parliamentary action could soften it. With the strong endorsement of the electorate, which had indicated its approval of the former House's position by returning a large majority of the members who had chosen to stand for re-election, the new House, which met in April, 1772, refused either to submit to any "Ministerial Instructions, dictating the manner in which Money-Bills must be framed," or to do business until there was some hope of passing a tax bill on its own terms. The Commons believed with Henry Laurens that it had "Justice and the Constitution" on its side and was prepared to "Elect–Suffer Dissolution–and Reelect–Stand firm." When it became apparent that the Commons intended to stick to its resolution, Montagu impatiently charged it with seeking to encroach upon the Crown's "just Prerogative" and again dissolved it.[55]

Before the second dissolution, the Commons, encouraged by Henry Laurens's reports from London that prospects were favorable for removing "the Stumbling Block in the way of our Carolina Tax Bills,"[56] again ordered the committee of correspondence to direct Garth to procure the recall of the instruction. No Commons House, the committee wrote Garth, could consent to that instruc-

---

[54] Hillsborough to Montagu, January 11, 1772, in Transcripts of Records Relating to South Carolina, XXXIII, 105–108; Laurens to John Hopton, January 29, 1771; Laurens to Williamson, November 28, 1771; Laurens to John Rose, December 5, 1771; and Laurens to James Laurens, December 12, 1771, all in Laurens Letter Book, 1767–1771, pp. 594–97; 1771–1772, pp. 74–79, 93–108.

[55] Montagu to Hillsborough, April 27, 1772, in Transcripts of Records Relating to South Carolina, 140–41; *South Carolina Gazette*, November 7, 1771, March 26, April 9, 16, 1772; *South Carolina American and General Gazette*, February 25, 1772; Laurens to Alexander Garden, May 24, 1772, in Laurens Letter Book, 1771–1772, pp. 286–93.

[56] See Laurens to William Williamson, November 28, 1771; Laurens to John Rose, December 5, 1771; Laurens to James Laurens, December 12, 1771, February 28, 1772; Laurens to James Habersham, December 20, 1771; and Laurens to Gabriel Manigault, March 2, 1772, all *ibid.*, 74–79, 93–108, 116–20, 198, 202–206.

tion "without, at the same time, absolutely surrendering" its "most fundamental Right of Originating all Grants to his Majesty." It pointed out that it still thought that "House fully justified by long usage and a multitude of Precedents, in ordering the Treasurers to pay that Money in the Manner" it did, but added that even if the House had erred it could never conceive of any Commons House submitting "to so unconstitutional a remedy as that insisted on by the Instruction." The Commons had now shifted its argument and was endeavoring to effect a recall of the instruction not because it was contrary to the House's right to order surplus moneys from the treasury without executive approval but because it violated the House's exclusive right to frame money bills. The committee ridiculed the Board of Trade's contention that the instruction was not intended to interfere with the Commons' privileges with regard to money bills. "This superlatively nice political refinement, tho' perhaps intelligible and distinguishable at St. Omers, and capable of being made so consistent with the Rights of the People thereabouts as to give it an easy passage amongst them," the committee declared, "we are well Assured, Notwithstanding all its gilding, that the Freemen of this province will suffer the greatest Extremities before they can be brought to stomach it."[57]

Garth did persuade imperial authorities to yield slightly. The letter from the committee of correspondence reached him at the end of May, 1772, when the ministry was ready to accept "a Drawn Game." In a memorial to the Crown he argued that the instruction "oppugned" the Commons' "most fundamental Right of originating all Grants to His Majesty." Hillsborough replied that it was intended only to prevent the Commons from ordering money from the treasury without consulting the governor or Council and not to interfere with its privileges in regard to money bills. He confided that he would favor a revision "if the Point in view could be effectuated in a way less exceptionable to the Commons House." The rest of the ministry shared Hillsborough's sentiments. Later in June he informed Garth that the ministry had agreed to revoke that part of the instruction requiring the insertion of certain provisions in all

---

[57] Committee of Correspondence to Garth, April 10, 1772, in "Correspondence of Charles Garth," *South Carolina Historical and Genealogical Magazine*, XXXIII (April, 1932), 136–38.

money bills if the Commons would pass a permanent declaratory
law stipulating "that no Monies in the Treasurers Hands . . . be at
any time issued by Order of any one Branch of the Legislature
singly and alone." By this concession the ministry hoped to remove
the Commons' grounds for complaining that the instruction interfered with its rights concerning money bills.[58]

It is doubtful that this slight concession would have satisfied the
Commons' leaders, but whatever good effect it might have had was
prevented by Governor Montagu's actions in South Carolina. Before he received notice of the ministry's concession, Montagu had
decided that the Commons would never accept the instruction as
long as it sat in Charleston, where the members who most heatedly
opposed it lived. He wrote Hillsborough in July, 1772, that he was
considering calling the Commons to meet at Beaufort in the southern part of the colony. This extreme tactic, which was probably
suggested by Gov. Thomas Hutchinson's similar maneuvers with
the Massachusetts House,[59] was a thinly veiled attempt at intimida-
tion. It would be not only a marked display of the political weapons
at Montagu's command but also a dramatic indication of his extreme disapproval of the Commons' conduct and his annoyance at
the colony's failure to find a suitable house for him in Charleston.
More important, Montagu hoped that the Charleston members
would remain at home and that the southern members attending
would be more moderate and comply with the instruction. Accordingly, despite the fact that he had by that time received news of
the ministry's concession on the instruction, he issued writs for the
election in mid-September of a new House to meet on October 8,
1772, at Beaufort.[60]

Montagu could scarcely have made a more serious political
blunder. He might have foreseen the results by considering the

---

[58] Garth to Committee of Correspondence, June 3, 25, 1772, and Garth's
Memorial to Crown, [June 2, 1772], all *ibid.*, XXXIII (July, 1932), 238–44;
Laurens to Peter Mazyck, April 10, 1772, in Laurens Letter Book, 1771–
1772, pp. 245–47; Hillsborough to Montagu, July 1, 1772, in Transcripts of
Records Relating to South Carolina, XXXIII, 164.

[59] The best discussion of this episode is Donald C. Lord and Robert M.
Calhoon, "The Removal of the Massachusetts General Court from Boston,
1769–1772," *Journal of American History*, LV (March, 1969), 735–55.

[60] Montagu to Hillsborough, July 27, 1772, *ibid.*, 167; *South Carolina
Gazette*, September 3, 1772.

tempest raised by Hutchinson in Massachusetts. South Carolina newspapers had followed that dispute with interest, one writer charging that—like the additional instruction—it was simply another attempt "to make even the mandate of the minister superior, in effect, to any American law."[61] This sentiment expressed what now became the position of South Carolina political leaders. They made every effort to frustrate Montagu's intentions by securing the election of representatives who would make the trip to Beaufort. In the *South Carolina Gazette and Country Journal*, Z. Z. warned the electorate that "the present Juncture of Public Affairs in this Province is critical and somewhat alarming," predicted that the *"Beaufort-Assembly"* might be "as important in its Consequences . . . as that of any assembly this Country ever saw," and urged that "Your own Welfare, the Welfare of Generations yet unborn, may in a great Measure depend on the Counsels and Conduct of the ensuing Assembly." The *South Carolina Gazette* reported that, because "the Existence of the *Beaufort-Assembly*, in all Probability, will be as *short* as, it is presumed, their Resolutions will be *spirited*," the electors seemed "determined . . . to vote for no Gentlemen but who are on the Spot and can give their personal Attendance—the present Crisis being looked upon as the most improper, to make the Choice a mere Compliment." "No Measure of any Governor," it declared, "was ever more freely and generally condemned."[62] The election resulted in another overwhelming endorsement of the Commons' opposition to the additional instruction. All but nine of the members of the dissolved April House were returned. At an informal caucus in Charleston the newly elected representatives resolved neither to pass a declaratory act nor to agree to a tax bill that either mentioned the additional instruction or failed to provide for the repayment of the Wilkes Fund.[63]

That Montagu had seriously misgauged the length to which Charleston leaders would go to prevent the Commons from accept-

---

[61] See *ibid.*, November 15, 1770, and *South Carolina American and General Gazette*, August 20, September 24, 1770.

[62] *South Carolina Gazette*, September 3, 17, October 8, 1772; *South Carolina Gazette and Country Journal*, September 15, 1772.

[63] *South Carolina Gazette*, September 17, 1772; Montagu to Hillsborough, September 24, 1772, in Transcripts of Records Relating to South Carolina, XXXIII, 173–80.

ing the additional instruction was apparent when it assembled at
Beaufort. The Charleston members attended in force and, already
highly incensed, regarded it, as the Commons later declared, as
"adding Insult to Injury" when Montagu kept the House sitting for
three days before he formally received it and then prorogued it to
meet at Charleston ten days later. Unknown to the Commons,
Hillsborough had ordered Montagu to encourage it to proceed to
business as quickly as possible, and the prorogation for the return
to Charleston was intended as a conciliatory measure. It had precisely the opposite effect. When the Commons reconvened in
Charleston on October 22, it immediately appointed a committee
on grievances headed by Christopher Gadsden and composed of
other leading members, including James Parsons, Thomas Lynch,
John Rutledge, Rawlins Lowndes, Charles Cotesworth Pinckney,
Thomas Bee, and Thomas Ferguson. The committee reported a
week later that Montagu's actions justified the Commons in breaking off relations with him completely but that urgent business made
such a course undesirable. It also recommended four resolutions
declaring Montagu's calling the House to meet at Beaufort an act
of "ill Will to the Body of the Free Men of this Province" and "a
most unprecedented Oppression, and an Unwarrantable Abuse of
a Royal Prerogative, which hath never been questioned by the
People of this Colony." Charging that his preventing the Commons
from proceeding to business at Beaufort was an "Evasion if not a
direct Violation of the Election Law" by which no period of time
greater than six months was to elapse between meetings of the
legislature, the committee recommended that Garth be directed
to petition the Crown either to reprimand Montagu or to remove
him from office.[64]

Montagu had anticipated such an action and prepared to meet
it by perusing the Commons' journals each day. But, when he asked
the clerk for the journals the evening after the committee presented
its report, he found that Speaker Rawlins Lowndes had taken them
home. Montagu then sent a note to Lowndes requesting the journals, but Lowndes, who was out for the evening, received the
message late and did not send the journals to Montagu until the

---

[64] Commons Journals, XXXIX, pt. 1, pp. 4–6, 11–12, 20–24 (October 10,
23, 29, 1772); *South Carolina Gazette*, October 15, November 2, 1772.

following morning. Montagu was greatly annoyed by Lowndes's delay and, when he discovered the committee's report in the journals, immediately sent for the House to prorogue it before it could adopt the report. But the Commons, after receiving the summons of the governor, finished debating the report and formally adopted it before attending him. Montagu was enraged by the Commons' actions, and, when its committee of correspondence wrote a letter to Garth after the prorogation directing him to procure Montagu's removal, his rage turned to fury. As soon as he could get a quorum of the House together, on November 10, he dissolved it and issued writs for a new election.[65]

To protect himself against a possible attack from the agent, Montagu immediately wrote the Earl of Dartmouth, who had replaced Hillsborough as colonial secretary in August, 1772, complaining bitterly that the Commons had made, in addition to its earlier attempt to dispose of public money by its sole authority, two other innovations in the colony's constitution. It had, he reported, continued to engage in legislative business after being summoned to attend the governor, and its committee of correspondence had continued to act after the House had been prorogued. How "dangerous it is," Montagu declared, "to allow Houses of Assembly to proceed, as it were daily in altering the usage of Parliament, thereby taking the power of the King in the most alarming manner and changing the very Nature of the Constitution." In the *South Carolina Gazette*, William Henry Drayton, returned from England and now a member of the Council, speculated whether such "unprecedented" innovations proceeded "from a *Malice propense*, designing to change, by Piece-Meal, the venerable Constitution of our Country." Montagu and Drayton had spotlighted the basic question in the long dispute: Could the Commons alter the constitution of the colony by its own action?[66]

---

[65] Commons Journals, XXXIX, pt. 1, pp. 20–29 (October 29, November 10, 1772); Montagu to Dartmouth, November 4, 1772, in Transcripts of Records Relating to South Carolina, XXXIII, 188–92; *South Carolina Gazette*, November 12, 1772; Committee of Correspondence to Garth, October 30, November 20, 1772, in "Correspondence of Charles Garth," *South Carolina Historical and Genealogical Magazine*, XXXIII (October, 1932), 262–64, 275–80.

[66] Montagu to Dartmouth, November 4, 1772, in Transcripts of Records Relating to South Carolina, XXXIII, 188–92; *South Carolina Gazette*, April

That it could was the verdict of the electorate, which in mid-December, 1772, returned all but nine of the innovating members of the previous House. No sooner had the Commons met the following January than it again disputed with Montagu, this time over his right to reject its choice as speaker. The Commons re-elected Rawlins Lowndes speaker, but Montagu, recalling Lowndes's conduct the previous November, ordered the House to select another. When the Commons unanimously refused to make another choice, Montagu prorogued it. Apparently because of embarrassment at having committed the technical error of proroguing only the Commons and not the Council, he dissolved the House a few days later for the fourth time since his return less than a year and a half earlier and called for new elections. "By an unparalleled Succession of Prorogations and Dissolutions, the Inhabitants of this Province have been unrepresented in Assembly about three Years," complained the *South Carolina Gazette*, asking "*Whether this is a Grievance*? And, *if it is*, Whether it is one of *the least Magnitude?*"[67]

Montagu had disputed with the Commons for the last time. His failure to cope with it prompted him to abandon the struggle and to return to England. The new House, composed mostly of the same men who had opposed Montagu through four different legislatures, was scheduled to meet on February 23, 1773, but the members carefully neglected to convene until March 11, the day after Montagu's departure. By this time the fiscal plight of the colony had become grave. No tax bill had been passed since 1769. Lieutenant Governor Bull urged the new representatives to consider the state of the treasury, although he refrained from mentioning the additional instruction for fear that it might "fix them more obstinately in their ill grounded opinion" as "is too much the spirit of popular Assemblies." But Bull's tact was of no avail. Montagu's

---

14, November 5, 1772. Drayton's siding with Montagu evoked some spirited abuse from South Carolina patriots, one of whom, in a veiled threat, suggested that Drayton's epitaph might conclude with the lines, "PREROGATIVE was my whole Aim,/ Whilst I had spirits to declaim.—/ Could I but sally forth anew,/ With Life of Scraps, patch'd up with Glue;/ That is the Theme I would insist on,/ Shou'd I be feather'd, tar'd, or pis'd on." *Ibid.*, November 19, 1772.

[67] *Ibid.*, November 26, 1772, January 7, 14, February 22, 1773; Montagu to Dartmouth, January 21, 1773, in Transcripts of Records Relating to South Carolina, XXXIII, 204–205.

behavior had goaded most Commons leaders to the point that they were willing to follow the suggestion of Christopher Gadsden, who was for letting "all go to the Devil" if Bull and the Council would not agree with the Commons. Again the Commons defied the instruction by preparing a tax bill containing a clause to repay the Wilkes Fund. When the Council rejected it, Bull permitted the Commons to adjourn until summer. Before breaking up, the Commons wrote Garth asking him again to request withdrawal of the instruction and Montagu's permanent removal from the governorship.[68] Garth did not have to seek Montagu's dismissal. The ministry was so displeased with Montagu's conduct that he had already resigned his post. Even before the committee's letter reached England, imperial authorities were preparing to replace him with Nova Scotia's Governor Lord William Campbell.[69] But it was nearly two years before Campbell would arrive in South Carolina, and in the meantime Bull administered the colony.

Bull was no more successful than Montagu in dealing with the Commons over the additional instruction. After the prorogation in March he optimistically wrote that, although some members were

---

[68] *South Carolina Gazette*, February 15, 1773; *South Carolina Gazette and Country Journal*, March 30, 1773; Commons Journals, XXXIX, pt. 2, pp. 4–6, 14, 17, 21–23 (March 12, 19, 20, 27, 1773); Bull to Dartmouth, March 30, 1773, in Transcripts of Records Relating to South Carolina, XXXIII, 225–27; Mark De Wolfe Howe (ed.), "Journal of Josiah Quincy, Junior, 1773," March 19, 1773, in Massachusetts Historical Society, *Proceedings*, XLIX (1915–1916), 452; Committee of Correspondence to Garth, March 27, 1773, in "Correspondence of Charles Garth," *South Carolina Historical and Genealogical Magazine*, XXXIII (October, 1932), 273–74. On the growing resentment to Montagu, see Committee of Correspondence to Garth, October 30, 1772, *ibid.*, 262–64, and Diary of John Joachim Zubly (Georgia Historical Society, Savannah), March 24, 1772. On Garth's proceedings against Montagu, see Garth to Committee of Correspondence, February 2, 25, April 3, 1773, and Garth's Petition to Crown, [February, 1773], all in Garth Letter Book, 1765–1775 (South Carolina Archives Department), 141–47, 150.

[69] On Montagu's resignation, see Garth to Committee of Correspondence, May 4, 20, 1773, and Committee of Correspondence to Garth, April 1, 1773, both *ibid.*, 139–40, 151–52; Laurens to John Laurens, March 9, 1773, and Laurens to James Laurens, March 11, 1773, both in Laurens Letter Book, 1772–1774, pp. 54–55, 59–62; Montagu to Barnard Elliott, May 1, 1773, in *South Carolina Historical and Genealogical Magazine*, XXXIII (October, 1932), 260–61; *South Carolina Gazette*, March 8, 1773; and Dartmouth to Bull, June 10, 1773, in Transcripts of Records Relating to South Carolina, XXXIII, 270–71.

"as tenacious as ever," others had softened "their language" about it. He suggested that the House might be persuaded to pass the declaratory act recommended by Hillsborough the previous year if it could be convinced that there was "not the least prospect or hope of the Royal Instruction's being revoked." Bull's optimism proved unjustified, however; a session in July failed to produce a tax bill. Bull reported to Dartmouth that the Commons seemed determined to adhere to its "right to be free from the influence" of the instruction, and Speaker Rawlins Lowndes wrote Peyton Randolph, speaker of the Virginia House of Burgesses, that the Commons would "never . . . Submit" to it.[70]

At a session in August and September, 1773, the Commons adopted a new expedient to replace the Wilkes Fund. It directed Attorney General Sir Egerton Leigh to sue the executors of Motte's estate for the money owed the colony. Although the amount due was £61,474.19/5 Carolina currency, the Commons specified that Leigh sue for only £49,140. By this expedient, Bull later wrote, the Commons hoped to carry its "Point, in making the Public Treasury pay the £10,500 equal to £1,500 sterling without inserting that exceptionable sum in any Money Bill." Bull thwarted this ingenious contrivance by ordering Leigh to sue for the entire sum. The House again tried to assert its power to issue money from the treasury on its sole authority by ordering the treasurers to advance £1,500 currency to provide carriages for newly arrived Irish Protestants. The treasurers refused to comply with the order, and they probably would have been committed by the House had not its attention been diverted by a dispute over whether the Council was actually an upper house of assembly.[71]

That dispute arose out of the Council's attempt to force the Commons to accept the additional instruction. The Council first

---

[70] Bull to Dartmouth, March 30, July 24, 1773, both *ibid.*, XXXIII, 225–27, 287–88; Rawlins Lowndes to Peyton Randolph, July 9, 1773, in Lowndes Papers (South Caroliniana Library, University of South Carolina, Columbia), P–1756/328.

[71] Commons Journals, XXXIX, pt. 2, pp. 39–40, 76, 92, 106–107, 115, 118 (August 13, September 3, 10, 1773; March 3, 10–11, 1774); Bull to Dartmouth, August 26, September 18, 1773, March 24, 1774, all in Transcripts of Records Relating to South Carolina, XXXIII, 292–94, 305–306; XXXIV, 21–22.

tried to excite public opinion against the Commons by publishing a report purporting to show the alarming state of the treasury. The Commons denied that the fiscal situation was as desperate as the Council had maintained, however, and replied that, although people might indeed lament that the failure to pass tax measures had seriously threatened the colony's public credit, its "Constituents would have had Reason for ever to lament the loss of their most valuable Privilege, the exclusive Right of Originating and Framing all Money Bills," had it passed a tax bill "in such a Manner as would have been agreeable to the Council." If the situation was not so grave as the Council insisted, the prospects were still far from bright, particularly because the general duty law—which had been bringing substantial sums into the treasury since the passage of the last tax bill in 1769—expired at the end of the session. Bull maintained that the Commons wanted it to expire because it would "flatter the bulk of the People" by temporarily relieving them from taxes and also create a serious situation that would bring pressure on the Crown to withdraw the additional instruction.[72]

But the Council was determined to force the Commons to revive the duty law, and a majority of its members decided not to pass any other legislation until that was done. Two of the councilors, John Drayton and William Henry Drayton, refused to agree to a "Measure so fatal to the Freedom of our Country," arguing that it put an undue "force" on the Commons. At William Henry Drayton's request, Thomas Powell published their dissent on August 31, 1773, in the *South Carolina Gazette*. Upset by Powell's printing a portion of its journals without its consent, the Council reprimanded Drayton, took Powell into custody, and, when he did not appear sufficiently contrite, sent him off to jail for "a high Breach of Privilege and a Contempt of this House."[73]

Powell's arrest provoked a formidable assault upon the Council's legislative authority. When Powell applied for his release

---

[72] Bull to Dartmouth, August 23, 1773, *ibid.*, XXXIII, 292–300; *South Carolina Gazette*, August 16, 25, 1773; Commons Journals, XXXIX, pt. 2, pp. 48–49, 51–53 (August 18, 20, 1773); Cooper and McCord (eds.), *Statutes*, IV, 264–65.

[73] *South Carolina Gazette*, August 30, September 2, 13, 1773.

under a writ of habeas corpus, Edward Rutledge, brother of John Rutledge and a rising young lawyer, represented him before Justices of the Peace Rawlins Lowndes and George Gabriel Powell —both members of the Commons. Rutledge denied the Council's power to commit people for a breach of privilege of a legislative body on the grounds that the Council was not an upper house of the legislature. Arguing that the Council was in no way comparable to the House of Lords, because it was not composed of independent men but only men "dependent on the Will of a King," Rutledge insisted that the Council was "Nothing more than merely a Privy-Council, to assist the Governor with their Advice." Both Lowndes and George Gabriel Powell agreed with Rutledge and set the printer free. When the Council asked the Commons to waive the usual exemption from arrest for Lowndes and Powell so that it could proceed against them, the Commons reviewed the case, approved the conduct of the justices, and resolved that the Council's committing the printer was "unprecedented, unconstitutional and Oppressive, and a Dangerous Violation of the Liberty of the Subject." The House then boldly requested Lieutenant Governor Bull to suspend those councilors responsible for the commitment and ordered the committee of correspondence to write Garth to ask for their removal.[74]

Bull was alarmed at these proceedings. He had repeatedly warned London authorities about the declining position of the Council. Now he added that the post of councilor had become "humiliating and obnoxious," that feeling against the Council was "at a great heighth and seems approaching to a crisis."[75] Just how far South Carolina patriots were ready to go in their attack on the Council was indicated immediately after the prorogation of the legislature in mid-September, 1773. Thomas Powell and Edward Rutledge brought suit for damages against Attorney General Sir

---

[74] *Ibid.*, September 2, 6, 13, 15, 1773; Commons Journals, XXXIX, pt. 2, pp. 77–79, 82–90, 93–94 (September 8, 11, 1773).

[75] For Bull's remarks on the declining position of the Council, see Bull to Hillsborough, October 20, November 30, 1770, and Bull to Dartmouth, April 9, September 18, 1773, all in Transcripts of Records Relating to South Carolina, XXXII, 342–45, 371–75; XXXIII, 256, 303–10. For a contemporary newspaper comment to the same effect, see *South Carolina Gazette*, October 18, 1770.

Egerton Leigh—the signer of the warrant to commit Powell. The suit failed, however, when Chief Justice Thomas Knox Gordon—one of Leigh's fellow councilors—ruled that the Council was "an *Upper House of Assembly*" and did therefore have the power of commitment.[76]

Gordon's decision put a damper on the campaign against the Council in South Carolina, although the controversy continued to receive some attention in London. Charles Garth dutifully, though pessimistically, presented to Dartmouth the Commons' request for the removal of the offending councilors. Reporting that Dartmouth had intimated that any application "denying the Council to be a Branch of the Legislature and an Upper House of Assembly" would be considered as an attempt "to subvert the Constitution" and that "no proceedings could be had upon it," Garth suggested in December, 1773, that any charges should be limited to challenging the right of the Council to imprison the subject for a breach of privilege.[77]

The dispute over the Council's right to act as an upper house was, however, almost immediately eclipsed by the storm over the Tea Act and the Coercive Acts. Crown officials, Garth reported in April, 1774, were so preoccupied with "all the Measures affecting Boston" that South Carolina matters had been pushed far down on the agenda.[78] Still, the Commons never abandoned its intention of getting around the additional instruction. South Carolina leaders inevitably looked at broader imperial measures in terms of their particular problems, viewing the Coercive Acts as a precedent by which the ministry could justify a law to "Cram down the Instruction of the 14th April and every other Mandate which Ministers

---

[76] Bull to Dartmouth, October 20, 1773, and Leigh to Bull, September 18, October 16, 1773, all in Transcripts of Records Relating to South Carolina, XXXIII, 325–33.

[77] Committee of Correspondence to Garth, September 16, 1773; Garth to Committee of Correspondence, December 27, 1773, January 9, March 11, 1774; Garth's Petition to Crown [December, 1773]; Garth to Privy Council Committee on Plantation Affairs [January, 1774], all in Garth Letter Book, 153–54, 158–65.

[78] Garth to Committee of Correspondence, April 21, 1774, in Garth Letter Book, 171. See also Laurens's remark that "the Complexion of the Times" would prevent a hearing on the dispute with the Council. Laurens to James Laurens, February 5, 1774, in Laurens Letter Book 1772–1774, pp. 198–201.

Shall think proper for keeping us in Subjection to the Task Master who Shall be put over us."[79]

The spring of 1774 marked the beginning of the fifth successive year of deadlock between imperial authorities and the Commons over the issues raised by the additional instruction, and there was little prospect of immediate solution. Bull reported in March, 1774, that the Commons still demanded as its "sine quibus non" that the £1,500 sterling be replaced and that no money bills be passed in the form stipulated by the instruction. Despite Henry Laurens's confident prediction as early as the spring of 1773 that the instruction would be recalled, Dartmouth and his colleagues in the ministry remained insistent that the Commons either adhere to the instruction or pass a declaratory act.[80]

Events in the spring of 1774 finally led to the Commons' devising a means to ignore the additional instruction altogether. Unrest among the Indians on the southern frontier made the need for defensive measures urgent. To provide some rangers to patrol the critical area, the Commons introduced a money bill without the clauses required by the additional instruction. It hoped that public opinion would force the Council to accept the measure and thereby admit the Commons' right to pass money bills without the objectionable clauses specified by the instructions. But the Council preferred to assume the blame for not defending the frontier than to offend the ministry by passing a revenue measure that did not conform to the instruction. By rejecting the bill the Council gave the Commons an excuse for adopting a radical measure. Taking matters into its own hands, the House proceeded to audit accounts of all public creditors to January 1, 1773, and without consulting either Bull or the Council ordered its clerk to issue certificates of indebtedness to pay those accounts. The Commons promised to

---

[79] Laurens to Gervais and Laurens to Thomas Savage, both April 9, 1774, both *ibid.*, 266, 268–73.

[80] Dartmouth to Bull, October 28, 1773, January 8, May 4, 1774, and Bull to Dartmouth, March 10, 1774, all in Transcripts of Records Relating to South Carolina, XXXIII, 335; XXXIV, 2–3, 15–19, 33–34; Laurens to James Laurens, March 11, 1773, and Laurens to Garden, April 8, 1773, both in Laurens Letter Book, 1772–1774, pp. 59–62, 96–97; and Garth to Committee of Correspondence, May 20, July 5, November 13, 1773, all in Garth Letter Book, 152, 155, 157.

redeem the certificates the first time it succeeded in passing a tax bill, and its members, along with the Chamber of Commerce, pledged to accept the certificates as currency. The Council vigorously protested this action, and Bull prorogued the legislature, but everyone in the colony except Bull—including even the councilors—accepted the certificates. The success of this measure made the passage of a tax bill less imperative, while at the same time it permitted the Commons to sidestep the issue embodied in the additional instruction.[81]

Ironically, at the very time the Commons was acting unilaterally to ameliorate the colony's fiscal plight, imperial authorities were modifying the controversial instruction. As early as June, 1773, Garth had urged Dartmouth to revoke the instruction because the bonds designed by Bull in 1770 to be signed by the treasurers prevented those officers from paying out money except through the formal passage of an ordinance or act by all three branches of the legislature. Garth had also persuaded South Carolina's new governor, Lord William Campbell, that withdrawal of the instruction was absolutely necessary. Upon Campbell's request colonial officials omitted the 1770 instruction from his instructions so that the South Carolina representatives would "have no longer any pretence to say that they are not left at liberty to frame their Money Bills as they think fit." At the same time, however, by inserting another instruction absolutely prohibiting Campbell to pass any bill to replace money ordered out of the treasury by the sole authority of the Commons, the ministry made it clear that it was neither recognizing the Commons' power to order money from the treasury without executive approval nor consenting to the repayment of the money sent to Wilkes.[82]

---

[81] Bull to Dartmouth, March 24, May 3, 1774, both in Transcripts of Records Relating to South Carolina, XXXIV, 21–22, 36–40.

[82] Garth to Dartmouth, June 16, 1773, Dartmouth to Bull, May 4, 1774, and Dartmouth and others to Crown, June 20, 1774, all *ibid.*, XXXIII, 277–78; XXXIV, 33–34, 47–52; Labaree (ed.), *Royal Instructions*, I, 210; Campbell to Dartmouth, April 2, 1774, in *The Manuscript of the Earl of Dartmouth* (3 vols. in 2; London, 1887–1896), II, 207; Garth to Lowndes, February 1, 1773, and Garth to Committee of Correspondence, November 13, 1773, March 11, April 21, July 19, 1774, all in Garth Letter Book, 141, 157, 165, 171–72, 178–79; Laurens to John Laurens, April 8, 1774, and Laurens to Gervais, April 9, 16, 1774, all in Laurens Letter Book, 1772–1774, pp. 261–62, 268–73,

It is highly unlikely that this arrangement would have satisfied the South Carolina Commons, but it never had an opportunity to either accept or reject it. The ministry did not inform Bull of the precise changes in the royal instructions, and by the time Campbell arrived in the colony in June, 1775, the Wilkes Fund Controversy had been pushed into the background by questions of greater moment.[83] War had broken out in Massachusetts, and the Carolinians had turned their attention to the broader questions of American rights.[84] The Wilkes Fund dispute ended in stalemate; neither the Commons nor Crown officials ever yielded on the issue of the right of the Commons House to issue money from the treasury by its single authority.

The Wilkes Fund Controversy brought a number of older political developments and issues to their culmination. The Commons' exclusive control over all financial matters had been the central issue in South Carolina politics from the introduction of royal government in 1721 until the mid-1750's. The antipathy of the Commons towards the royal instructions and the denial that they were binding derived from the 1720's and had acquired increasing currency in succeeding decades. The Council had been declining in prestige and in political effectiveness since the 1740's, and the denial of its legislative authority was a reiteration of an earlier suggestion.[85]

The controversy was also instrumental in bringing South Carolina politicians to a full realization of the nature of the political challenge involved in Britain's new colonial policy. One of the

---

283–84; Laurens to John Laurens, April 19, May 10, 1774, both in "Laurens Correspondence," *South Carolina Historical and Genealogical Magazine*, IV (April, 1903), 101, 107. Two long official reports, one dated 1773 and the other without date, were prepared for Dartmouth and may be found in the Dartmouth Manuscripts (William L. Salt Library, Stafford, England), 777.

[83] See Dartmouth to Bull, December 10, 1774, and Alexander Innes to Dartmouth, May 1, 1775, both in Transcripts of Records Relating to South Carolina, XXXIV, 222; XXXV, 92–99; Innes to Dartmouth, May 16, June 3, 1775, in B. D. Bargar (ed.), "Charles Town Loyalism in 1775: The Secret Reports of Alexander Innes," *South Carolina Historical Magazine*, LXIII (July, 1962), 127–31; and Commons Journals, XXXIX, pt. 2, pp. 180–81 (January 25, 1775).

[84] *Ibid.*, 293, 302–305 (July 11, 24, 29, 1775).

[85] For an earlier airing of this same question see *South Carolina Gazette*, Supplement, May 13, 1756.

central issues of the American Revolution was the threat to assembly rights, and no other single event was so important in bringing that fact home to South Carolina political leaders and in convincing them of the seriousness of the imperial challenge as the Wilkes matter. Henry Laurens correctly interpreted the broader aims of British policy and the additional instruction as a "Scheme . . . to reduce us to the State of a Country Corporation." In attempting to curtail the Commons' authority to order money from the treasury without executive consent, the ministry was challenging a power that the Commons had exercised without contest for two decades, and the additional instruction seemed to be a blatant symbol of the slight regard imperial authorities had for the rights of American lower houses. The South Carolina Commons shared Henry Laurens's belief that "the Representative Body of the People in Carolina, when regularly Assembled, have and ought to enjoy all the Rights and Privileges of a free People—or in other words—all the Rights and Privileges, as a Branch of the Legislature, which are held, enjoyed and exercised by the House of Commons in Great Britain."[86] Its stubborn resistance indicated how vital those rights were to American legislators and how far they would go to preserve the political structures they had built over the previous century.

For five crucial years beginning in December, 1769, the Wilkes grant was the central issue in South Carolina politics, interrupting the normal process of government and contributing to the rise of an intense bitterness toward the ministry among South Carolina politicians. For them the description in the *Gazette* of a statue of Lord Hillsborough inscribed with the motto "Massachusetts is my wash-pot and South Carolina my Footstool!" was no idle jest. "What Shall we Say," lamented Henry Laurens in April, 1774, on the eve of the modification of the instruction, "of the Injury done to a province by a Ministerial Mandate held over that province and totally Stagnating public business for four Years." In October, 1774, after one of the frequent prorogations, the *South Carolina Gazette* complained that "we *still continue* in the Situation we have been for some Years past . . . with little more than a *nominal* Legis-

---

[86] Laurens to James Laurens, December 12, 1771, in Laurens Letter Book, 1771–1772, pp. 95–104.

lative Representation."[87] No annual tax bill was passed in South
Carolina after 1769, and no legislation at all after February, 1771.
For all practical purposes royal government in South Carolina
broke down four years earlier than it did in any of the other
colonies. There was no period of quiet in South Carolina. While
the flames of revolution cooled elsewhere in the colonies after the
repeal of most of the Townshend taxes, there was no relaxation in
the broader objectives of the new colonial policy. With the exception of parliamentary taxation no other issue was so important as
the Wilkes Fund matter in persuading South Carolina politicians
that their political fortunes would never be secure so long as they
were subject to the whims of a group of politicians over whom
they had no control and from whom they could expect no sympa-
thetic treatment of their grievances. In this sense, the Wilkes Fund
Controversy was the bridge to revolution in South Carolina.

I I I

The pamphlets reprinted here—the only publications of any
length produced by the Wilkes Fund Controversy—were a direct
result of the assault on the Council's legislative powers in the fall
of 1773. On January 20, 1774, the London bookseller Thomas Cadell published without any indication as to the author the *Considerations on Certain Political Transactions of the Province of
South Carolina*,[88] an 83-page review of the Wilkes Fund Controversy that employed irony and ridicule to condemn both the
original vote to Wilkes and the behavior of the Commons at every
stage of the dispute, especially its denial that the Council was an
upper house. Cadell claimed that the pamphlet "was the production of" a "person of Emenince" in England. But Henry Laurens,
still living in London, quickly recognized that it was the work of

---

[87] Laurens to Gervais, April 16, 1774, *ibid.*, 1772–1774, pp. 283–84; *South
Carolina Gazette*, September 6, 1773, October 24, 1774.
[88] The pamphlet was first advertised in the *Daily Advertiser* (London),
January 20, 1774. For this information I am indebted to Mr. Thomas R.
Adams of the John Carter Brown Library.

Sir Egerton Leigh, attorney general, surveyor general, and president of the South Carolina Council.[89] Although no one—Leigh, Cadell, or anyone else—in a position to know ever openly admitted Leigh's authorship, there can be little doubt that Laurens was right. Laurens had not only been an intimate friend of Leigh, who was married to his niece, but had felt the sting of Leigh's caustic invective during a heated pamphlet exchange in 1768–1769. Internal evidence, moreover, makes it absolutely clear to anyone familiar with Leigh's role in South Carolina politics since the Stamp Act crisis that he was the author. The author's frank admission at the beginning of the pamphlet that he was "a downright *Placeman*" and had been "for nearly twenty years"—Leigh's multiple office-holding had earned him the reputation in South Carolina as the placeman par excellence—and his treatment of his own role in the Council's commitment of the printer Thomas Powell in September, 1773, point directly to his authorship.[90]

When Laurens first saw the *Considerations* in Cadell's book shop, he vowed that these, "Specious, partial fallacious Considerations" should "not pass unnoticed." As soon as he realized that the *Considerations* was "the insidious production of Sir Egerton," however, he had some misgivings about "interfering in the Case," not merely because of his falling out with Leigh during the earlier pamphlet exchange but also because of a bitter personal quarrel of the previous year over Leigh's sexual involvement with his wife's sister, also Laurens's niece.[91] But Laurens finally concluded that he could not permit "such hellish Machinations" to destroy his

[89] Laurens to Gervais, January 24, 1774, Laurens to James Laurens, January 27, March 2, 1774, and Laurens to John Laurens, January 28, 1774, all four in Laurens Letter Book, 1772–1774, pp. 191–92, 194–96, 202, 218–21, 238–40.

[90] For a perceptive analysis of Leigh's role in South Carolina politics; his friendship with, estrangement from, and pamphlet exchange with Laurens; and the internal evidence in the *Considerations* that so clearly indicates Leigh's authorship, see Robert M. Calhoon and Robert M. Weir, "The Scandalous History of Sir Egerton Leigh," *William and Mary Quarterly*, 3d ser., XXVI (January, 1969), 47–74.

[91] On the details of this episode, see *ibid.*, 63–64, and Laurens to Leigh, January 30, 1773, and Laurens to Gervais, November 26, 1773, Laurens Letter Book, 1772–1774, pp. 36–39, 137–42. For Laurens's vow that the *Considerations* would be answered, see Laurens to Gervais, January 24, 1774, *ibid.*, 191–92.

"country's peace & Welfare." Determined to present the "Case of So[uth] Carolina . . . in a light of Truth and Justice," he enlisted Ralph Izard, Jr., another South Carolinian then living in London, "who Zealously took up the Cause." Izard persuaded his friend, Dr. Arthur Lee, scion of the Virginia Lees, to write an answer. A "pretty writer" and "firm friend to his Country's Cause," Lee was widely known to have been the author of a number of anonymous pro-American pamphlets and newspaper essays published in London.[92]

To supply Lee with the necessary information on a dispute about which he must have known but little, Laurens busily collected materials from Charles Garth and James Crokatt, respectively the present and former agents for South Carolina, and spent his mornings "rummaging . . . at the Plantation Office, and elsewhere," for relevant documents. Together with Izard, Laurens arranged with bookseller John Almon for publication and assumed the financial costs, including a sum for Lee, for which they hoped to be reimbursed by the South Carolina Commons. Although Lee had apparently finished the pamphlet by late February and the printer had run off a first impression shortly thereafter, publication was delayed for over a month until April 8, while Laurens, against "Some opposition," expunged "many Severe Articles" of "personal Censure against Leigh" and made a few additions.[93] Entitled *Answer to Considerations on Certain Political Transactions of the Province of South Carolina*, the pamphlet, 140 pages in length, was a detailed point-by-point answer to the *Considerations* and a slashing attack both upon the role of the ministry in the dispute

---

[92] Laurens to Gervais, January 24, 1774, Laurens to John Laurens, February 18, 1774, both in *ibid.*, 191–92, 217.

[93] Although Laurens sent a copy of the first impression to his brother James so that he might "See how freely I used my pen—as well as what additions are made," no copy of it apparently survives. On the preparation and printing of the *Answer*, see Laurens to Gervais, January 24, April 9, 1774, Laurens to James Crokatt, February 16, 1774, Laurens to James Laurens, February 17, April 13, 1774; Laurens to Alexander Garden, April 13, 1774, all six in *ibid.*, 191–92, 211–16, 268–79. According to Laurens, he insisted upon exorcising some of the personal abuse of Leigh because it was "incongruous with the principal Subject." But it is clear that he was also worried that people in South Carolina would attribute such abuse to his personal animosity against Leigh to the detriment both of the pamphlet and of his own reputation.

and, despite Laurens's editing, upon its author. In "point of Style & . . . keenness of . . . ridicule," it was perhaps not, as Reverend Alexander Garden of Charleston remarked, "a Match for the . . . *Considerations*," but it was, nevertheless, as one reviewer declared, "an answer with a vengence!"[94]

Largely because their publication coincided with the passage of the Coercive Acts, neither of these pamphlets seems to have attracted much attention or had any impact on political events in either London or South Carolina. The *Considerations* received a long and highly laudatory review in the *Monthly Review*, in which the reviewer complimented Leigh on his "good sense and impartiality," endorsed his views on the Wilkes Fund dispute and "the form of colony government," and reprinted lengthy extracts.[95] But the pamphlet seems to have sold few copies. Similarly, George III may—as Laurens was assured he would—have read the *Answer*,[96] but few others did. The *Monthly Review*, in a short and hostile notice, described it as "coarse and Virulent,"[97] and during the first month it sold only 42 copies; Laurens reported with extreme disappointment that its sale could "only keep pace with that" of the *Considerations* and that there was little prospect that more copies would be sold. "The Sale of Such Papers," he wrote to his brother James, "is always made upon the first publishing or not at all."[98]

In South Carolina there was, if anything, even less interest. Leigh's pamphlet was not even noted in the Charleston newspapers until September; the *Answer* was not mentioned at all,[99] and Laurens received only one response from the various friends in the colony to whom he had sent copies of the *Answer*. As late as February, 1775, Laurens, then back in Charleston, wrote Izard that "not a single Syllable has been imparted to me upon the subject of the ANSWER," and it is doubtful that Izard and Laurens

---

[94] Laurens to Ralph Izard, Jr., September 20, 1774, *ibid.*, 365–68; *Monthly Review*, L (June, 1774), 486.

[95] *Monthly Review*, L (March, 1774), 208–12.

[96] Laurens to John Laurens, April 8, 1774, and Laurens to Thomas Savage, April 9, 1774, both in Laurens Letter Book, 1772–1774, pp. 261–62, 266.

[97] *Monthly Review*, L (June, 1774), 486–87.

[98] Laurens to James Laurens, May 12, 1774, Laurens Letter Book, 1772–1774, pp. 305–308.

[99] Extracts from Leigh's pamphlet were published in the *South Carolina Gazette*, September 19, 1774.

ever were repayed "the hundred Guineas" they had put up for writing and publishing expenses.[100]

I V

However profound their disagreements, the authors of the *Considerations* and the *Answer* agreed upon one point: the ultimate issue in the Wilkes Fund Controversy was the nature of colony constitutions. Both saw the constitution of South Carolina as under attack by malignant forces bent upon its destruction. For Leigh the guilty parties were the *"Popular Member[s] of the Community"* who ever since the Stamp Act crisis had been fomenting resistance to and attempting to usurp the legitimate powers of British authority, following every new claim "by another, which, generating [still] more, . . . multiplied like the encreasing power of numbers, in a course, as it were, of *Geometrical Progression*." Initially, in South Carolina, these popular leaders had been content merely to follow the example of New England, but at length they grew so "Insolently Saucy and Arrogantly Vain" that they determined "to find" their "own Feet" and to demonstrate their *"Originality"* by the Wilkes Fund vote, an act of such *"vast Reach, profound Depth, and uncommon Boldness"* that none of their *"Northern Tutors"* dared follow the example. By that single act, South Carolina's popular leaders had pushed the power of the Commons House of Assembly, their primary base of operations, far beyond that even of the British House of Commons. Together with the Commons' declaration that the Council was not an upper house in 1774, this act had so subverted the existing civil order that the very "bands . . . of Society" were "loosened, the plan of his Majesty's Government [was] totally disordered, and the Commons," like its English

---

[100] Laurens to James Laurens, May 12, 1774, and Laurens to Ralph Izard, Jr., September 20, 1774, both in Laurens Letter Book, 1772–1774, pp. 305–308, 365–68; Laurens to Izard, February 10, 1775, in "Izard-Laurens Correspondence," *South Carolina Historical and Genealogical Magazine,* XII (January, 1921), 1–3; and Ralph Izard, Jr., to Edward Rutledge, May 25, 1775, in A. I. Deas (ed.), *Correspondence of Mr. Ralph Izard of South Carolina . . .* (New York, 1844), 77.

counterpart in that "unhappy area of 1648," became "the *vortex* which swallows all the power."[101]

That a conspiracy of power was indeed threatening to overturn the existing constitution of South Carolina Lee had no doubt, but he located it not in the actions of the colony's popular leaders but in the sinister behavior of the British ministry, spurred on by misrepresentations from deceitful and interested wretches in the South Carolina Council. "Ever watchful for Opportunities to advance their own Importance," they "worked under Ground" through "some secret Emissary" with Hillsborough to gratify their mutual "Lust of absolute Dominion." It was well known, said Lee, that it had long been "the Study of Ministers . . . to invade the Liberties of the People, especially in America." Of all the "dark and midnight" schemes undertaken by the ministers in pursuit of this malevolent design, however, none seemed to Lee so "entirely futile and splenetic," so "Vain and absurd in its Object; unjust and injurious in its Consequences; violent and unconstitutional in its Principle," as the additional instruction of April, 1770. Nor could there be any greater proof of the sinister intent of the instruction than the total refusal of the ministry to consider any of the "several Applications and Petitions" made by the Commons against it in an attempt to clear up the misrepresentation on which it was based and to secure its withdrawal.[102]

To a large extent, these opposing conceptions of the nature of the controversy turned around contradictory ideas about the character of the South Carolina constitution. Leigh's position was that the constitution was entirely "*derivative*" from the Crown, "wholly *ex gratia*," and "that, without the King's Grace, we had been destitute of any Constitution whatsoever." Leigh did not argue that the king could give the colony any form of constitution he chose. Because the colonies were not "conquered Countries" but "parts and parcels of the British Empire, and settled by British Subjects," he could give "no other Constitution . . . than one resembling that of England," one that was both in accord with traditional British "Constitutional Principles" and "agreeable to the Laws and Practice of his own Kingdom." Thus, although the British constitution,

---

[101] *Considerations,* 3–4, 6, 20–22, 60–61.
[102] *Answer,* 1, 3, 12, 16, 23–24, 29, 38–39, 43, 60, 123.

and not the king, was the original source of whatever rights and privileges the colonists might enjoy, Leigh was careful to insist that it was the king—and the king alone—who actually extended those rights and privileges to the colony by the royal commission to his governor. Because the constitution of South Carolina was therefore entirely derivative from the king through the royal commission, it followed both that the authority of all segments of the government—the Commons House of Assembly as well as that of the upper house and the administration—flowed exclusively from that commission and from no other source whatever and that the constitution itself was always "subject to such modifications upon Constitutional Principles, as His Majesty shall . . . see proper and expedient." As long as he was careful not to violate the basic principles of the British constitution, the king could change the colony's constitution at will and by his sole authority. No binding contract between the king and the inhabitants of South Carolina required their consent to such changes. Only in cases involving positive "subsisting Laws" formally ratified by the king and the people through their representatives was the approval of the colonists required. With no authority which did not derive through the king, the colonists could never alter their constitution without the king's authorization.[103]

One of the central principles of the British Constitution—the very basis, said Leigh, quoting the eminent lawyer Sir William Blackstone, of the "true excellence of the English Government"—which the king had originally sought to incorporate into the constitutions of the colonies was the concept of balance whereby "all the parts" of the government formed "a mutual check upon each other." Thus, in the British Parliament, the House of Commons, representing the "People," acted as a "check upon the Nobility" in the House of Lords, while the king functioned "as a check upon both." In trying to fashion legislatures for the colonies after this model, the king, because there was no colonial nobility, had had to resort to the appointment of a small group of prominent men in each colony to form an upper house to serve as the middle branch. Like the House of Lords, the primary function of this body was to

---

[103] *Considerations*, 35, 37, 42, 53–54, 56, 63.

act as a "*Barrier* to withstand the Encroachments of the Lower House," to use its "Negative and Controuling Power, in all Legislative Acts" to maintain "a due Balance in the Constitution."[104]

"Owing to an *Original Error*" in the constitution of the upper houses, however, they had proved unable to perform this function adequately. Appointed only during the king's pleasure and lacking, therefore, the permanency and total "*Independency*" that were the distinctive hallmarks of the Lords, the upper houses had neither the strength nor the status within their respective communities to resist the lower houses' voracious appetite for power. The result in South Carolina was that the authority of the "People's Representatives in General Assembly" had increased so much that the "due equipoise" of the constitution had been "in a great measure lost, and the weight of power" had come to center almost wholly "with the People." Until the Crown saw fit to correct this "*Error*" by giving members of the upper houses life tenures and thereby conferring upon them that "*Independency* which is so necessary to this station, and so agreeable to the Constitution of the Parent-State," the task of restraining the lower houses and preserving the balance of the constitution, Leigh strongly implied, necessarily devolved upon the king. So weak was the authority of the upper houses that the old balance no longer obtained, and, as Leigh correctly sensed, a new de facto balance between king and people had taken its place.[105]

The total inability of the king's governor and the upper house to prevent the South Carolina Commons from ordering money from the treasury by its sole authority thus made it absolutely essential for the Crown to intervene to check such a radical "departure from the Constitution" by the additional instruction of April, 1770. Opponents of the instruction had of course grounded their arguments upon custom, arguing that "usage . . . for a series of years, without controul or interruption" made the Commons' exercise of that authority thoroughly constitutional. But Leigh argued that "the Precedents . . . of new Communities are of very little weight" and, in any case, that "Time gives no sanctions to Acts illegal in them-

---

[104] *Ibid.*, 24–25, 36–37, 44–45, 50–51, 67–69.
[105] *Ibid.*, 24–26, 60–61, 67–69.

selves." That the practice in dispute was precisely such an act Leigh had no doubt. Because it derived all of its authority from the Crown, the Commons obviously could never make so fundamental an alteration in the constitution of the colony on its own, could never extend its "Rights beyond the original views and intention of those" who were responsible for its very being without explicit authorization from the king. The "*political,* as well as the *corporeal* System," Leigh declared, "stands in constant need of correction," and such "uncommon tumours" as the Commons had introduced into the "Body Politic" had to be "speedily removed and wisely managed" before the whole constitution was deformed and destroyed.[106]

Predictably, in the *Answer*, Lee took issue with Leigh on virtually every important point. Leigh's assertion that "the Constitution and Liberties of the Provinces" were "merely *ex gratia,* flowing wholly from the Bounty of the Crown, that they should be abridged or modelled" in any way the Crown and its advisers saw fit, was the very "Extremity of Wickedness." That "courtly and convenient Doctrine," Lee declared, reached "back somewhat more than a Century, into the Days of omnipotent Prerogative," and was scarcely compatible with the free constitution of Georgian Britain. To say, as Leigh had, that the British constitution was the source of the colonists' constitutions and rights while at the same time asserting that they were entirely derivative from the Crown was, for Lee, a blatant contradiction. Lee agreed that colonial liberties sprang directly "from the Rights and Privileges of *British* Subjects" but denied that the king had any role whatever in extending them to the colonies. They were, he said, "Coeval with the Constitution" of Britain and could neither be "created, nor . . . abolished by the Crown." Far from being the source of those privileges, the king's original charter to South Carolina "was only a Recognition that emigrating could not work any Forfeiture of the undoubted Rights of the Subject"—rights, Lee carefully emphasized, which were "equal, not inferior, to those of the Crown." Nor could the Crown's subsequent commissions and instructions to its governors after it had assumed administration of the colony from the proprietors in

---

[106] *Ibid.,* 18, 24–28, 71.

any way abridge or modify those rights, much less constitute their legal foundation, as Leigh had argued. Himself a "Creature of the Constitution," the king obviously had no more "Power of making, modelling, and controuling the Constitution" in the colonies than he had in Britain itself. Thus, whereas Leigh thought it necessary only for colonial constitutions to be consistent with the British constitution—a conception that gave the Crown considerable latitude in shaping them—Lee contended that the colonists were entitled to all rights of Britons and that the embodiment of those rights in the colonial constitutions was automatic and obligatory— an argument which accorded the Crown no role in determining either the form or the content of those constitutions.[107]

Perhaps the most fundamental liberty the colonists thus inherited, and the most sacred feature of their constitutions, was the right to a free representative government. As the representatives of the people of South Carolina, the South Carolina Commons, Lee believed, stood upon precisely the same legal foundations, performed exactly the same functions, and had the very same relationship to the Crown and to its constituents as did the House of Commons in Britain. Just as the king had no authority to give "a Rule of Conduct" to either house of the legislature in Britain, so he could not "direct, instruct, or dictate to" the assemblies in the colonies without manifestly destroying that "mutual Check and Balance" which Leigh had admitted was "the very Essence of the Constitution." The additional instruction of April, 1770, was pernicious precisely because it attempted to extend the power of the Crown beyond its legitimate sphere. By seeking to "limit the Uses, or prescribe the Purpose, for which the People, or their Representatives, are to give their own Money," that instruction was a manifest violation of the constitution, "an arbitrary and dangerous Interposition of Prerogative" in a matter which was "the peculiar and incommunicable Power of the Commons."[108]

Lee's lengthy objections to the Council's acting in a legislative capacity rested on a similar base. The Council's abject dependence upon the Crown, especially the precarious and impermanent tenure

---

[107] *Answer*, 3, 101–104.
[108] *Ibid.*, 29–30, 48, 52–53, 59, 62, 103–104.

of its members during the king's pleasure, rendered it so "totally different from the House of Lords" that it was impossible for it to play a corresponding constitutional role because it would never act as a "Check upon the Crown." For the Council to function as an upper house merely tipped the balance of the constitution greatly in favor of the Crown by giving it control of two-thirds of the legislature. Indeed, Leigh had inadvertently admitted as much when he had written that the Council's primary concern as an upper house was to assist the royal governor in resisting the continual trespasses of the Commons upon the rights of the Crown. But, Lee asked, who was going to protect the rights of the people against "dangerous Usurpations" on the part of the Crown? "No Judge living," Lee declared, "can maintain, upon constitutional Principles, that the Council, constituted as it now stands, is, or ought to be an Upper House of Assembly."[109]

In direct contrast to Leigh, who had argued that the Council had to function as a middle branch of the legislature to preserve the equilibrium of the constitution, Lee thus contended that the constitution could never be properly balanced until the Council had been eliminated completely from any share in the legislative process. The only suitable distribution of power in the colonies was an equal division between Crown and people, with the latter having "One-half of the legislative Power."[110] This was the "established Constitution" the king found when he took over South Carolina, said Lee, in a blatant historical error, and the king had no authority "to alter the Constitution, and invest a Council of his own Creation with Rights and Powers which he *does not possess.*" He could, of course, "vest the Powers of Government, *which he does possess* [by virtue of his purchase from the proprietors], in his Instrument the Governor" through his royal commission and instructions. But insofar as those documents had sought to endow the Council with legislative powers, they were "clearly unconstitutional or irrelative." That the Council had in fact functioned as an upper house for over half a century since South Carolina had

---

[109] *Ibid.*, 102–103, 112–14, 120–22, 125.

[110] *Ibid.*, 98–99. For a similar line of argument in South Carolina almost twenty years earlier, see the article signed T——s W——t, May 6, 1756, in *South Carolina Gazette*, Supplement, May 13, 1756.

become a royal colony did not adequately establish its right to do so because, said Lee, quoting Sir Edward Coke, "*Consuetudo nunquam prejudicat veritati*"—custom at no time prejudices truth. "No Antiquity" could legitimate any practice that was unreasonable or inconsistent with the principles of the constitution.[111]

The authority of custom in connection with the Commons' vote to Wilkes was, however, an entirely different matter. For one thing, the Commons' power to issue money from the treasury without executive consent was simply a logical extension of its power over the purse and a necessary counterbalance to the preponderant weight of the Crown in the South Carolina constitution. Moreover, as everyone understood, the authority as well as many of the specific powers and privileges of the British House of Commons rested in large part upon custom and usage, the *lex parliamenti*, and, because the South Carolina Commons corresponded so closely to its British counterpart in virtually every respect, Lee was absolutely certain that "the Sanction of long Usage" was sufficient to justify its exercise of that power. Thus, the vote to Wilkes was "not Novel," as Leigh had claimed, but *"constitutional in its Mode"* because it *"was agreeable to the Usage and Practice, both antient and modern, of the Commons House of Assembly in the Province of* South Carolina." "There are some old-fashioned People," Lee asserted, in a direct challenge to Leigh on the most fundamental and crucial point in dispute, "who will be constant in thinking, that what has prevailed from the Beginning of the Colony, without Question or Controul, is part of the Constitution; and that [such] ancient and undoubted Rights are of all others the most sacred and valuable." What Lee was contending, of course, was that the South Carolina Commons, like the British Commons, had its own peculiar *lex parliamenti*, a cluster of powers, privileges, and precedents firmly grounded in custom and in the implicit acquiescence of the Crown. No mere *"Indulgence"* or *"Tenure at Will,"* these customary powers, Lee believed, were a vital part of the constitution

---

[111] *Answer*, 98–99, 104–105, 111, 113–15, 134–35. A year later Lee used this same argument and cited the *Answer* in objecting to the alteration of the Massachusetts Council by the Massachusetts Government Act in his *Speech Intended to Have Been Delivered in the House of Commons* . . . (London, 1775), 14–15.

that could never be abridged or altered by the unilateral action of the Crown. "The Boast, the Blessing of *English* Subjects," wrote Lee, was that they were "governed by Law and not by Will," and among the essential ingredients of that law the customs and usages of parliaments—including colonial lower houses—were among the most important.[112]

By thus reducing the issues to one of will versus law, Lee, no matter how sincerely, had somewhat misrepresented the major point in contention between Leigh and himself. Leigh had never argued that the royal will was not circumscribed by law. On the contrary, he had been careful to specify that the king was bound in all of his actions by the fundamental law of the parent state. What he had contended was that the king had originally prescribed a constitution for South Carolina based on British constitutional principles, that, therefore, the colonists derived whatever rights and liberties they were guaranteed by that constitution through the king, that the king could alter the constitution *at will* as long as he did not violate the precepts of the British constitution, that the South Carolina Commons could not change the constitution through custom and usage unless those changes had the *explicit* consent of the king, and that any usage that was contrary to British constitutional principles was automatically void and unconstitutional even if the king had explicitly consented to it.

In opposition, Lee had argued that the South Carolina constitution—as well as the rights and liberties embodied in it—derived not from the king but directly from the colonists' inherited rights as Britons, that the king, far from having prescribed the constitution, had done no more than merely recognize its existence, that the king could not alter the constitution under any circumstances, except possibly with the consent of the colonists, that any local custom of long standing that had not been explicitly rejected by the king was, ipso facto, an inviolable part of the constitution, and that both the South Carolina Commons and its constituents could through usage modify particular practices or aspects of the British constitution to meet new and different conditions in the colony. The major point of disagreement, then, was not whether the colo-

---

[112] *Answer*, 12, 24, 43–46, 51–52, 68, 77, 115.

nists were to be governed by will or law but what the respective roles of the king and local custom were in determining the shape and content of the South Carolina constitution.

V

Whether the constitutions and liberties of the colonists derived from the will of the Crown or from the colonists' inheritance as Britons, whether those constitutions were fixed according to an a priori design modeled on the British constitution or were perpetually adapting to new circumstances through local custom and usage, and the precise relationship of the Crown, on the one hand, and the lower house of assembly, on the other, to the constitutions of the colonies—each of these questions about the extent and character of colonial self-government had been a major, if often only an implicit, source of tension in imperial-colonial relations since the middle of the seventeenth century. They were rooted in the seventeenth-century English debate between the Crown and the House of Commons over whether, as J. G. A. Pocock has written, "all laws, customs and privileges were derived ultimately from [the king's] . . . will" or were traceable to "ancient custom and consequently . . . not derived from his will."[113]

In this debate, *will* "came to be thought of as a power divorced from custom and standing over against it," while the concept of *custom*, as it was developed by a long line of legal theorists from Sir Edward Coke to Sir Matthew Hale, came to mean "either law in perpetual adjustment or law as unchanging and immemorial." The latter meaning often implied "a static and unchanging content," while the former connoted "that custom was constantly being subjected to the test of experience, so that if immemorial it was, equally, always up to date, and that it was ultimately rooted in nothing other than experience." This latter conception of "immemorial custom in perpetual adaptation" received its most sophis-

---

[113] *The Ancient Constitution and the Feudal Law: English Historical Thought in the Seventeenth Century* (2d ed.; New York, 1967), 233–34.

ticated formulation in the hands of Hale and "presented custom, the gradual process by which men adjusted their institutions to their needs, as the origin of all law and the ultimate reason why laws could not be derived from the sovereign's will." The emphasis in this formulation was thus not on the necessity for the periodic return to first principles recommended by Machiavelli and his intellectual descendents, but upon "gradual process, imperceptible change, the origin and slow growth of institutions in usage, tacit consent, prescription and adaptation"; and law, constitutions, and institutions were conceived of not as the sudden and ingenious creations of men, but as the accretions of history, which was itself seen as "an unceasing and undying process, in which the generations are partners and in which men perpetually adapt themselves to new needs and new situations."[114]

In Britain, this conception of custom fell into decay after the Restoration. Under the later Stuarts, as Pocock has shown, parliamentary thinkers tended to reduce it to little more than the "crude dogma that there had always been a Parliament," and there was a strong tendency following the Glorious Revolution of 1688 to shift the emphasis away "from ancient custom and precedent to unhistorical reason." To the great extent that the original, ancient British constitution was thought by the vast majority of the British political nation to have been restored by the Revolution and, therefore, to have been once again fixed, now hopefully for all time, in its pristine form, men were inclined to stress the timelessness and rationality of the original principles on which the constitution was founded and to de-emphasize the role of custom as the process of perpetual adaptation in shaping the constitution. The result was that "the concept of custom, and of English institutions as founded on custom, ran underground," as it were, from the Revolution until it was once again given major emphasis by Edmund Burke during the reign of George III. One consequence of this de-emphasis seems to have been that the potential tension between the older conception of the constitution as rooted in custom and the newer

---

[114] *Ibid.*, 15, 19, 233–36, 242, and J. G. A. Pocock, "Burke and the Ancient Constitution: A Problem in the History of Ideas," *Historical Journal*, III, No. 2 (1960), 131–32, 136.

idea of the fundamental law as derived from rational and eternal principles remained almost wholly implicit and rarely rose to the surface of public life in early Georgian Britain.[115]

The story was entirely different with the colonies, where imperial officials in Britain still claimed for colonial governors many of the prerogatives that had been challenged by the House of Commons under the Stuarts and had subsequently been relinquished by the Crown during the Revolution settlement. Because royal governors inevitably based their claims for these prerogatives upon the royal will as expressed in their commissions and instructions, while lower houses defended colonial privileges on the basis of the colonists' rights as inherited through the custom of the ancient constitution and the common law, the conflicts between prerogative and liberty invariably called forth the rhetoric of the seventeenth-century English struggle between Crown and Parliament and thus came to be conceived of as contests between *will* and *law as custom*.[116] Increasingly, during the mid-eighteenth century, however, governors grounded their opposition to the encroachments of the lower houses upon their assigned prerogatives less upon the commissions and instructions per se, and less, therefore, upon the royal will, than upon the original and fundamental principles of the British constitution as embodied in the commissions and instructions. At the same time, the lower houses were more and more forced to justify the often idiosyncratic "privileges" they had developed as a defense against the exaggerated claims of the governors by an appeal to local usage and custom.[117] As a consequence, the conflict between *reason* and *custom* that had remained largely only implicit in British constitutional thought since the Glorious Revolution became increasingly explicit in the colonies during the 1740's and 1750's and was superimposed upon and fused with the older dichotomy between will and custom.

---

[115] *Ibid.*, 135, 141; Pocock, *Ancient Constitution*, 234–35, 241–43.

[116] On this point see my "Political Mimesis: A Consideration of the Historical and Cultural Roots of Legislative Behavior in the British Colonies in the Eighteenth Century," *American Historical Review*, LXXV, No. 2 (1969), 337–360.

[117] See Greene, *Quest for Power*, 16–17, for a brief discussion of this development.

This fusion tended to obscure the essential issues in the debates over the character and extent of colonial self-government, and the tendency was strongly reinforced by the failure of Crown officials in Britain to give any more than sporadic support to the royal governors in these debates during the half-century prior to 1765. The results were that neither of the two opposing conceptions of the constitutions of the colonies was ever fully articulated and that the constitutional relationship between Britain and the colonies remained thoroughly ambiguous. From the perspective of the Stamp Act crisis and the debate over Parliament's authority over the colonies, however, older questions about the Crown's relationship to the colonies and the nature of the colonial constitutions acquired a new and heightened urgency, and they became the central issues in several bitter contests between the Crown and colonial lower houses, including the Wilkes Fund Controversy. Attacking these questions with an intensity and a thoroughness they had never before received, the antagonists in such controversies, as the two pamphlets here reprinted so pointedly illustrate, made it abundantly clear for the first time that the primary point at issue was whether, as the Crown contended, the constitutions of the colonies had been set by the Crown for all time according to the unchanging principles of the British constitution or, as the colonists asserted, they were in a perpetual state of change as institutions and law adapted through usage to new conditions.

The full exposure of the wide divergence over this question represented a major escalation of the pre-Revolutionary debate between Britain and the colonies. In opposing the Stamp Act and the Townshend measures, the colonists had denied Parliament's jurisdiction over the internal affairs of the colonies—a sphere in which Parliament had not, prior to 1765, been very active. Now, by arguing explicitly that the Crown's authority over the colonies was limited not only by its obligation to conform to the canons of the British constitution but by local usage and custom, they were issuing a fundamental challenge to the Crown's traditional conception of its constitutional role in the colonies. For the ultimate implications of the argument were that sovereignty over the Empire resided not in the Crown, much less in the British Parliament, but rather in the separate constitutions of each of the colonies as they had emerged from the colonists' inherent rights as Britons and from colonial usage and custom, and that the local legislatures played just as dynamic a part in this process as the House of Commons did in shaping the British constitution.

The importance to the pre-Revolutionary debate of this challenge to the Crown and of the colonists' reliance upon their local constitutions as a defense against measures taken by both Parliament and the Crown in its executive capacity has often been underestimated, as historians have emphasized the more visible and more immediate quarrel over parliamentary authority and the colonists' use of the more generalized concepts of rights of Englishmen and natural rights to support their position. The two pamphlets that follow do not suggest that this emphasis ought to be reversed; they do suggest, however, that the Crown's relationship to the colonies and the nature and integrity of the constitutions of individual colonies were issues of considerably more significance in the period from 1763 to 1776 than has usually been supposed. Because they illuminate those issues so fully and illustrate their integral relationship to the pre-Revolutionary controversy, as well as because they contribute to an enlarged understanding of the emotional intensity and the specific intellectual issues involved in the Wilkes Fund dispute per se, these tracts deserve the serious attention of all students of the American Revolution.

A NOTE ON THE TEXTS

This edition of the *Considerations* and the *Answer* is the first since the original. In reproducing the texts, I have carefully maintained the original spelling, capitalization, italicization, and punctuation, though a few typographical errors by the original printers have been silently corrected. The original footnotes appear at the bottom of the page and are indicated by the asterisks and other symbols used in the original texts, while my notes are designated by arabic numerals and are printed together at the end of the two texts. All references to the pamphlets in the introduction and in both the original and my notes to the texts are to the original pagination of the pamphlets as designated, in this volume, by brackets inserted in the text. The *Considerations* is reprinted from the copy in the Michigan State University Library, and the *Answer* from the copy in the Rare Book Division of the Library of Congress. I am grateful to both institutions for permission to use their copies as the basis for this edition. Professor Majorie E. Gesner of Michigan State University helped me to solve several puzzles in connection with the many legal annotations, and my colleague Professor John W. Baldwin and his wife Jenny aided me in translating one long, difficult Latin passage from the *Answer*.

CONSIDERATIONS
on certain
POLITICAL TRANSACTIONS
of the
PROVINCE of
SOUTH CAROLINA

CONSIDERATIONS

on certain

POLITICAL TRANSACTIONS

of the

PROVINCE of

SOUTH CAROLINA:

containing

A VIEW

of the

COLONY LEGISLATURES

(Under the Description of That of CAROLINA in Particular).

with

OBSERVATIONS,

Shewing their RESEMBLANCE to the BRITISH MODEL.

—*In Vitium Libertas excidit, et Vim Dignam Lege regi.*
Horat.[1]

·o❧ By Sir Egerton Leigh ☙o·

LONDON:
Printed for T. CADELL, in the Strand,
MDCCLXXIV.

CONSIDERATIONS, ETC.

It is the Duty of a Good Citizen and a Loyal Subject, to promote, as far as in him lies, the Public Service; and one step towards it is, candidly to examine those Principles and Tenets which divide Men's Minds, and inflame one part of a Community who glory in adopting, and the rest in opposing and rejecting them.

Opposite Sentiments, long remaining unexplained, always engender Disputes; and as it is a nice and delicate concern to discuss the Causes of Public Discontent, the business often is neglected.— Hence it is that prejudices naturally arise; loose opinions steal into Men's hearts; and That is held for Truth which flatters the present Humour; besides, there is a Fashion in the Mode of *Thinking*, as well as in the Mode of *Dress*.

The great aim of a Worthy Writer ought to be directed to the search of Truth.—He may be permitted to express himself with so much warmth as will convince his Reader that he feels: but intemperance and passion mock all serious disquisition, and must be carefully avoided; for *over-heated Zeal never helps a bad Cause, and seldom serves a good one.*

Under this kind of influence and persuasion I take up the pen; but with that modest fear, that trembling awe, and mistrustful apprehension, which almost shake my resolution. I therefore [2] humbly bespeak the candid attention of my Readers, and those liberal allowances which the Generous Public are ever ready to make, when modestly implored, and not arrogantly or self-sufficiently demanded.

The best proof of my own candour is to avow my connection with the Crown; that I am a downright *Placeman;* have been so for nearly twenty years; and that I owe more to the Royal Favor, than any merit I possess can justly claim. And now, methinks, I may fairly be allowed to say, according to the Maxim of the Times, that I have given a most Disgustful Figure of myself—a monstrous Portrait!—the painting whereof is coarse, the colours glaring, and the whole Piece obnoxious to the sight. I fear the number of my Readers will be greatly lessened.—Not a Person out of Place will, probably, peruse me; and the Patriots will, one and all, avoid me: for according to modern Acceptation, a Man in Place is a perfect *Basilisk* to a *Patriot* out of Place; it being now very manifest to all Mankind, that this single circumstance alone, *the being in or out of Place,* defines and gives the difference, between a *Popular Member* of the Community, and a *Courtier* at St. James's. No matter—The Ill-favoured Figure is before the Public Eye; and they are welcome to use it with all the Gothic Freedom of their Ancestors, and to censure or approve.

It is not my intention to enquire into the Policy of imposing Stamp-duties on the Subjects in America; neither do I presume to determine any thing respecting an Act so extremely offensive to the Colonies in general; but I beg to offer a small conjecture, That the Repeal thereof will prove to be an *Epoch* in the Annals of British Story; for, since that Memorable Period, the Public Affairs of these Countries have been in a state [3] of almost ruinous Distraction; and what was probably meant to inspire Gratitude and Love, has rather kindled Rancour and Disgust.—The affection of the Parent State seems to be considered as the effects of aged fondness and impotent attachment: and sorry I am to say that Concessions have daily produced Usurpation and Resistance; one claim has been followed by another, which, generating more, have multiplied like the encreasing power of numbers, in a course, as it were, of *Geometrical Progression.*

By slow, and almost imperceptible degrees, Jealousies and Distrusts have fastened upon Men's Understandings; and the Tone and Temper of the People's Minds have undergone some Fatal Changes. Man is not born for a series of indulgence—and Human Nature teaches us, that we cannot bear a constant Tide of flattering Success, without becoming Insolently Saucy, and Arrogantly Vain. It is as necessary that some Line should limit and ascertain the exact Boundaries of our Political System, as that Landmarks should be made to determine the extent and figure of our Lands. Dormant Rights likewise, and supposed Titles, are eternal sources of Confusion! And such is the strange Contradiction of our Nature, that we never complacently yield a clear Right with so good a grace, as when it is powerfully demanded. Thus we may be justly stiled,

"Children of a larger Growth;" for Children lose their temper when too much humoured and caressed.

It is not my design at present to carry my Observations beyond the Boundary Line of the Province of South Carolina; though I must take notice by the way, that when American Disputes ran very high, some years ago, and all the Men of Genius in our Sister Colonies strained every [4] nerve, and summoned every power, to support the favorite Doctrine of the Times, *we* stood *gazing* with a silent Admiration; and, like the stupid Devotees of old at the Mystic Oracles of Delphos and Apollo, waited for a Breath of Inspiration from the Renowned Town of Boston! In short, we had just so much Understanding as enabled us to Copy, with tolerable accuracy, those Lessons of Political skill, which were kindly wafted to us *from the Land of Vision* (as a decent Writer prettily enough stiles the Province of New-England). This, however, was our *Ultima Thule*[2] for some time.—The power of Mimickry baffled all the powers of Genius, and our Ambition was well satisfied; partly under the persuasion of being good Scholars, and partly under the flattering hope that we might in due season become Masters of the Art. Practice ever gives confidence—and as a Child, by frequent essays to walk, is encouraged to lay aside his *go-cart,* and quarrel with his *leading-strings,* so we, in like manner, began to take Courage, to feel our own Strength, and to find our own Feet. There is something very soaring in the Human Mind; and an Idea of *Originality* is flattering to a great degree. Hence it is, that I date those Memorable Exertions, which never once entered into the Heads of our *Northern Tutors*: and what adds to their Value and Importance is, that the Acts, which I propose to celebrate, retain, in every sense of the word, their *Originality* to this day; not one Copy having been made by a single Colony on this Wide-Extended Continent.

The first Fancy which cast forth its irradiating beams upon the Minds of our Assembly, signalized the Annals of the Year 1766.—It was then discovered, that the *"American Stamp Act was not transmitted to the Governor by the Secretaries of* [5] *State, or Lords of Trade:"*[3] and although the Lieutenant-Governor,[4] who was then in Administration, had been furnished by the Attorney-General[5] with the Act printed by His Majesty's Printer, yet it was not deemed by the Assembly to be such a Notification thereof, as to oblige a Governor to enforce the Execution of it.

It is difficult to say, to whom they were indebted for this Wonderful Discovery: whether to Lawyers or Laymen, is very immaterial, inasmuch as nothing of the *kind* was ever hinted by any other Provincial Senate. Perhaps our Neighbors recollected what my Lord Coke says, that *"before Printing and till the Reign of Henry the Seventh, Statutes were Engrossed in Parchment, and by the King's Writ proclaimed by the Sheriff of every County,"[6] and therefore, they might possibly conclude, that this practice was not only out of use, but since the Art of Printing was an unnecessary caution. Be this as it may, it is sufficient to observe, that the Honor of this *State Juggle* belongs to *us* alone.

I mention this by the bye, as being an *Effort* of our own; and yet not so much for the Credit which it gives, as to convince Mankind, what astonishing advances we have made, from the first moment we abandoned our Political Teachers, and stood like Men upon our own proper legs.—Besides, there is both Instruction and Delight, in tracing the displays of Human Understanding, from the early budding forth, to a more advanced stage of culture and improvement. When we proceed step by step, tracing, as it were, the several gradations, marking the stealing progress of Man's inventive skill, and keep a steady eye on the several Operations, we naturally ac-[6]quire a regular System of Reflection, and we find our Judgement ripened, in proportion to the attention we have given, and the admiration we have paid.

The Reader will perceive, that the first commencement of Carolina Politics on our own proper bottom (after most Servile Imitations about the same period), is dated upon the Introduction of the Stamp-Act into the British Colonies: and, having said as much as the Importance of our *first Walk* in the wide field of Political Science, merits at my hands, I proceed to state and consider a *Second Effort* of the Assembly, which, for its *vast Reach, profound Depth,* and *uncommon Boldness,* challenges the first Rank in the Annals of Modern Story.

That the mind may be duly prepared to receive a becoming

---

* 2 Inst. 526, 644, 670.

impression of this matter, it is proper to premise, by way of excuse for that lapse of time between the *first Stroke* and the *second*, that our advances, though slow, and after a long pause, are nevertheless extremely regular and sure: and though we cannot boast any great rapidity of Genius, it is evident that we sufficiently atone for the defect by the *solidity*, the *comprehensiveness*, the *novelty* of the Plan, and the *immensity* of its Object.—For my own part, I always prefer a superstructure upon an old and settled foundation—I hate all sudden and flashy operations; they have nothing either permanent or secure about them: then, again, they supply little for the mind to dwell upon; for travelling like a ray of light, they both dazzle and confound; whereas the *sober*, the *cool*, the *long digested Plan* commonly bids fair to secure both Approbation and Applause. Let us now bring this Business to a proper Test; try it by its own intrinsic worth; examine its tendency; view the [7] measure through the purest speculum; and, provided the Enquiry is conducted with singleness of heart, and with an eye to Truth, we shall neither repine at the labour, or retire from the contemplation of the subject with disgust.

On the eighth day of December, 1769, a full House of Assembly passed an Order in the words following:

"ORDERED, That the Public Treasurer do advance the Sum of 10,500 1. Currency (equal to 1500 1. Sterling), out of any Money in the Treasury, to be paid into the hands of certain Members therein mentioned, who are to remit the same to Great Britain, for the Support of the Just and Constitutional Rights and Liberties of the People of Great Britain and America.

"RESOLVED, That this House will make Provision to reimburse the Public Treasurer the said Sum.

"By Order of the House."[7]

This Sum was remitted by Bills of Exchange, drawn by some merchants[8] there, in favor of the late Public Treasurer[9] of the Province, on certain Gentlemen[10] in London and Bristol.

This being the plain and simple state of the Case, it is but just that the Assembly's inducements for adopting this measure should accompany the fact. After a repose of about three Years, from the date of the last Transaction, the Assembly had been, no doubt, ruminating upon the situation of Public Affairs, both at home and abroad: and as Men of liberal sentiments disdain to confine their Benefactions to the Members of their own soil and climate; and, like Citizens of the World, taking a wise and extended range, and wisely contemplating the rise and fall of Empires, and, probably, reflecting that the Consti-[8]tution of Great Britain was apparently going to decay, and that only one faint dawn of hope remained from a *Club of Patriots*, who had then lately formed themselves into a Society for Supporting *The Bill of Rights*: I say, from some of these considerations they voted the Sum stated in the Order. It appears, likewise, very clear to me,* that they were convinced "how nearly the Americans must be affected by any attacks upon the Constitutional Rights and Liberties of their Fellow-Subjects residing in Great Britain; and that they, perceiving the Oppressions they and the Colonies actually suffered proceeded from the same cause; and also feelingly sympathizing with those *noble Spirits*, who had stood, and were then standing, as it were, in the Breach, fronting the whole collected Fury of Ministerial Vengeance; therefore they gave this free and liberal aid, that the same might be applied in Defence of the Constitutional Rights of all the Subjects of the British Empire; and particularly for Supporting such of their Fellow-Subjects, who, by asserting the just Rights of the People, become obnoxious to Administration, and suffer from the Hand of Power.

"I am also persuaded, that this Assistance was given upon an idea, that those noble Purposes could not be carried into execution in any measure so effectually as by placing the Money in the Hands of the *Gentlemen Supporters* of *The Bill of Rights, that truly Patriotic Body of Men;* so that Peace, and Happiness, and Constitutional Security, might thereby be extensively and freely enjoyed by every Subject throughout the British Empire."[11]

[9] No Man can deny that these were the ostensible reasons for this extraordinary Gift; and as all our present Distractions spring from this single source; and as the tendency of the measure makes this subject a point of some concern; I shall take the liberty to examine it with all that spirit of Freedom, which it seems to have been the ambition of the Assembly, in other cases, to cultivate and

---

* The Committee's Letter to the Agent.

Considerations

improve. I fly to the great Bulwark of our Liberties—the Press;—
and as it is the peculiar privilege of a free-born Subject of Great
Britain to consider the legality, justice, and propriety of Public
Measures, no Man, with any face of reason, can blame my conduct
in this respect. I purposely avoid every personal reflection; neither
is it my design to cast a slur on a single Individual, or to point at
the characters, principles, or tenets of Private Persons.—It is the
act of the whole Body which alone engages my attention; and,
therefore, if any word or phrase can be tortured to import private
reflections, let them call to mind, that I profess to treat of *Measures*,
not *Men*.

I believe it will be readily allowed, by every Person of common
Understanding, that the *Purity* of an Intention is not of itself alone
a substantial reason for a measure grounded thereon; and it is a
point alike obvious and admissible, that whatever Acts, for the
advancement of the Public Good, are proposed to be adopted by
a Legislative Body, must have their foundation in the Constitution, or ought to be rejected: because, under imaginary notions of
doing *good* upon false principles, they may be insensibly led to
commit great *evil*: it is, therefore, incumbent upon all *Bodies
Politic*, to examine with the utmost nicety and precision, the true
bottom and foundation of every proposition, lest they should be
unwarily [10] betrayed to wound that Constitution, which it is
their Duty to support. Legislators must never do any thing, merely
because they *dare;* for this is a base and ignoble maxim:—they must
always Virtuously Dare to do what is *Right*, that they may be cau-
tiously fearful of doing what is *Wrong*.

The Money being thus voted and remitted, was actually paid to
the Illustrious *Supporters of the Bill of Rights,* or to the Secretary[12]
of that Society for their use, according to the intention of the gift:
how the same has been applied is a kind of secret, which will probably remain so; and it is very foreign to my present purpose, to
pass even a conjecture on this head.

About the month of March, 1770, the Lower House sent to His
Majesty's Council (being the Upper House of Assembly) the Annual Tax-Bill, to defray the Charges of the Government from the
first day of January to the thirty-first day of December, 1769, both
days inclusive, and for other Services therein mentioned; and on

the second reading thereof, and also of the Schedule thereto annexed, the Council discovered the following Charge: viz. "To Jacob Motte, Esq. advanced by him, to certain Members of the House, by a Resolution of the House of the eighth of December last, 10,500 1."[13] and the Council, by a message to the Lower House, dated the fifth day of April, 1770, declared, That the Grant of the Sum before mentioned did not appear, in any sense, *honourable, fit,* or *decent*: not Fit or Honourable, as they conceived the Assembly's Jurisdiction was merely local, and for Provincial Purposes; and not Decent, as the Grant by the Tax-Bill was expressly declared to be for His Majesty, and yet contained a provision highly affrontive to His Majesty's Government, which [11] they declared to have ever been, in their opinion, Gracious, Mild and Good, to all His faithful People.[14] The Message was temperate; and calculated to persuade the Lower House to remove that obstacle which prevented them from giving their concurrence to the Bill.

The Assembly sent an Answer two days after, returning the Council's Message for their Calm Re-consideration; which was immediately followed by another from the Upper House, expressing that the Assembly's Proceedings were neither Parliamentary or proper; and that they were determined to adhere to their former sentiments.[15] About this time, a Prorogation took place;[16] and thus ended the Business of this Session.

The Legislature again sat in August following, when the Honourable William Bull, Esq. Lieutenant Governor, communicated a Copy of His Majesty's additional Instruction to the Governor, which had then lately come to his Honour's hands, bearing date the fourteenth day of April, 1770.[17]

This Instruction recites, "That the *Lower House* of Assembly in South Carolina had lately assumed to themselves a power of ordering, without the concurrence of the Governor and Council, the Public Treasurer of the said Province to issue and advance, out of the Public Treasury, such Sums of Money, and for such Services, as they had thought fit.—It next states the Case before rehearsed, which was the very occasion of this new Instruction; and after deeming it just to put a stop to such dangerous and unwarrantable Practices, and for guarding against such unconstitutional Application of the King's Treasure, Chearfully Granted to His Majesty, for the public Uses of the Province, and for Support of the Government thereof, His Majesty is pleased to direct the Governor, on Pain [*12*] of Removal, not to give his Assent to any Bill that shall be passed by the Lower House of Assembly, by which any Sum of Money shall be appropriated to, or Provision made for, defraying any Expence incurred for Services or Purposes not immediately arising within, or incident to, the said Province, unless upon the King's Special Requisition; nor to any Bill for Granting any Sum to His Majesty, etc., in which Bill it shall not be Provided, in express Words, that the Money so to be Granted, or any Part thereof, shall not be Issued or Applied to any other Services than those to which it is by the said Bill appropriated, unless by Act or Ordinance of the General Assembly of the said Province.

"The Proclamation next forbids the Governor to give his Assent to any Bill passed by the Lower House, by which any Sum shall be Granted to His Majesty, etc. generally, and without Appropriation, unless there be a Clause inserted, Providing, that the said Money so to be Granted, shall remain in the Treasury, subject to such Appropriation as shall thereafter be made by Act or Ordinance as aforesaid.

"It contains also a Provision, that in all future Bills for Raising and Granting Public Monies, a Clause be added, subjecting the Public Treasurer, etc. in case he shall Issue or Pay any such Money otherwise than by express Order contained in some Act or Ordinance of the General Assembly, to a Penalty in Treble the Sum so Issued contrary thereto, and declaring them to be *ipso facto* incapable of holding his said Office, or any other, Civil or Military, within the said Province."[18]

On the thirtieth day of August, 1770, the Commons House of Assembly made another ex-[*13*]periment, by sending a like Tax-Bill and Schedule, containing the same obnoxious Item as the former, which the Upper House rejected on the first reading; a thing seldom done, and perhaps only allowable in certain cases;[19] however, this Session ended like the preceding one, by a Prorogation to the 16th of January 1771.[20]

On the 15th of February following the Lieutenant Governor communicated to the Council the following paragraph of a Letter which he received the same day from the Right Honourable the

Earl of Hil[l]sborough: "I must not omit to acquaint you, that the becoming manner in which the Council have exerted themselves in support of his Majesty's Measures, has not escaped the King's Observation; and I am commanded to signify to you his Majesty's Pleasure, that you should express to them his Majesty's Approbation of their Conduct;" which his Honour the Lieutenant Governor did accordingly.[21]

It would be tedious and unprofitable to set down the many Meetings of Assembly since this period, or to mark the several Prorogations and Dissolutions which have taken place from time to time; it being sufficient for the present purpose to observe, that the several Tax-Bills since August 1770 have been rejected by the Upper House upon the same principle that influenced them to reject the former bills; and the same obstruction to public business still remains; the same firmness in the Council in opposing what the Assembly insist upon as a Right, tho' disallowed by the King's Instruction; and the same obstinacy in the Commons House to maintain the Right contended for; every season has produced warm resolutions and messages in a stile of contempt and intemperate resentment.

[14] I cannot omit taking notice in this place, that in October 1771 another Tax-Bill was brought to the Upper House, and in November following was returned to the Lower House, with a message grounded on the original objection; and as they in the course of this Session proceeded so far as to commit the present Public Treasurers[22] for a non-compliance on their part with a new order of the House for payment of money for a public use upon their *own Authority alone,* and in the face of the King's Instruction providing against any such attempts, the House was immediately dissolved.[23] In April 1772, when Lord Charles Montague[24] was in the Administration of Public Business, he took occasion in his Speech at the opening of that Session, to acquaint the Commons House of Assembly, that his Majesty "had lately again signified to him, that it was his pleasure, That he should adhere with firmness to the directions contained in his additional instruction of the 14th of April 1770; and that it was his firm resolution to adhere to the Constitution."[25]

The Provincial Agent[26] has been instructed to apply to the

Crown, requesting his Majesty to reconsider the said Instruction; and also to withdraw the same. A Petition was accordingly presented for that purpose; but the Instruction has neither been vacated or withdrawn;[27] the Reader will therefore clearly perceive that a solemn confirmation of the Royal Order in his Majesty's Privy Council places the dispute at so great a distance, that there is not the least shadow of expectation that the Crown will revoke an Act framed upon mature deliberation. Besides, after the most gracious condescension on the King's part to the ardent wishes of the Com-[15]mons House of Assembly, the said Instruction having been ratified and confirmed on a revision of the merits, it is the most unpardonable presumption to look for further concessions from the Crown.

It is not foreign to the point to observe, that the King's Ministers have been, from time to time, furnished with every plausible argument in favour of the Vote and Resolution, and with every precedent from their Journals, that by any construction can be considered as a plea for such a practice; and therefore the case has been in as fair a train as possible, and must be presumed to have undergone the strictest scrutiny and enquiry. But notwithstanding all these advantages on the side of the Commons House, and that nothing urged by them has ever been opposed or contradicted by any other body of men before the Privy Council, the same obstacle stands in the way; and not a single public debt has been provided for since the commencement of this dispute on the fatal 8th of December 1769. And that we may form some idea how the Royal Mind stands affected in relation to this subject, so late as the month of June 1773, I give you the following Extract from my Lord Dartmouth's Letter to his Honor the Lieutenant Governor, relative to the Council's having in March last rejected the Tax-Bill, which he communicated to the Council the 6th day of August last, viz. His Lordship acquaints him, "That the said proceeding of the Council was considered by the King as a fresh mark of their zeal and duty; and his Lordship was further commanded to desire, that his Honor would not fail to signify to the Council his Majesty's Approbation of their Conduct;"[28] which his Honour then did with great pleasure.

[16] Thus have I most dispassionately and candidly stated every material circumstance attending this important subject, nearly in

73

the words used by the several parties in the course of the transaction; and, as far as I can judge, in no shape contradictory to their genuine sense and meaning. I am not conscious that any thing is omitted which can give light or information in the case; and tho' I have been necessarily obliged to trespass upon my Reader's Patience in order to collect the substance of every Legislative Act, and bring it into a clear point of view, so far as relates to the Vote and Order of the Commons House of Assembly, yet I trust that the matter in dispute will be now more clearly understood.

The true points of debate, then, may be comprehended in a few plain positions, arising from the above detail of facts, viz. That the Commons House of Assembly signalized themselves in favour of a Club called the *Supporters of the Bill of Rights*, held at the London Tavern, by voting in December 1769 1500 l. Sterling for their use, and ordering the Public Treasurer to pay the same out of any monies in the Treasury.

That this Order was made by their own *Sole Authority*, independent of, and without the privity or consent of the other two branches of the Legislature.

That when the first Annual Tax-Bill was sent to the Upper House in the month of March 1770, with a Schedule annexed containing the following charge, viz. "To Jacob Motte, Esq. advanced by him to the persons named by a Resolution of the House 10,500 l. (being of the value of 1500 l. Sterling)" the Council rejected the said Bill, and several sub-[17]sequent ones have since met with the like fate for the very same reason.

That the conduct of his Majesty's Council has not only been twice highly approved by the King himself, but the dispute has been taken up by the Crown; and by an additional Instruction to the Governor, such Orders have been declared to be unconstitutional; and the like practice has been thereby fully provided against in future.

That the Assembly, tenacious of their Rights as conceived by them, and obstinate in adhering to the measure which had given so just cause of offence, have repeatedly persisted in the justice and propriety of the original Vote and Order, notwithstanding his Majesty's royal interposition in the case.

Considerations

Thus stands this important Contest between the Crown and the People's Representatives of his Majesty's Colony of South Carolina.

Let us now proceed to consider the Act of the Commons House with a *bold* and *manly freedom*, and in all the different views in which it can be placed.

First, then, the measure was originally bad, in every sense of the word. For granting the power, for argument sake, to be in the Assembly to pass such a Vote and Order, independently of the other two Branches of the Legislature; still the exercise of such a power, in the case stated by the Order, was *idly* and *unnecessarily wanton*; the appropriation of the sum for the purposes mentioned, *arbitrary* and *unjust*; the objects of their benevolence, *laughable*, *ridiculous*, and *absurd*; and the pretended cause of the Grant, a *gross* and *palpable affront* to his Majesty, as also to his Government.

That the Act was both *idle* and *wanton*, may appear from a consideration of the Royal pre-[18]dilection in favor of this Colony on numberless occasions. The King's Ministers have ever been open to access, and almost every proposition from the Agent has been attended with remarkable success: in war, we have been peculiarly protected by an early appointment of Convoys; and Government has afforded its best aid to procure liberal Bounties on the various products of the country; in short, the Colony of South Carolina may be considered as one of the most favourable soils in his Majesty's American Dominions. That the measure was *arbitrary* and *unjust*, I appeal to any man of common sense and understanding. The Delegates of the People may raise money; it is, perhaps, their immediate province to originate Supply Bills, and to lay Duties, Taxes, and Impositions upon the People, with the concurrence of the other Branches of the State: but under pretext of these Constitutional and inherent Powers, they ought not to extend these Rights beyond the original views and intention of those from whom they derive their whole authority. There is a line of Jurisdiction for every order of men in a civilized state, beyond which they cannot pass; and fit it is that Public Bodies should have boundaries, restraints, and limitations, since they are equally liable with Individuals to be misled by passion, fancy, or caprice.

With what colour of justice could the Assembly tax their Constituents, and apply their money for purposes altogether foreign, under pretence of a power to raise money upon the People, for services or purposes immediately arising within or incident to the Provinces? Their Authority is *local*; and as their Laws are only made for their own internal Government, and extend not beyond the Jurisdiction to which they refer, so [*19*] in like manner must every Legislative Act bear a local reference, and every Grant or Appropriation of Money must, generally speaking, be made for real and substantial services performed to the Province. They have no more right to raise money upon *constructive* ideas of benefit and service, than the Judges have to declare *constructive* Treasons: No; the Law has defined and clearly pointed out the crime of Treason, and the Constitution has as precisely ascertained the power of the Commons to give and grant.

It may be said, that the Assembly have many times voted sums, by way of Relief to their Sister Colonies labouring under any general Calamity; and hence it may be inferred, that they have a right to dispose of the People's Money, and apply it to other uses than for their own immediate service. I readily allow the first part of the position, but I deny that so general a conclusion can be fairly drawn from it. The misery and sufferings of our fellow-creatures demand our aid; Humanity dictates the lesson; Nature pleads for it; and Gratitude requires it; and therefore this case is necessarily excepted out of the general maxim: besides, what one Colony gives to another is in some respect a kind of loan; inasmuch as the like return is made to our benevolence when Distress visits our own borders. Neither this case, nor a Grant of Moneys upon a Royal Requisition, can afford the least pretence for a Vote, grounded upon merely an *ideal* benefit, such as the Order states.

It is true, that the Commons are to judge and determine in what cases they will or ought to give and grant; but surely it is implied, that they shall not arbitrarily and injuriously appropriate the Public Treasure, and thereby abuse the confidence reposed in them by the People. [*20*] Surely it will not be contended, that they have a right to impoverish the Members of the State, when the necessities of Government require no such exertions. Admit, for a moment, that the Assembly are possessed of a power to apply the Money of their Constituents to any purposes generally, and we must also admit, that they may do so to any Amount and Extent whatever; and then, I think, the *Represented* are in a state of absolute Vassalage and ruinous Dependence.

Is it not an Arbitrary Act to tax the Estates of the Subjects in this Colony to support a *private Club*, a *Tavern Club*, a *factious Club*, upon any specious pretence or colourable excuse?—Is it just, fit, or reasonable, that Burthens should be laid upon the People, to serve a job or gratify a whim?—Can Men suffer themselves to be so deluded, and amused, to their loss as well as shame?—Are chains more tolerable, because imposed by our own consent?—Can Men tamely surrender their Reason, and the power of Judging for themselves, by a single *act of Delegation*?—Was it their sense and meaning, to furnish their Constituents with rods for their own backs; and are those whom they chose to represent and to protect them, to be their Executioners?—Is the Colony arrived to full *maturity*?—Has it no wants of any kind?—Does it stand in need of no Supplies for Beneficial Establishments; for the Encrease and Advancement of the Products of the Soil; the Extension of its Commerce, and the Promotion of useful Knowledge? Are the several Counties so well supplied with Churches, Chapels, and Spiritual Teachers and with Schools for the Instruction of Youth; or, Are the Public Roads, Bridges, Causeways, and Fortifications, in such perfect state and condition; and are the circumstances of the Colony in general so extremely easy, that the [21] Treasury meet only to *receive*, and not to *pay*? If these things are so, we may overlook, for once at least, the *idle prodigality* complained of: but if these questions cannot be favourably answered, Every Man in the Community is injured to a certain degree; and every Sum diverted from their Service, is an Act of real Tyranny and Insolent Oppression.

For my own part, I must candidly confess, that I never reflected in my mind upon this subject, but I found two very different passions excited in my breast, *mirth* and *resentment*. The comical part of the story is, That a Collective Body of Men, in their *grave* and *senatorial stations*, should persuade themselves, that *Magna Charta*, the *Habeas Corpus Act*, and the *Bill of Rights*, stood in need of a little propping from a Club of Men whose standard was set up at the London Tavern. That the King, Lords, and Commons of England were either remiss in their Duty to the State, or indifferent about it; that all the Virtue and Public Spirit in the Nation had *squeezed* itself into the London Tavern; and that nothing could save Britain and America, but a *little ablution* at that sacred spring; are such absurd and laughable circumstances, that no Age or Nation can furnish a Precedent so superlatively ridiculous and weak! Enjoy the laugh for a moment—suppress your anger, and image to yourselves a set of sedate sensible Politicians, with big wigs and grave faces, unanimously passing such a Vote, and such an Order, by the plenitude of their own power.

View the case in a serious light, and it is impossible to sit calm and unmoved at the relation. What could influence Men to step forth, and, by an unconstitutional and unwarrantable stretch of Power, to misapply the Public Money, and at [22] the same time offer so gross an insult to His Majesty's Government both at home and abroad?

The House of Commons have never gone farther than passing a Vote of Credit upon a requisition from the King; and That for Public and Beneficial Purposes, and on Great and Emergent Occasions: but this Order can never be considered in the nature of a Vote of Credit; for it is literally issuing Money out of the Treasury, the application whereof has either been directed by Law, or the same is part of certain Surplusses arising from different Funds, which though raised, exceeds the Necessity for which the same was granted, and therefore remains in the hands of the Treasurer, to be accounted for as the respective Laws limit and appoint. It is therefore extremely evident, that such Surplus Money is a kind of *sacrum depositum*[29] in the Treasurer's hands, which only the United Branches of the Legislature can appropriate or issue. What is once granted to His Majesty, cannot be diverted from the uses to which it is meant to be applied.—No one in his senses can contend that it may: and it is equally absurd for one Branch of the Legislature to touch Surplus Money; not only because the same has been actually granted, and to the perfection of which Grant the Three several Branches of the Legislature had unitedly concurred, and, therefore, the like Powers only can direct a different appointment respecting the same; but also because a Grant, till vacated by as solemn an Act, must stand good, and will continue to bind the Money, so as to prevent any appropriation whatsoever, till a Law directs it. And it is a joke to say, that Surplus Money may be borrowed in this loose way, upon an idea, that what is not wanted revests, as it were, (by a kind of ingenious fiction) in the People, or in their Representatives in their [23] behalf. For, How can this fiction operate as a sort of virtual Repeal of the Law which granted the Sum? or, At what moment of time, and by what kind of *secret Magic*, was the same effected?—For, being once vested in the King, by Law, how can any part thereof become divested by a mere partial Order of only the Lower, and most subordinate, House of Legislature? Weak men will dispute any point, however idle and absurd; wise men will both reason and dispute; and fools will dispute, and refuse to be convinced. That His Majesty's Council have something to do in the Money-concerns of the Colony, appears by an Act of Assembly, passed the twentieth of September, 1721, entitled, "An Act for Appointing a Public Treasurer, and other Public Officers;" by which they are made liable to be called to account by each, and either, House of Assembly, and their bonds put in suit by the direction of either House, etc.[30]

Now, to shew that the Ordering Surplus Monies to be paid upon a direction of the Commons House alone, cannot be altogether proper, I must take notice, that divers Laws make provision in such cases; and particularly the General Duty Act, passed the fourteenth of June, 1751, respecting the Duties imposed thereby, viz. That "whatever Surplus shall be remaining of the said Duties, after paying the several Demands and Outgoings by this Act directed, every such Surplus shall be carefully retained by the said Public Treasurer, until appropriated by the General Assembly."[31]

Similar Provisions are made by divers other Acts; which demonstrably prove, that Surplus and unapplied Monies in the Treasury cannot be drawn thereout by a Vote and Order of the Commons House alone.

[24] A little reflection must convince every Man, that the Power contended for by the Commons House is of so dangerous a nature in itself, as affords a strong argument against the existence of such Power; for if the Lower House may so Vote and Order Monies out of the Treasury, which are granted to His Majesty, and that by their own Authority, may not the same Power be assumed by a Governor, or the Council, or both unitedly, to answer a Job, or to

accomplish a favourite Plan, independent of the People's Representatives?—and the rather, when it is considered that, by the
King's Twenty-second Instruction, as entered in the Council Journals, the Governor "is directed not to suffer any Public Money
whatsoever to be issued and disposed of, otherwise than by Warrant under his Hand, by, and with, the advice and consent of the
Council."[32]

If the matter is taken up on ideas of common sense, it is doing
no violence to our understandings to suppose, that a Governor
may issue Monies by his own Order, as representing His Majesty,
to whom the same were granted; but that the Commons, who
have granted the Money, shall still retain a power over it, re-
possess themselves of it, and apply it at their pleasure, for a good
reason or a bad one, or for no reason at all, surpasses all human
comprehension.

Happy, however, is our case, that the present subject does not
rest upon Opinion merely, but is determinable by the Principles
of that Constitution, which ought to be the pride and glory of all
the Subjects of His Majesty's Dominions. The true excellence* of
the English Government consists in this, "that all the parts of it
form a [25] mutual check upon each other.—In the Legislature, the
People are a check upon the Nobility, and the Nobility a check
upon the People, by the mutual privilege of rejecting what the
other has resolved; while the King is a check upon both; which
preserves the executive power from encroachments."[33]

In this view it is, that His Majesty has interposed His Royal Authority, by an *Additional Instruction* to His Governor, grounded
upon an actual, dangerous, and unconstitutional Encroachment of
the Commons House of Assembly, in the manner stated in these
sheets.—This has been done by way of *check*; and in order to prevent a practice so unwarrantable, and that the wound thereby
given to the Constitution may be healed, the Instruction must be
viewed in the light of a *timely Correction* by the Executive Power,
and as a *call* and *admonition* to a Third Branch of the Legislature
to return to first principles, from which they had so improperly
departed; and is also intended to prevent in future, what seems, to

---

* 1 Blackst. 154.

the Royal Judgement, an undue Encroachment: it is, therefore, injurious to consider this Act of Government merely as a Direction to the Commons House of this Colony, how, and in what manner, they shall frame and originate a Money Bill; because the King only tells them of their departure from the Constitution; points out the proper practice, as grounded thereon; and, by thus interposing, and prohibiting His Representative from giving His Assent improperly, and upon unfit occasions, as also to remedy the evil complained of with so much justice, His Majesty has done no more than exercised *that Act* of Sovereignty given Him by the Constitution, for the purpose of maintaining the Just Balance of the State.

[26] The distinction is extremely obvious, between an Instruction given as a rule of conduct to the several Branches of the Legislature, upon a point of departure from acknowledged principles, and an Instruction which contains new-fangled ideas, not warranted by, or known to, the Constitution.—The one is only a *Remembrancer*, as it were, reminding them what the Constitution is, and giving them a rule for adhering to it; which is the regular check lodged in the King's hands to prevent Encroachment; whereas the other would be irregular, and savour of the nature of a trespass: and a *novel Invention*, from whatever quarter, is an innovation upon the other Branches of the Legislature. Keeping these observations in view, every popular argument against the King's Instructions, as being only a rule to His *Governor*, and that the People are not to be *Instructed*; must fall to the ground, as inconclusive and foreign to the point.

I know that many People, finding no warrant for the practice contended for by the Assembly, either in the Proceedings of Parliament, or in the Constitution of our Country, have immediate recourse to the usage of the Province for a series of years, without controul or interruption; and to those who skim over a dispute, without weighing the force of the several arguments, this assertion may be considered as a good plea in favour of the practice; and therefore I think it my duty to offer a few words on the only feasible pretence which the advocates for it can set up.

It is very true, that, for several years antecedent to the year 1737, the Commons House have ordered Monies to be advanced by the Treasurer, without the concurrence of the Council and assent of the Governor; but from that period, no such mode prevailed, till the year 1751, or [27] 1752; and since that time many Orders occur, some sent for concurrence, and many not. This difference of proceeding points out a distinction; for where they have ordered Monies arising from appropriated Funds which have not been wanted, the Council's concurrence and the Governor's assent have been applied for; but where the Orders have been general, they have gone upon a sort of Idea, That there were Surplusages and Balances sufficient to satisfy the Order without any intermediate Inconvenience, till the same could be replaced by a Public Tax-Bill; and I cannot in any other way account for the course of practice which has at different times prevailed.

In order to combat these Facts, let us previously reflect what slow advances *Infant Societies* of Men make towards Regularity or Perfection; that in the first outset they are occupied in providing for their necessary wants, and securing their protection; the niceties and punctilios of Public Business never enter their heads, till they have brought their Colony to such an outward state that they feel some *Self-conceit* has crept into their hearts; then it is that Men begin to give the polish to their Acts, and to be emulous of Fame: the Precedents, therefore, of new Communities are of very little weight; and whatever rank they bear, the influence they ought to have must be proportioned to the prevailing Uniformity of Practice, which is the true badge of their Importance; for when there is any long Interruption to, or Discontinuance of, a Practice, the fluctuation creates Embarrassments, and puzzles the Understanding, without leading the Mind to any determinate conclusion on the point.

But granting for once, that a particular model has been adopted for a series of years without [28] interruption or controul, Time gives no sanctions to Acts illegal in themselves; and when Inconveniencies arise, and the *Blot* is hit, the Merit of the Practice is then called in question, and it is tried and must be determined by the Laws and Constitution of our Country. In like manner Public Rights, of what nature soever they are, (tho' dormant for a time) can never be extinguished, except by the Power that first created them; and the continuance of a practice on no better foundation than *Indulgence*, confers no permanent and durable title; mere permission being a tenure at will: the Man is in possession one month; and the Lord of the soil may eject him the next.

The instances wherein the pretended practice has prevailed may be safely admitted, to shew the impropriety of the like practice in the present case; for every one will readily allow, that altho' it may be pardonable for Public Bodies to relax somewhat in favour of the State, yet it by no means follows; that they may do so on occasions unworthy of Indulgence. The instances which the Assembly can cite for granting Orders by their *sole Authority*, refer to Payments to their Governor for Indian Uses, Local Services, Salaries of Clergy advanced on particular occasions, Furniture for the State House, Books for the Assembly, for the Silk Manufactory, and the like. And shall such Precedents be urged in defence of *Orders* made in like form on behalf of *Clubs*, and *idle fantastic Measures?* for conceits of flimsy Politicians, and to indulge a Spirit of Faction and Disorder in the Metropolis of our Sovereign's Kingdom? Can we with any face plead Precedents of honourable tendency to support the most wanton acts of passion and intemperance? Is it possible for men to be so blinded by prejudice and passion, that Prece-[29]dents for doing real and substantial *Good* shall be urged in argument to promote the cause of *Evil?* Alas! Reason has but little influence in the favourite schemes of State Intrigues! All the kind and benevolent affections are at rest; the souls of men are perturbed! Disorder and Distraction take the lead! and every faculty is awakened to breed confusion and distrust! It is amazing to reflect what baneful effects are wrought by Political *Manoeuvres!* the Social and Benevolent Spirits retire; and men for the most part lose their Humanity together with their Sense and Understanding. Oh *Politics!* how ye deform the Human Soul! blunt Natural Affection! sow the foul Seeds of Hatred and Ill-will! confound the Laws of Right and Wrong, making our Journey through Life a painful Pilgrimage indeed!

It is a matter of doubt with me, whether the folly of the Vote, or the folly of persisting in it after conviction of its impropriety, is the greatest. There is something very singular in the whole of this affair; for I have been told, that those who adopted the measure, and decline the defence of it; who frankly own, in their private situations, that nothing of the like kind will be done in future; who

very unreservedly admit it was an hasty business, and that they
heartily repent it; are of sentiments expressly opposite to these
declarations, in their Public Station; and with the utmost ve-
hemence declare, that they never will give up the point, or pass a
Tax-Act whilst the Royal Instruction stands as an obstacle in the
way. If the measure cannot be justified upon the Principles of the
Constitution, common Prudence directs us quietly to relinquish
what we cannot hold; and it is no disgrace for Public Bodies of
Men to retract any Tenet [30] especially when it is either dangerous or improper to maintain it. The dispute lies between the King
and the Delegates of the People; and the question now is simply
this: Whether the King is to recall or vacate his Instruction; or
the People submit to a check for an unconstitutional Application
of the Public Treasure? Justice as well as Prudence require us to
yield the point. On firm ground we may safely tread, but to persist
in opposition to a timely and regular interposition, is to me an
obstinacy highly culpable, and altogether unbecoming. Perhaps to
high Spirits, concessions of any kind are mortal stings; but if there
must be a degree of condescension in some quarter, before tran-
quility can be restored to an afflicted Province, surely it is most
reasonable to expect, that Duty to the King should influence the
People to make the first advances; and the rather, as an opposition
in the present case will inevitably affect the most essential Interests
of the Colony, by retarding its Growth, weakening its Credit, and
encreasing its Distractions.—No part of the King's Dominions can
be injured by this local difference, nor is the great Machine of Government in the least affected by it; the punishment is as local as the
dispute itself; the People of the Colony alone suffer in the cause,
which no wise man can think a good one.

It is rather an odd circumstance, that we have no certain information what became of the 1500 l. after it was paid into the hands
of the *Patriotic Club*. That it was spent remains no doubt; but How,
is the great mysterious Question. Whether it was applied to pay
the *Tavern Score*, or to satisfy the hungry Creditors of some *half-
starved Patriot*, are problems to puzzle the wise heads of those who
gave it; but to me nothing [31] is more strange and unaccountable
than the great reserve which all Parties have maintained respect-

ing this *unprecedented Benevolence.* I have not been able to learn what the venerable Supporters seriously thought in relation to this Gift. That they laughed at it, and enjoyed the joke, I can readily suppose: that they passed a sneer upon it, and pronounced it an *idle Affair;* that they ridiculed the Credulity of the Donors, and admired their Faith, I can easily believe; but it is not possible to carry our conjectures any farther.

Some inquisitive folks have been very restless to know what sort of grateful acknowledgements the Club have paid to the House of Assembly for this generous Donation; but it is as curious to reflect, that the *Silence* is equally as *sullen* on one side of the water, as it is on the other. I cannot learn from authority, that even the poor *unavailing Tribute* of Thanks has been returned for all this *Legislative Kindness.* There is a great shamefacedness on both sides, in the course of this Transaction. The Club either knew not how to express their sense of the Favor; or their sincerity, as men, would not allow them to pay a sacrifice which (tho' gainers by the Grant) their Hearts must disapprove; and I am firmly persuaded in my own mind, they were afraid to expose themselves by returning thanks: and the House, I have reason to believe, are better pleased without them.—Thus it is when Public or Private Bodies of Men play a loose Game; both sides are always shy, and the only way to avoid a total rupture is to preserve, if possible, the same kind of happy distance that has been between the House and the Club; there being no real Danger, except when jarring Bodies meet in contact.

[32] The money has been voted and spent, and the Society which received it is now no more! The *Great Charter,* the *Bill of Rights,* the *Habeas Corpus Act,* the *Constitution itself,* are left to the wide World to fight their own Battles, and maintain their own Ground! The *Supporters* have given way, and their strength is as exhausted as their Purse! Their Friends the House have nothing more to give; and 'tis thought they have long repented what is given! What a melancholy state of things is this! But how blessed a condition, compared to the miserable and forlorn situation of a Colony which now feels the evil effects of ill-directed Zeal!

I come now to consider a new stroke of Provincial Politics, and the last-distinguishing Effort of the Colony of South Carolina, in the great attempt of establishing a Character of Originality; an idea so very flattering to the Human Mind!

The Legislature stood prorogued to the Month of August 1773: and the old obstacle still being in the way, and the Lieutenant Governor seeing little prospect of doing business, opened the Session by a Message to each House, to save a piece of idle pageantry, and the formality of a public Speech.[34]

A few days passed, and one or two Bills were sent by the Lower to the Upper House, which were ordered to lie upon the table for the most cogent and prudential reasons.—The Upper House, anxious for the Public Credit, and deploring the miserable state of the Colony Affairs, owing to the above unhappy dispute, judged it highly expedient to enquire into the true state of the Public Treasury, in order to guard against Accidents, and to provide in due time for the Public Safety. One of the Treasurers being ex-[33]-amined, gave such a melancholy detail, that the Upper House addressed the Governor upon the subject, for the purpose of calling in 50,000 l. Currency, in order to keep the Treasury in a proper course of circulation.[35] As this Enquiry discovered the weakness of our State, the Commons House entered into some violent Resolutions; and by a message to the Governor on the subject of the Council's Address, attempted to charge them with having given an improper state of the Treasury Accounts: but the Upper House not choosing to submit to the imputation of having deceived the Public, prosecuted the Enquiry still further, and demonstrated the Truths contained in their Address,[36] which the Assembly have not since attempted to disprove.[37] In the course of this Session, a Protest of an extraordinary nature was entered in the Upper House Journals by Two Members;[38] which having a manifest tendency to reflect upon the Proceedings of the House, and the same being printed by one Thomas Powel[39] in the South Carolina Gazette, without any leave or permission from the House, this matter was taken up as a gross Contempt, and Breach of Privilege; and the Printer being sent for and acknowledging the fact, and declining to give proper satisfaction to the House, he was thereupon committed by virtue of a Warrant under the Hand of the President, Sir Egerton Leigh, Baronet, the 31st of August 1773; which Warrant was by the express Order of the House.[40]—On the 3d of September the said Thomas Powel was discharged from his confinement, upon a return of the Cause of Commitment by the Sheriff[41] on the back of an Habeas Corpus, issued by the Honourable Rawlins Lowndes, Speaker,[42] and George Gabriel Powel, Esq. another Member of Assembly,[43] pursuant to an Act of Assembly [34] passed on the 12th of *December* 1712, empowering Two Justices (*Quorum Unus*)[44] to put in force the Habeas Corpus Act to all Intents, Constructions, and Purposes, as fully as the same can be put in execution in his Majesty's Kingdom of England.[45] The Justices judicially declared the Council to be no *Upper House of Assembly*, and therefore held the Commitment illegal, and of course discharged him.[46] The Council applied to the Assembly for redress against their Members; but they, instead of complying with the request, entered into several pointed Resolutions, avowed the same Doctrine which the Justices had broached, approved their Decision, returned the Thanks of the House to them, for the same, and agreed to address the Governor to suspend those Members who had voted the Commitment; and also to address His Majesty for their Removal: and on the 13th of September they addressed the Governor accordingly, who very properly judged the subject too important to be determined by him; and the rather, as the affair is to be laid before the King.[47] The Council, finding such new Doctrines adopted by the Lower House, and perceiving that the Constitution was, in effect, subverted by their proceedings, lost no time in stating these Grievances in a suitable Address to His Majesty; they likewise addressed his Honour the Lieutenant Governor the same day, and requested him to transmit the Address, and other papers referred to, to the Secretary of State for the American Department, in order to be laid before His Majesty. The Lieutenant Governor, by his answer, undertook to transmit them according to their request;[48] and this Session being a most *noisy* and *disturbed one*, and every popular subject being brought to a happy conclusion, though somewhat interrupted by the Lieutenant [35] Governor declining to Suspend, agreeable to the modest expectations of the Lower House, they desired leave to adjourn till January next, to which time they stand adjourned accordingly.

Having given a Narrative of the Proceedings of this extraordinary Session, I shall now examine the pretensions of the Council to take upon them the Powers of an Upper House in the Legislature of this Country, and make some general Observations on the Constitution of the Colony, as formed on the British Model.

Upon the absolute Surrender of this Soil by the Lords Proprietors to his late Majesty, in the year 1729, for the Considerations agreed on; and confirmed by Act of Parliament, the Colony of South Carolina vested in His Majesty, and consequently he had a full right to give a Constitution; and to form such Establishments as were agreeable to the Laws and Practice of his own Kingdom. He was pleased therefore to appoint a Governor by Commission under the Great Seal of England, by which his Powers were precisely ascertained, and whereby he was authorized to call Assemblies composed of the Freeholders of the Colony, etc.; and the very last Commission, which was to Lord Charles Montague so lately as 1766, contains the following clause, viz.

"And that you, etc. with the consent of our said Council and Assembly, or the major part of them *respectively*, shall have full Power and Authority to make, constitute, and ordain Laws, Statutes, and Ordinances, for the Public Peace, Welfare, and Good Government of the said Province, and the People thereof, and such others as shall resort thereto; and for the Benefit of Us, our Heirs and Successors, which said Laws, Statutes, [36] and Ordinances, are not to be repugnant, but, as near as may be, agreeable to the Laws and Statutes of this our Kingdom of Great Britain."[49]

The King's Pleasure is also more largely and specially set forth in a Body of Instructions, containing every necessary Power and Rule of Direction for the better Government of his Colony; and the Names of all the Council are particularly specified in the said Instructions.

The Members of the Council are severally appointed by the King's *Mandamus*; or *Letter* to his Governor, directing him to swear in, and admit such a one to be of His Majesty's Council of the said Province; and by virtue thereof, they are merely Counsellors of State, to whom the Governor for the time being applies for advice in cases of weight and moment.

This Council of State, consisting of Twelve Persons, are named in the King's Instructions to his Governor, as expressed in the

Clause above-mentioned; and this additional plan of Duty pointed out by His Majesty, is surely no more inconsistent or incompatible, than the power given to the Governor and Council by Act of Assembly to be a Court of Chancery can be so deemed. One sett of men may have various Jurisdictions; and the circumstance of the same People acting in separate and distinct situations may be as easily reconciled, as that a Priest shall be at one time in the *Desk*, and at another in the *Pulpit*; the nature of the Offices differ in the *Mode* of performance, but the *End* is just the same.

The Clause above-mentioned almost in positive words declares Three distinct and separate Branches of the Legislature: "That you, (meaning the Governor) with the consent of our said Council and Assembly, or the major part [37] of them *respectively*, shall have power and authority to make, ordain Laws, etc." which terms, as *individually* distinguish, and mark out, Three independent and distinct States, as language can express.—Besides, these different Powers are derived to them by distinct Instruments: those of a Privy Council, by Mandamus; and those of a Legislature, by the King's Commission and Instructions to His Governor. I never was able to comprehend, how the Commons House of Assembly presumed to liken themselves to the House of Commons of Great Britain, and then drop all sight of that Model from which the other Branches of our Subordinate Legislature are manifestly taken; for it is by virtue of the Governor's Commission that the Freeholders of the People are called in Assembly, and by the King's writ, signed by the Governor and the Members of His Majesty's Council; and therefore all those eminent Rights they so much value themselves upon, were, in fact, originally conveyed to them through the very same medium, as those of the Council in Assembly, which are now fixed and established by Laws suited to our local circumstances, and which were framed under the King's Royal Prerogative and License. Our Constitution is *derivative*, and entirely flows from the Crown, is wholly *ex gratia*,[50] and, therefore, subject to such modifications upon Constitutional Principles, as His Majesty shall, from time to time, in His Royal Wisdom, see proper and expedient; provided, also, that they are not repugnant to any subsisting Laws.

The Rights and Privileges of the Commons House are neither

created nor recognized by any Statute of Great Britain; they arise, as it were, by grant from the Crown; their Legislature owes its establishment to the King; and every claim [38] they set up, springs to them from the same medium through which the Council derive theirs. This being the true state of a plain fact, it follows as a consequence, that when the Crown gave permission to call an Assembly, they surely might appoint a Council; and lawfully invest them with the powers expressed in His Majesty's Commission and Instructions; and the rather, when we call to mind that the People of this Country made humble suit to His Majesty King George the First, in the year 1721, to take them under His Royal Protection and Government, by renouncing their Charter Rights under the Proprietary Constitution; and this change being effected at their own instance, and afterwards by a clear purchase on the part of the Crown for a valuable consideration, and by an absolute surrender by the Lords Proprietors, in 1729, the Power who embraced them in order to protect them, could alone give motion and activity to them, as a Colony, or distant Member of the Parent State.

When the Crown had thus taken the Government of this Colony upon them, and had appointed Francis Nicholson,[51] Esq. Provisional Governor thereof, the Assembly passed an Act of Recognition, on the 18th of August, 1721, which recites, that "whereas His Most Sacred Majesty had been graciously pleased, at the humble desire and request of His faithful Subjects of this Province, to take the same under His Majesty's most gracious and immediate Government and Protection; and had also been pleased to Commissionate, under the Great Seal of Great Britain, Francis Nicholson, Esq. Governor, etc. over the same, *with full Powers to call a General Assembly, etc.*, and that they with one voice and heart did acknowledge His Ma-[39]jesty's *most lawful and undoubted Right* to the said Province; therefore, in gratitude, they prayed, that it might be enacted by His Majesty, by, and with, the consent of the Governor, Council, and Assembly, that they do recognize His said Majesty to be of right, and, by the Laws of Great Britain, is Sovereign Lord and King, etc. etc."[52]

This Act of Recognition expressly shews, that the *Powers to Call a General Assembly*, originated with the King himself. With what face, then, can Gentlemen deny those Rights to His Majesty's Council (who bear a share in the Legislature of the Country under the same Authority by which they themselves are allowed to sit), so essentially necessary to support their proper dignity and consequence as Legislators?

By the eleventh section of a Provincial Act, passed in 1721, it is enacted, "That the Members of Assembly chosen by that Act, shall have as much Power and Privilege, to all Intents and Purposes, as any Members of Assembly theretofore had, provided the same are such as are according to His Majesty's *Thirty-fifth Instruction*."[53] Can any thing more decisively point out the sense of that Dependence upon the Crown, which the People at that time of day entertained, than this extraordinary Provision, which virtually declares the Power of the Crown to bind us by Instructions?—And the Act in a manner incorporates the same, by excepting those cases of Privilege which this Instruction so flatly disallows; and in points, too, of the most delicate nature, and which remain undecided upon to this day, between the Lords and Commons of Great Britain.

The Thirty-fifth Instruction to Governor Nicholson, which I believe is continued to the pre-[*40*]sent day, runs in the following words: "And whereas the Members of several Assemblies in the Plantations, have frequently assumed to themselves Privileges no ways belonging to them; especially of being protected from Suits at Law, during the term they remain of the Assembly, to the great prejudice of the Creditors, and the obstruction of Justice;—and some of the Assemblies have presumed to adjourn themselves at pleasure, without leave from our Governor first obtained; and others have taken upon them the sole framing of Money-Bills, refusing to let the Council alter or amend the same; all which practices are very detrimental to our Prerogative: If, upon your calling an Assembly in South Carolina, you find them insist upon any of the abovesaid Privileges, you are to signify to them, that it is our express Will and Pleasure, that you do not allow any Protection to any Member of the Council or Assembly, further than in their persons; and That only during the Sitting of the Assembly; and that you are not to allow them to adjourn themselves otherwise than *de die in diem*,[54] except for Sundays and Holidays, without leave from you, or the Commander in Chief for the time, being first obtained.—It is also our further Pleasure, that the Council have the like power of framing Money-Bills as the Assembly; and you are expressly enjoined not to allow the said Assembly, or any of the Members thereof, any Power or Privilege whatsoever, which is not allowed by Us to the House of Commons, or the Members thereof, in Great Britain."[55]

The Privileges expressed in this Instruction were enjoyed by the Council, without Interruption, till 1735, when the Assembly claimed a [41] sole and exclusive Right of framing Money-Bills, and which they have, at different periods since that time, continued to assert and maintain.[56]

This Instruction relates entirely to Legislative Business, and the Privileges of the Members of Assembly, and forbids the Governor to allow protection to any Member of the Council or Assembly, further than in their Persons, etc. Now, as mere Counsellors protection is out of the case, neither has the framing of Money Bills anything to do with their station, as Members of the Privy Council; from whence it is evident beyond a doubt, that the Council form one Branch of the Legislature of this Country, and must be viewed as a separate and distinct Body, both from the Governor and Assembly, because the Council have a concurrent power with the Assembly to frame Money Bills, etc.; which shews a *distinctiveness* of Legislative Jurisdiction; and the Governor (till Assent is necessary) has no part allotted him to act, except that he is to keep the Members within due bounds of Privilege under the terms of his Instruction.

Privilege is a term inapplicable to the Council sitting as a Privy Council; for in that character they possess not a single privilege by their Constitution, and very few by the Laws of the Province; and all the privileges of His Majesty's Privy Council at home, consist in that security which certain Laws give them against attempts and conspiracies to destroy their lives. The term Privilege, therefore, in this Instruction, points directly to the Members of Council exercising Legislative Duties; in which station alone, the Council apprehend they are entitled to any privilege or personal protection.

[42] That no man may entertain a conceit, that in reciting and

discussing this *Thirty-Fifth Instruction,* I thereby mean to set up the King's Instructions generally to His Governors in America, as Laws and Constitutions by which the Colonists are or ought to be governed; I shall plainly tell my Reader all I wish to infer, viz. That the King, when he gave Power to call an Assembly, at the same time, and by the same public Instruments, established in His Council a Right of Legislation, as a distinct Body from the Commons House: That the whole scope of the King's Commission and Instructions manifestly shews, that the Assembly derive their powers from the same fountain that the Council do; that our Government is clearly derivative; and that, without the King's Grace, we had been destitute of any Constitution whatsoever: That our Provincial Legislature, by the first Election Act, passed in 1721, after His Majesty had taken this Colony under his own immediate protection, plainly shews, that they entertained this sense of the matter, by declaring that the Members shall have as much privilege as heretofore, provided the same are such as are according to His Majesty's Thirty-fifth Instruction. What is this exception, or saving, but a clear acknowledgement that the King, by his Instruction, might direct in the way stated, that the power of modifying the Government of His Colony was in His hands? And I appeal to the uniform practice, from 1721 to 1735, as an irrefragable argument in support of the Council's Legislative Rights, when they were allowed to frame, alter, and amend Money Bills, by virtue of this Instruction.

[43] It is a rule in construing a Statute,* to pay great regard to the construction which the Sages of Law, who lived about the time, or soon after, it was made, did put upon it; because they were best able to judge of the intention of the Makers thereof: for it is a maxim, that *Contemporanea expositio est fortissima in Lege.*[57] Now I produce the King's Commission and Instruction, upon the establishment of this Colony as a Royal Government, to prove His Power over it in the instances mentioned; and agreeable to the above maxim, I give you not merely judicial decisions, but the judgment of the Legislators themselves who lived at that time, implored the protection of that Power, which they afterwards

---

* 2 Inst. 11, 136, 181.

expressly acknowledged, who adopted the Instruction which so limited and restrained them, and so mightily enlarged and extended the powers of the Council, and who submitted to these Royal Regulations by conforming their practice wholly to them.

That the Council have a Legislative Right, as a Second Branch, appears, not only from constant experience, but also from the stile and expression of our Laws.

In 1722 was passed an Act with the following title: "An Estimate† of the Charges of the Government, that is and will be due on the twenty-fifth of March next, 1723, to be provided for by the General Assembly, and agreed to by the Committee of *Both Houses* appointed for that purpose."[58]

An Act of Assembly passed the fifth of February, 1736–7, for laying an Embargo on Ships or Vessels; and the Preamble opens in the following words: "Whereas the *Legislative Powers* of this Province have received Advice, that a [*44*] dangerous Scheme is formed by certain Subjects of the King of Spain, etc."[59]

Many of the Laws passed at that time in the Enacting part say, "By the Governor; by and with the Advice and Consent of the Council and the Representatives;" and others express, "by the Governor and the Council, and the Representatives convened in General Assembly."

If we examine the King's Disallowance, or Repeal, of the Acts of Assembly, about the same period, this point will be more clearly established. The Repeal opens thus:* "Whereas by Commission under the Great Seal of Great Britain, the Governor, Council, and Assembly are authorized and impowered to make, constitute, and ordain Laws, etc. for the peace, welfare, and good government of the Province, etc."[60]

The Governor has an Instruction requiring him to observe, that in passing all Laws, the stile of Enacting the same be, *by the Governor, Council,* and *Assembly.*—And to what end was such a direction given, but to preserve *that stile,* which so clearly expressed the distinct Bodies, whose respective concurrence and assent were

---

† Trott's Carolina Laws, p. 405.
* Trott's Carolina Laws, p. 397.

Considerations

declared necessary for making Laws, etc? The Governor is likewise
enjoined to transmit home all Laws, with the several dates, or
respective times, when the same *passed the Assembly*, the *Council*,
and received *his Assent*. Is it possible to express the *Individuality*,
if I may be allowed the phrase, of the several Branches, in more
clear and positive Terms? Do not the words denote Three separate
and distinct Parties; and That too as precisely as any Deed tripar-
tite in Law? Is it not evident beyond a doubt, that [45] every Act
must pass the Assembly, pass the Council, and have the Governor's
Assent to the perfection of it? These different stages strongly point
at the *Model* from which our Subordinate Legislature is taken; and
the features bear as strong a resemblance to the Constitution of
our Mother Country, as those of an Infant can be likened to the
stronger lines of an aged Parent: the similitude may be traced in
both cases, with only certain circumstantial Differences; such as
must necessarily distinguish Infancy from Age, Maturity from
Childhood, Strength from Weakness.

By an Act of Assembly passed in the year 1736, for ascertaining
Public Officers Fees, those of the Clerk of the Council are also
enumerated; and in a separate Division next immediately following
is this Title:

"*The Clerk of the Council in Assembly his Fees.*" Among the
several allowances are, for "a *Warrant of Contempt*, Ten Shillings;
and a *Releasement* therefrom, Five Shillings."[61]

By another Fee Law passed the 7th of May 1743, the like provisions are made for the same Officer, with an Increase of Ten Shillings on a Warrant of Contempt. True it is, that this Law has never
been confirmed by his Majesty, but it proves as strongly what it is
cited to shew, viz. the Sense of the People's Representatives in relation to the Rank and Condition which the Council hold in the
Legislature of the Colony.[62]

Many of the Acts of Assembly sufficiently evince, that the Council were till lately ever considered as one Branch of the Provincial
Legislature; and the language of the Lower House on different
occasions confirms this Doctrine, if any thing is wanting to support
it. I appeal to their own Journals of the 11th of May 1754, wherein
it will appear, that the Assembly, in [46] their Address to the Gov-

95

ernor, take notice of his Affection and Regard for the Welfare of the Province lately expressed in his Excellency's Speech to *both Houses*.[63]

I must here desire my Reader to go back some pages, and take another view of the King's additional Instruction to his Governor, and he will there find that his Majesty, throughout the same, denominates the People's Representatives by the stile of the *Lower House*; which, *vi termini*,[64] implies an Upper House or Superior Body, to which that Title must bear immediate reference, and respect. Upon the whole, I think these Conclusions may be fairly drawn from the several Facts above-stated: That it was His Majesty's Intention to assimilate the Constitution of this Colony to that of Great Britain, so far as the local circumstances and situations of things could possibly admit: That it was his Royal Will to establish Three distinct States, in the Persons of a Governor, a Council, and Assembly: That divers Acts of the Colony Legislature maintain the same Distinction: That Uniform Experience hath preserved the like Idea; and that the Legislative Powers of the Council have been virtually, and almost expressly, recognized and declared by positive Laws, and by the Language and Stile of Public Papers, as appears by the Journals of Assembly.

It may be proper further to observe, that Bills have originated in the Council, as well as in the Assembly; though it must be owned, the practice has not been frequent: however, the Assembly, after a second reading of a Bill, always send it to the Council by two of their own Members; and when twice read, and perhaps altered and amended, the Council return it by the Master in Chancery. When it has undergone a third reading, and been passed by the Assembly, it is in like [47] manner brought up again to his Majesty's Council, who, upon the third reading, either pass or reject the same; and if passed, it is carried back to the Commons House, who direct the same to be ingrossed: and at the end of the Session the Three States, viz. Governor, Council, and Assembly, meet in the Council Chamber, when the Speaker of the Assembly reads the Title of the Act, and then presents it for the Governor's Assent: this being given, the Speaker signs it, as also the Governor, who likewise seals it.

Thus it manifestly appears, that there are Two separate Bodies of Men, who, in a Parliamentary way, mature the several Laws which concern the welfare of the Province; and though, perhaps, the mode of doing Business may differ in certain circumstantial points from the practice of both Houses of Parliament, yet true it is, that, in substance, the Proceedings are the same, and as all Bills, for the most part, take their rise in the Lower House, the Council, by the Practice which prevails, have a negative in every case, upon the several Acts of the House of Representatives; as *they* would have upon those of the Council, which might originate with them; and as the Governor, in his Executive Situation, *has* both upon Council and Assembly.

This is a Picture not unlike to the British Plan of Government; and the Resemblance is so striking, that men have been led to compare it to that great Model of Perfection—not urged thereto by arrogant Presumption, but excited by the Love and Veneration which they bear to the most glorious Constitution in the World; from an honest pride to claim alliance to *it*; from a firm persuasion of the Blessings flowing from *it*; from a pleasing reflection that we are the genuine Sons and Daughters of Britain, Descen-[48]dants from the Loins, and kindred Members of the same State; from a full conviction, that our own Happiness will be best secured by adopting the same Maxims, and embracing the same Laws. Hence it is, that a Governor is said to represent the King; the Council, the House of Lords; and the People's Representatives, the House of Commons of Great Britain. And where is the Arrogance of this innocent and natural Allusion? Every Man of Sense must know, that the Powers and Extent of Jurisdiction belonging to the King, Lords, and Commons, are so immensely great, and so inexpressibly transcendent, that none of the works of Man can be properly compared to this stupendous Machine, so knit and so connected as to animate and sustain a System of its own.

No man of common understanding can draw the comparison, without perceiving most sensibly the immense differences and distinctions that arise upon the comparison; but when we consider ourselves as Members of one great Empire, and that our Colonies have a Legislature of their own to regulate their interior Polity, we are struck with admiration of the British Plan in this little epitome thereof exhibited in ours. We view a Governor, and find, upon

97

examination, that his Power flows from the King; that he represents Him, and exercises certain Acts of inferior Regality, and is possessed of the whole Executive Power of Government in our contracted sphere. We proceed, and find that a Council named by the King, act Legislatively, as a Second or Middle Branch, between the Sovereign and People; and we instantly figure to our minds a House of Lords. We behold a House of Representatives chosen by the People, engaged in framing Laws, laying Taxes, and regulating the Affairs of this [49] Community with the concurrence and consent of the other two Branches; and we as readily form an idea of the House of Commons. The Outlines of Government agree in both cases; and I defy any Man to say, They are not substantially the same, so far as local circumstances will admit, and a narrow circle of Duty will allow; and saving also, certain eminent Distinctions which can only belong to the Sovereign State.

Judge BLACKSTONE,* speaking of the Colonies, thus expresses himself: "The Form of Government in most of them is borrowed from that of England; they have a Governor named by the King, or, in some Proprietary Colonies, by the Proprietor, who is his Representative, or Deputy. They have Courts of Justice of their own, from whose Decisions an Appeal lies to the King in Council, here in England. Their General Assembly, which are their House of Commons, together with *their Council of State*, being their *Upper House*, with the concurrence of the King, or his Representative the Governor, make Laws suited to their own Emergencies."[65]

Having, I hope, satisfactorily proved, that the Council of this Colony are a Second or Middle Branch of our Provincial Legislature, and in fact an *Upper House* of Assembly, I propose to answer the several Popular Arguments suggested by a Spirit of Faction in some, and by Ignorance in others.

It is asserted, that the Council cannot be an Upper House of Legislature, in nature of a House of Lords, because they are appointed by the King, may be suspended by the Governor, and are removeable at the King's pleasure; because [50] they are not endued with the same Rights and Privileges as the House of Lords; and because they are not a permanent Body, and Inde-

---

* 1. Blackstone, 108.

pendent of the Crown. I do not recollect that anything more has ever been urged against the pretensions of the Council, but what falls under one or other of the points above suggested.

I conceive that the Council being appointed by the King, is an objection both idle and absurd because the Hereditary Counsellors of the Kingdom, the House of Lords, (which the pride of our Plebeians will not allow this Body to compare themselves to, even *distantly, restrictively,* or *metaphorically*) are raised to those dignities by the immediate grace and favour of the Crown. It is the King who places Coronets on the Heads of his Subjects, and at a risk whether they will fit the Heads proposed to wear them; all Honour flows from thence; and if the appointment of the King lessens the consequence of One of his humble Council of South Carolina, it must operate equally against Coronets and Mitres. But it is said that the Council may be suspended, and removed at pleasure. This situation, I must own, is precarious, and liable to great objection: however, when we reflect that it is merely *honorary,* attended with no profit, but much trouble, and more vexation; when we consider, that scarce an instance can be found of any wanton or arbitrary exclusion, by the King's Governors, of a Member from his Seat in Council, and that the difficulty for the Crown to supply these Vacancies, under the various discouragements which attend the situation, is extremely great; we shall have reason to conclude, that the Appointment is not altogether as Dependant, as suits some Men to represent. But granting it were as contended for, the power of the Counsellor remains the same; [51] his *Tenure* is precarious, and on that score his Virtue may be put to a severer trial; but still he has a clear Constitution to govern and direct him; and the Argument is no stronger against the Provincial Council, than against Provincial Judges: till very lately, the Judges of England were in little better condition themselves; and yet their Judicial Power was never questioned, or their Authority disputed.

A man may have as good an estate for years, during the term, as another who boasts a Fee Simple; and though the Council have no stated and determined duration, still I do insist, that the Power vested in them is just the same; it may be exercised with as much independence, as by a Peer of the Realm; and though in a more precarious way, and with greater peril to the Party, yet the objection stands good only against the *Tenure*, not against the extent of Power or Jurisdiction.

For my own part, I have ever been indifferent about the Stile and Title of the Council in their Legislative Rank, and have always thought it a matter of small moment, whether they were called His Majesty's Council, The Council, The Board, or The Upper House. Names may be proper in some cases to signify Things, but Names can never confer Rights, or give a line of Jurisdiction; and therefore I have been satisfied with contemplating, that this Body enjoy Substantial Rights, and by their Negative and Controuling Power, in all Legislative Acts, are to be looked upon as maintaining a due Balance in the Constitution of our Minor State: it is therefore weak, nay, childish, to contend, that they are merely a Privy Council, when the whole Course and Order of the Legislative Proceedings distinguish them as one Superior Branch.

[52] Many people argue, that although Bills are sent to the Council, and Public Business is transacted with them in a Parliamentary way, that still they are only a Council: they admit, indeed, their power to do certain Mechanical Acts, and to give their Concurrence or Dissent; but they flatly disallow them to be an Upper House, or that they are entitled to any of those Parliamentary Rights, Privileges, or Distinctions, which of necessity pertain to the several Branches of the State; they will graciously allow them all the drudgery and toil of a House, with a large portion of scurrility, invective, and abuse; but they cannot condescend to admit, that they enjoy any badges or ensigns of Authority, or that they possess, of right, a co-ercive power to punish in any case whatever.

The Council, considered merely as such, must consent as well as advise; and consequently their judgments are to be informed of every fact necessary for them to know, previous to their giving such consent. Now, if it is acknowledged, that Parliamentary practice is the most eligible mode of doing business, what reason can in justice be assigned, why they should not be allowed to hold a Legislative consequence; in fact, as well for their security, as for maintenance of their dignity, since they formally carry about them every appearance of a Legislature, by concurring in or rejecting, by altering or amending Bills, and by strictly pursuing the several modes of Parliamentary procedure? It seems pretty clear to me, that under these circumstances, it is more for the honour and credit of the Colony, to view the Council as an Upper House, in imitation of a Constitution which every one affects to admire; and nothing can be more absurd or unjust than to suppose, that His Majesty ever meant to im-[53]pose burthens upon Persons, without intending at the same time to give them all necessary powers for their protection and support. And can any thing be more unreasonable than to contend, that the Members of Assembly, sitting on Legislative business at the West End of a Public Building, have, and enjoy, the Privileges of Members of the House of Commons; and that the Council deliberating on the same Business at the East End of the same House, in the same way, and to the same general end, and in every stage of which Business they have an equal Concurrence, and ultimately an absolute Negative on every Act of the Commons House; and yet *they* shall have no Privileges or Power of an Upper House, or Second Branch of the Legislature, but are to lie open and exposed to every species of insult, without the least shadow of power to punish or correct? The inequality under such a situation is so glaring, that the due equilibrium would be lost, and all Power would center in the House of Representatives.

In the course of my observations, I have been obliged to mention certain Instructions from the King to His Governor, as proofs of His Royal Intention, that the Constitution of the Colony should be assimilated to that of the Mother-Country; and it is my wish that I may be understood to mean that, in general, Instructions are mere Directions for the Governor's Conduct; but sometimes they are in addition to the Commission, and contain a more full explanation of the King's Pleasure, respecting the powers given in, and by, the said Commission, under the Great Seal; and therefore such Instructions may well be argued from, provided they are framed upon the principles of the English Constitution. And this naturally leads me to view the present subject in [54] another light, and I think it must add greatly to strengthen the foregoing reasoning.

I lay it down as an undeniable proposition, That the King can give no other Constitution to His American Colonies, than one resembling that of England; no other plan of Civil Government can be instituted by virtue of any power under the Great Seal of that Kingdom; for when the Subjects of the Parent-State repaired to the Western World, they did not renounce their Connection with it.—The Colonies are not to be considered as conquered Countries, being parts and parcels of the British Empire, and settled by British Subjects; and they are the King's Plantations, but not His Conquests. By the *22d and 23d Car. II, c. 26*, they are through the whole Act called the King's English Plantations: and in the tenth paragraph 'tis said, "Inasmuch as the Plantations are Inhabited with His Subjects of England."[66]—And so in *15 Car. II. c.7 s. 5.*[67] and *12 Car. II, c. 34*[68] they are called Colonies and Plantations of this Kingdom of England.

No Man will be so hardy as to declare, that when the Subjects repaired to America, they therefore quitted the Laws and Constitution of their Country:—they could not relinquish their Natural Allegiance, and it was not in their power to do the other.—This is a Dominion belonging, not only to the Crown, but to the Realm of England, though not within the Territorial Realm. *Vaughan,* 350, says, that they follow England, and are a part of it.[69]

That Allegiance continues, let the Subject go to the remotest Region of the King's Dominions, every one must readily admit; for which reason, the Laws must govern and protect him†[70] *unum* [55] *trahit alterium.*[71] Besides, the Great Seal extends to America, and a Writ of Error lies to all subordinate Dominions, of which the Plantations are held to be a part. Not to shew that this intimate Connection, this continuing and subsisting Dependance, were clearly understood about the time of the first Settlements in this Quarter of the World, I cannot omit taking notice, that in the Reign of Charles II, one of the Articles of Impeachment against Lord Chancellor Clarendon was, *"that he had introduced an Arbitrary Government into his Majesty's Plantations."*[72]

From these general Observations it seems very evident to me, that the Civil Establishments of this Colony, being made by the King *Jure Corona,*[73] must be looked on as Authorities respectively bearing the Image of the like Powers in the Mother Country, and

---

† Vaugh. 402.

operating in all respects as such, as nearly as the local Condition of a subordinate and dependant Colony can enable them to do.

The Resemblance is still more striking when we take a View of the different Departments. We have Courts of Common Pleas and King's Bench, of Oyer and Terminer, of Chancery, as also a Court of Admiralty, and Ordinary for Probate of Wills and granting Administrations. We have Circuit Courts, Sheriffs, Coroners, Constables, and Justices of Peace; and these several Jurisdictions subsist by the same Authority, and for the same great ends, as the like Courts in England. Our Laws are principally those of England, in all the great Branches of Liberty, Property, and Personal Security; and the Mode of Practice is the Mode observed in England in all substantial Points. Our Legislature consists of the Governor, who represents the King; and he is Head of the Community. Our Council, con-[56]sisting of Twelve Members (for want of a Nobility) form an Upper House; and the Lower House, which answers to the House of Commons, is composed of the Representatives of the People. These Three Bodies do the most important Acts of Legislation: they raise Money, impose Duties, and pass Laws, extending to the Lives, Liberty, and Property of the Subject; and many persons have suffered death by Laws of our Provincial Legislature, before the Royal Assent has been obtained.

By an Act of the Assembly, passed the 12th of December, 1712, entitled, "An Act to put in force in the Province of South Carolina, the several Statutes of the Kingdom of England, or South Britain, therein particularly mentioned; the Acts enumerated are not only declared to be in as full force, as if they had been specially enacted, and made for the said Province," or by any Assembly thereof, but also the Statutes referred to, or explaining such enumerated Statutes, and all the Statutes relating to the Allegiance, or declaring the Rights and Liberties of the Subjects, are made of the same Force.

The several Civil Officers are likewise declared to have the same Power and Authority of the like officers in England. The Common Law itself is also made of force; and it is ordained, that the Courts of Record shall have the power of the King's and Queen's Court, mentioned in any of the said recited Acts.[74]

This Civil Order of Government is surely a true Copy of our

Mother-State, so far as the same can suit our dependant Situation; and what cruel Hand will attempt to spoil a single Feature of the Picture?

[57] Upon a critical Survey, and nice Comparison, it must be owned, that the Piece, though it has merit, is not perfect: but the same objection will lie, with very great force, against the Original itself; for, though much has been done to give strength and stability to the Constitution, much is still wanting to secure it. Every man knows the Faults of the one; and therefore I shall briefly hint at the Imperfections of the other—with this humble request, That an Argument on the score of a Defect, may have no other byass than to shew, that the Copy wants some correction and amendment.— The grand Flaw in our Civil Establishment is, the Want of that Independence, so necessary to preserve the true, Political Balance; but when we regret this Want, let us patiently reflect, whether such a State of Independence can properly subsist, or, in the nature of things, suit our particular condition. The Governor holds the first Rank in our Legislature; and though he represents the King, it will be found impossible that he can possess so large an Independence; for he is but a *Delegate*, is only cloathed with certain limited Portions of the Royal Prerogative. His Consent to Laws is rather provisional, than final; and, even in his Legislative Station, he is controuled by Instructions; and, therefore, is a two-fold Character, as *Judge and Minister*.

The uncertain Tenure by which the Council hold their places, points out, likewise, the same want of Independance; but is it a sound Argument to say, that because these two Bodies differ so widely, on comparison, from the King and House of Lords, that, therefore, they are no Branches of our Provincial Legislature? This, indeed, is not asserted in relation to the Governor; but it would hold equally strong against him, as against the Body to whom it is opposed; and con-[58]sequently, by proving too much, it actually proves nothing to the purpose. The question, properly put, is not, Whether each Body has as much Power as the like Bodies possess in the Kingdom of England, for this is neither possible, or necessary to our dependant State; but the true question is, Whether they do not respectively act in points of Legislation; and Independently too, of each other; and without one controuling, or unduly influencing the other? And I will be bold to say, They do; for they sit apart; and the Acts of the Council are not considered as the Acts of Individuals, but of the Body at large. The Independance, therefore, is decently enough maintained in a Constitutional View, between the several Powers acting separately within the Jurisdiction of the Colony; and the dependance is, strictly speaking, only as finally resting upon the King himself; or, in other words, both Governor and Council hold their places at the Will of the Crown, and yet, acting distinctly in the Colony, are independent of each other. I lay very little stress upon the circumstance of a Governor having it in his power to Suspend; because this is, in some degree, provided against by his Instructions; and arbitrary removals so seldom occur, that they can scarce be supposed to influence the present subject of dispute.

It is by no means necessary, that our Legislature should enjoy the same Extensive Rights, and Honorable Distinctions, as the Legislature of Great Britain; because we are subordinate to, and dependant upon, the Sovereign State. We move in a narrow Circle, and have little more to do than to take care of our Estates, preserve a decent Police, repair Churches, clear Cuts, make Drains, mend Roads, and Bridges, and Ourselves, which much require it, and to thank God for his Boun-[59]ty; and the King for his Protection. And if we will but modestly see what a contracted Scheme this is, compared to the immense objects of a great Commercial Kingdom, having Territories in every Quarter of the Globe, we shall be better satisfied with our Condition, and find less fault with the several Orders of our little State, the importance whereof is proportioned very properly to the small and circumscribed circle, within which we have any part to act.

By this time I hope my Reader is convinced, that our Colony Constitution is borrowed from the English Model; and as all the parts bear so near a resemblance; as the King could give no Civil Government incompatible with, or repugnant to, His own; and as Reason points out, that the respective Branches of our Subordinate State, are intended to act in imitation of those from whom the whole plan is apparently derived; that therefore no exception will be taken to deprive the Body of Men of those Rights, which they ought to hold under the same Authority by which all the other Members of our Civil State hold and enjoy theirs.

Upon the whole of this enquiry, I think it must appear, that His Majesty's Council are a Middle Branch, or rather an Upper House of Legislature of the Colony of South Carolina.

When I seriously reflect, that the nearer we can resemble Ourselves to the Mother-Country, the more Honor will redound; and when I call to mind, that it ought to be our Glory and Ambition to preserve a good Understanding in that Quarter; I am amazed, beyond measure, to find such a spirit of Contradiction, and such untoward Sentiments prevail.

I cannot now entertain a doubt, that the Council are an *Upper House*; I am well convinced they [60] stand in that relation; and I must say, that the daring denial of this Power is a bold step towards a Dissolution of our Civil Government. It must be confessed, that the House of Assembly have pressed so sorely for many years upon this Second Branch, that it has made many respectable Persons *shy* of accepting what was formerly esteemed a Seat of Honor and Distinction. When the General Opinion proclaims, that a Place in Council is a kind of alienation from the concerns and interest of the People; that the Members are said to possess Rights which every Person in the Community is called upon to question; when they are represented as arrogating to themselves, powers which never were intended to be bestowed upon them, and there is no Tribunal on the Spot to decide the difference; when the part allotted them to act is made a mockery, and the Populace are encouraged to believe, that the Council are *mere Tools* and *Engines* to the Crown, from whom they pretend to derive *Powers*, which are wantonly stiled Usurpations; what security can such a Branch of the Legislature have, when they are neither formidable by Numbers, nor important in the course of Jurisdiction?

The Assembly have now declared to the People, that there is no Upper House, and that a Commitment for Contempt by the Council in that character is Illegal, Unconstitutional, and Oppressive; and so I must allow it to be, if they are not a Second Branch of the Colony Legislature. This is a melancholy Judgment, big with danger, and subversive of all Civil Order: The bands of our Society are now loosened, the plan of his Majesty's Government totally disordered, and the Commons are the *vortex* which swallows all the power.

[*61*] We are surely going back to the unhappy era of 1648. History informs us of the *Evils* of those days; and we may guess what ill effects will flow, if such doctrines are revived; especially if there is no Middle State to restrain the exorbitances of Democratical Oppressions. Methinks I see the beautiful copy of our English Constitution much altered and defaced; yea, the *vitals* of our Civil State have received a mortal wound: but my hands are not embrued in this cruel murder, and though I behold strong men, like *Sampson;** taking hold of the middle pillars, oversetting by one bold effort the fabric they support,[75] I will sooner be buried in its ruins, than be a sorrowful spectator of a Factious Triumph.

If the Council are no Upper House, though they do the business of one, and have no authority to Commit in any case; if they are destitute of every Parliamentary Right and Protection, I see nothing to oppose the Sons of Violence and Disorder from intruding into the Council-chamber, overawing their proceedings, obstructing the Members in their Legislative deliberations, and committing every act of disrespect and insolence; and under all these pungent aggravations, his Majesty's Honourable Council must either submit to the affront, or exert a power which two Justices will under colour of Law evade, and for which the Assembly will bestow their highest commendations. What Man of Spirit and Reputation will condescend to this inhuman treatment? The Subject who owes a duty to the King likewise owes a duty to himself; and if he neglects to support his own honour and dignity, it is much to be feared he will add little to his station.

[*62*] Men who seriously contemplate this important subject, and who have no private interest to serve, or favourite passion to indulge, who search for Truth as *a Pearl of great price*, and wish the prosperity of every Member of the Empire, must silently bemoan the unhappy and deranged state of Public Affairs in one of the most flourishing Colonies of North America.

I have briefly sketched out the wide difference between the

---

* Judges xvi. ver. 29.

House of Lords and the Council of our Province, and I have also hinted that our dependant situation makes it neither suitable nor proper that our Privileges should approach a literal comparison with those of the Parent-State; but surely so much power and weight must vest in this Middle Branch, as will answer the ends and purposes of their original institution. Every one admits, that their consent is absolutely necessary to the enacting Laws and Statutes; and it is *this consent* which gives them a Legislative Capacity, and entitles them to such rights and privileges of Parliament as are immediately essential to their existence as one distinct Member of the State. The power of Commitment for Breach of Privilege and Contempt, is that kind of authority which is necessary to their existence as a Body; for without it, every thing they do is a mockery and farce, and they are a mere *Tub* to the Whale, to sport and play with. Judges, Justices, and Courts of Justice, enjoy, and daily exercise this power; and if deprived of it, they could not subsist a moment, or answer the end of their appointments. And if Magistrates, when persons are brought before them by Habeas Corpus, take upon them to discharge Prisoners committed for Contempts, because no Act of Parliament is produced to warrant the Commitments, I am inclined to believe, that the Court which Committed would devise some plan [63] of punishment for such an insolent offense. Perhaps some ignorantly suppose, that this power of Commitment, the Privileges of Parliament, and the Right which Courts sometimes practise of giving Protections in certain cases, all spring as concessions from the Crown: but this is not the fact; for the Prerogative has no such powers to give. Perhaps others believe, that they are derived from some old Statute, deep buried in the Rolls of Parliament. This neither is the case. No; these powers arise by the necessary operation of Law, as incident to the respective Courts and Offices which exercise the same; they are entwined, as it were, in the Constitution itself, and are as much a part of the Law of the Land, as Magna Charta, or any other venerable Statute. The King cannot make Law, or create Privilege; but it is the Constitution itself which conveys peculiar and acknowledged Rights, and Privileges, and Protections, to the Parliament, to certain Officers of Trust, and to the Courts and Ministers of

Justice. Their origin, perhaps, cannot be traced to the springhead, any more than many principles of Law; but immemorial usage, general consent, and urgent necessity, have given them as deep and good a root, as written Laws or Statutes possibly could do.

The Ninth Article of Rights insisted upon at the time of the Revolution is, "That the Freedom of Speech, and Debates or Proceedings in Parliament, ought not to be impeached or questioned in any Court out of Parliament."[76] Now, comparing our Legislature, for the purposes of our own interior Polity, to the great Original from which the same is evidently copied, it seems unjust to the last degree, that the Proceedings of a Provincial Council should be impeached and questioned, nay over-ruled by Inferior Magistrates; [64] and that persons should be absolutely set at liberty, Committed by them acting legislatively; and that the Assembly shall also be permitted to interfere, censure the Middle State of the Colony, and give marks of applause to their own Members who presumed to decide so nice a question. And this is the more extraordinary, when it is considered, that the Act of Settlement at the Revolution, gives no new and unknown Rights, but merely declares such as the People then claimed to be their indubitable Rights and Liberties; and likewise when we farther reflect, that our Patriots are always happy to point at periods which have been so conducive to the establishment of Public Freedom.

No man can give a good reason, why the Assembly should have such Rights, and deny them to the Council; for they can only claim them as bearing a relation to that body which enjoy them in England, and the Council can only do the same; and it cannot admit of doubt, that the power is as necessary and essential to the one Branch, as it is to the other. Perhaps it may be said, that the Council are few in number, and that the power may be abused. To this I can only answer, That Popular Assemblies are most likely to be hurried into acts of precipitation, as well as violence, and that the objection to Power, merely because the same may be abused, is weak to a degree; and when I assure my Reader, that the Power of Committing has never been exercised by the Council more than twice from the first Settlement of the Colony, no great stress can be laid upon the danger of intrusting the Upper House with such a Power. But to shew my candour, I must frankly own, that this argument is as strong to prove the People very *good*, as to prove the Council either temperate or wise.

[65] The whole scope of the argument against the Council's power as an Upper House is, That they are not as Independant as the People wish, and of course do not possess that degree of Freedom which befits the Legislative Body of a Free Country; that is, the Council are not the Hereditary Counsellors of the King, nor do they possess many of the high privileges which pertain to that illustrious body. They are no Court of Judicature, nor do they try their own Members on life and death; they derive nothing from prescription or time immemorial; and their tenure is at the pleasure of the King, or at the will of a Governor. And because these things are so, shall this Branch have no privilege whatever? Because they are not wholly Independant, are they on that score to be Dependant altogether? Is there no intermediate state between the most extensive and the most limited authority? And because the Council are not a House of Lords, are they destitute of all Legislative Rights? This kind of reasoning is presumptuous to a great degree; because, granting we possessed those ample powers, they must be useless burthens. We have neither Finances to maintain the dignity, or Objects to deserve the splendor, our State is narrow, and our wants are few; we have no prospect beyond the limits of the Colony, and therefore the Nobility would be *idle affectation, foolish pageantry* and *insensible parade*. But these circumstances by no means exclude such incidental and concomitant powers as are necessary to support a certain degree of dignity and weight suited to our case, and requisite for the maintainance of due order and distinction. When time shall ripen, and make us Independant, we may aspire to *Dukedoms*, and pant for *Lordships*; but at present, we may content ourselves [66] with the power we *have*, which is nearly equal to the power we really *want*.

I take it for granted, that I have said sufficient to convince my Readers, that the Council are an Upper House, and have a right to Commit for a Breach of Privilege and Contempt; I shall therefore only cite a few Cases to convince them, that a Man cannot be legally discharged by any Power whatever from a Warrant of Commitment by a Legislative Body, during the sitting of both Houses.

Considerations

In the Case of one Sheridan, who, in 1680, was in custody by Order of the House of Commons, and who applied for a Habeas Corpus, which was denied, the matter was agitated in the House; and one of the soundest Lawyers in those days, Sir *William Jones*, in express terms declared, that the Habeas Corpus Act doth not extend to Commitment by either House of Parliament; that it relates merely to Cases bailable; that Commitments by the House are in the nature of Judgments; and that no Commitment on a Judgment is a bailable Case.[77] This happened about two years after the Habeas Corpus Act passed, which makes it a strong argument in point.

The celebrated Case of the Aylesbury Men has settled the matter beyond a doubt,[78] and the only Case which has occurred since that Determination, is that of the Honourable Alexander Murray, about twenty-two years ago, who being Committed by Order of the House of Commons, and a Habeas Corpus being issued, the cause returned by the Goaler was only an Order of the House of Commons, without *any crime alledged*; and the Judges declared they could not "Question the Authority of that House, or Demand the cause of their Commitment, or Judge the same;" and they remanded the Prisoner: this great point [67] is therefore clearly settled, and *now* is become the Established Law of the Land.[79]

Some people object, that the Council are a mixed Body, and that it is improper to vest the same persons acting as Advisers to the Governor with the Legislative Powers of an Upper House; but I see no great weight in this Objection; as there is, in fact, no connection between the respective Duties, they being altogether distinct, and seldom bearing the least relation to each other; however, granting that a Case may arise in the Legislature which had been in some degree under the consideration of the Council of State, it cannot be supposed that the Members of the Council will counteract *Legislatively*, what they had before done or advised as a Board of Privy Council, because these different situations create no separate interests, neither do they subject the Members to any *invincible necessity* of acting in a manner contradictory or repugnant to themselves.

This Body, by their very constitution, are intended to maintain a kind of Balance between the Crown and the People; for "the

111

two Houses* naturally drawing in two directions of opposite interests, and the Prerogative in another, still different from them
both, they mutually keep each other from exceeding their proper
limits."[80] The Council are a sort of *Barrier* to withstand the Encroachments of the Lower House; and by the experience of a
Century at least, the Institution has been found to answer extremely well the purposes of our Subordinate Jurisdiction. The great
mistake in which men find themselves involved upon the subject,
is wholly owing to an *Original Error*. We are apt to argue from the
situation of a great and mighty Kingdom, without perceiv-[68]ing,
that *political fitness* and *expediency*, such as are suited to the
Rank, the Wants, or Necessities of an Empire, cannot be applied to
our *limited condition*. The *fitness* must undergo various changes
and modification; and though we may retain certain features sufficient to preserve a kind of resemblance, and mark our *Filiation*, it
is impossible we can literally copy the whole piece.

The Establishment of Provincial Councils in their present form,
has till lately given satisfaction both to the Crown and People, and
the opposition which has been stirred for several years past, is owing to some Alterations which Time has produced, the most material of which is the encrease of the People's Representatives in
General Assembly, whereby the due equipoise is in a great measure
lost, and the weight of power centers with the People. *Like causes*
will in all Countries produce *like effects*; and whenever that nice
equilibrium which the different Branches of the Constitution are
intended to preserve, is lost, by an accession of too much power
to either Branch, the one will of course swallow up the other. Thus
it happened, the last Century, when the Commons had resolved
upon the Downfall of Monarchy, they likewise voted the *House of
Lords* to be useless and dangerous.

The Colony suffers in no respect by the twofold character of a
Council; but if a Privy Council were to be formed promiscuously
from the Members of both Houses, this would weaken the weight
of the Crown, and add greatly to the scale of the People, which
stands in need of no addition. But, in my apprehension, it seems
absolutely necessary that the Numbers of the Council should be

---

* 1. Blackst. 155.

encreased; and for this plain and obvious reason, Because a body of Twenty-Four Counsellors, for instance, appointed by the King from the First [69] Rank of the People, most distinguished for their Wealth, Merit, and Ability, would be a means of diffusing a considerable Influence through every Order of Persons in the Community, which must extend very far and wide, by means of their particular connections; whereas a Council of Twelve, several of whom are always absent, can have little weight, nor can their voices be heard amidst the clamour of *prevailing* Numbers.

I think this Body, acting Legislatively, ought to be made independent, by holding that station during the term of their Natural Lives, and determinable only on that event, or on their intire departure from the Province. But the same Person might nevertheless, for proper cause, be displaced from his Seat in Council; which regulation would, in a great measure; operate as a *Check* to an arbitrary Governor, who would be cautious how he raised a powerful Enemy in the Upper House by a rash Removal; at the same time that the power of Removal would keep the Member within proper bounds. The Life-Tenure of his Legislative Capacity would likewise sufficiently secure that *Independency* which is so necessary to this station, and so agreeable to the Constitution of the Parent-State. I know some folks will raise both scruples and fears; but for my own part, I think without much reason; for if we attend to the workings of human nature, we shall find, that a certain degree of Attachment commonly arises to the Fountain from whence an Independent Honor flows. Opposition seldom settles upon the persons who are raised to Dignity by favor of the Crown, it having so much the appearance of Ingratitude, one of the most detested vices; and it ever acts a *faint* and *languid* part, till a Descent or two are past, and the Author of the Elevation is extinct. From this reasoning it seems tolerably clear to me, that [70] the Legislator being for life, and deriving his consequence from the Crown, will, rather incline to *that scale;* and it is not probable that his opposition could in any instance be *rancorous* or *factious,* inasmuch as, though his Life-Estate is secure, he would not wish unnecessarily to excite the resentment of the Crown, or exclude his Descendants or Connections, perhaps, from succeeding afterwards to such a Post of Honour and Distinction in their Native Country: in short, this idea seems to admit such a *qualified Dependency,* as will attach the Person to the side of the Crown in that proportion which the Constitution itself allows, and yet so much *real Independancy,* as will make him superior to acts of Meanness, Servility, and Oppression. Whether these sentiments are well founded, or not, I submit to the impartial judgment of my Reader; what I principally mean to infer is, that the Happiness of these Colonies much depends upon a due *blending* or *mixture* of Power and Dependence, and in preserving a proper Subordination of Rank and Civil Discipline.

Some few distinctions it might be proper to annext to this situation, as an inducement to Men of Family and Fortune to accept the trust; for, in its present *impotent* state, it is a real burden; and as being overborne by the force of Numbers in the Lower House, is rendered obnoxious to the People, and oppressive to the Party.

These hints I venture to throw out as a kind of temporary or provisional expedients, such as may suit our present state and condition, and in conformity, in some degree, to the original plan sketched out on the First Settlement of our American Colonies. What may be fit and proper for each Province upon a change of the System altogether, and upon a more enlarged and comprehensive plan, I do not presume at present to sug-[71]gest; the subjects of this Pamphlet being principally confined to one particular Colony; and therefore an entire new scheme, or plan, upon untried ideas, is rather foreign to my present purpose. When the Colonies have made further advances in Population, Trade, and Science, some other mode of Government may, at a future day, become necessary for the safety and security of the American Dependencies, and for the permanent establishment of British Rule and Sovereignty over these distant and remote Members of the Empire: at present, the old Original *Draught* will probably answer every purpose, with the aid of a few occasional improvements, such as time, and a change of circumstances, naturally suggest, without doing the least degree of violence to the present System. In every human work, we find so much work of the *Moment* prevail when it was first fabricated, that a few years often convince the Original Projectors, how short-sighted and imperfect their ideas were, how unequal to answer any material vicissitudes, or to sustain the weight which it was intended to bear. Daily experience must convince every thoughtful man, that the *political*, as well as the *corporeal* System stands in constant need of correction; that the motions of the one are frequently affected by foreign and accidental causes, as well as the other; that a due and orderly circulation may be wanting in both; that gross humours oftentimes arise, and threaten danger, unless speedily removed and wisely managed; that as excrescences do many times deform and afflict the natural body, so, in like manner, uncommon tumours invade the Body Politic, and render it diseased and infirm; therefore Art must supply the want of fore-sight, and such physical skill must be exercised, to remove mala-dies, and restore to soundness, as the prevailing symptoms may re-[72]quire. Idle Quackery must be totally avoided; for no Cure less than *radical*, can be of material moment, whether the machine be *human or political*.

I cannot close this subject without expressing my sincere con-cern, that such unhappy disputes divide men's minds, and distract the Public Councils of this Country; and I have presumed to offer these considerations to the world, that the subject may be fully understood, and that the Colony as well as others may judge of it with the greater ease and certainty, by seeing every fact fairly stated and candidly discussed. But I must again repeat, that Twelve Members of the Council bear no kind of proportion to the numbers of the *Lower House*, which consist of Forty-eight Mem-bers: and what still adds to the defect is, that as several of the Council are frequently and necessarily absent on their own private concerns, and it often happens, that others are either absent from the Province, or, through sickness, are unable to attend, the Coun-cil seldom consist of more than *five* persons; and commonly only *three* assemble to dispatch the most weighty concerns. This cir-cumstance lessens the real and constitutional dignity which this Body are intended to maintain, and the People cannot be taught to reverence or respect an institution, the Business whereof is trans-acted, like a Court of Quarter Sessions, by three Justices of Peace! Hence it is, that the *Middle Branch* is in a manner overwhelmed by the force of numbers in the Lower House, and that they fall into Derision and Contempt for the want of *Numbers* in their own. I therefore most ardently wish to see this evil remedied, by such an addition to the number of his Majesty's Council, as that Twelve Members at least may always be assembled on the Business of the State; then, and not till then, will this middle Branch be able to maintain a proper [73] Balance to support their own Constitutional importance, and to withstand the overbearing attempts, and the haughty encroachments of the Lower House.

I sincerely wish the lasting happiness of the Colony of South Carolina; and I am firmly persuaded, that nothing is so likely to promote it, as a timely and speedy interposition on the part of the Crown, and a decisive settlement of these uneasy contentions upon the sound principles of the English Constitution.

Although it is not the immediate design of the present Publication to consider American Affairs at large, it may possibly be expected, that something should be said concerning the general relation which the Colonists bear to the Mother-Country; and that having traced the Constitution of the Colonies, and observed upon its resemblance to the British Model, it may not be altogether foreign to offer a few thoughts on their Common Rights, as the remote Children of Great Britain.

So much has been said on the right of *Taxation*, and likewise on the idea of *Virtual Representation*, that I forbear to offer one sentiment about them; and the rather, as I am inwardly persuaded, that the grand security of the Colonists against unreasonable Burthens, Taxes, or Impositions of any kind by the Mother-Country, (granting the Right to do so to be unquestionably clear) consists in this: That the Interests of both Countries are so blended together, and so entirely intermixed, that it is not possible for the Parent State to oppress her Colonies, without sensibly feeling at the same time, and also partaking of a proportionable share of the evils arising from any false measure whatsoever. Colonization cannot thrive under hardships and discouragements, and [74] when the Colonies begin to languish, Britain may begin to tremble. America therefore has, seriously speaking, nothing to fear; for Interest alone, without the principle of love springing from such a near and dear alliance, will always bring matters right, and prevail against bad policy and evil machinations.

The following ideas form a part of my American Creed: The

happiness and prosperity of Great Britain and her Colonies depend *solely*, under God, on a firm and *indissoluble Union;* and therefore every man who wishes well to his Country, ought to lay aside all narrow and contracted notions, and should exert his utmost abilities to remove idle Prejudices, ill-grounded Jealousies, Vulgar Errors, and misconceived ideas; and by resorting to the Principles of our Constitution to rectify Political Mistakes, he will thereby promote the Public Good, and enforce a *uniting, conciliating*, and *strengthening System.*

The King's regal power is as extensive as his Territory; and as there must be in every State one *supreme Legislative* Jurisdiction, so the same, in like manner, has a right to an occasional exercise thereof, over the most distant and remote Branches of the Empire. And this one over-ruling Power is implied in the nature of things; for there cannot exist, at one and the same time, in the same Empire Two supreme Jurisdictions; because *Equals* can on no score controul *Equals*, and Two supreme Directions imply two distinct and separate States: I therefore hold, that in our Government this One *Supreme Legislature* is the *British Parliament*, which clearly possesses *summum imperium*;[81] whilst our Colonies, at the same time, possess certain Subordinate Powers of Legislation, as essential to *their* Political Existence.

[75]The Colonies are not Conquests, but English Plantations; they are the Genuine and Legitimate Offspring of Great Britain, and are, beyond all doubt, well entitled to *jus publicum*,[82] and *jus privatum*.[83] That they are part and parcel of the King's Dominion, and were intended to be united thereto as intimately as possible, appears from the spirit and sense of all the Charters, from the express words of the several Acts of Navigation, and from all the Statutes wherein any mention is made of America, from the first foundation and settlement of the Colonies to the present day; it is therefore idle to question this superintending and over-ruling power of the British Parliament, or its right to extend to these remote Countries, as parcels of one great State, to which they are united. "Truth," as Dr. Cudworth says, "is the most unbending and uncompliable, the most necessary, firm, immutable, and adamantine thing in the world."[84]

That the Union between the two Countries may be the more compleat, I earnestly wish the Colonists to see *their happiness* in that *very Dependence* on the Mother-Country, which is their best security, both against Foreign and Domestic Foes; at the same time I as sincerely wish, that the British Rule over these distant and valuable Territories, may always be mild, temperate, and just, and that so much of the English Constitution as can consistently be interwoven into these Subordinate Jurisdictions, may be from time to time added, to complete the Image of that model, which it is intended to represent.

There is not a maxim of Religion, Morals, or Politics, more evident to me than this: That America is a *Hen* that lays her *Golden Eggs* for Britain; that she must be cherished and supported as part of the great Family of Britain; then will [76] her Trade encrease; and in return she must promote and augment her Commercial connection with the Mother-Country, and "†cling to her like as the vine curls her tendrils, which implies subjection."[85]

It is certainly proper that the Colonists, in consideration of protection, should, on their parts, maintain a becoming reverence and esteem for the Supreme Power of that Empire, of which they are Members. Their Allegiance, Honour, Gratitude, Faith, and every thing else are pledged in conscience to the Parent-State; it is their Duty to give strength to the Commonwealth, and to use their Liberty, not as a *Cloak* for Licentiousness, but for the maintainance of Civil Order. They should always remember that Liberty is best supported by a settled plan of Government, and that contumelious treatment of the Mother-Country is at all times a bad lesson to the Members of their own Subordinate State: In short, they should lay aside Jealousies, and nourish a spirit of Trust and Confidence; always keeping in remembrance what a celebrated Writer hath long since said, "§This is not the Liberty which we can hope, that no grievance ever should arise in the Commonwealth: That, let no man in this world expect; but when Complaints are freely heard, deeply considered, and speedily reformed, then is the utmost bound of Civil Liberty attained, that wise men look for."[86]

---

† Milton.
§ Ibid.

[77]

POSTSCRIPT

Since the foregoing Sheets were finally compleated, Mr. Thomas Powel the Printer, (whose Name has been already mentioned, page 33, and who had been so fortunately relieved from his Confinement by Two Magistrates under the Habeas Corpus Act, as before related) attempted by his Attorney,[87] on Tuesday the 18th of September last, (being the Return-day for the Process of the Court of Common Pleas in the Colony of South Carolina) to file a Bill against Sir Egerton Leigh, President of the Council, (he being likewise one of the Lawyers of that Court) to answer to the Complaint of the said T. Powel, for Assault and false Imprisonment of his Person, to his Damage 1900 l. currency; and that Gentleman being present when a Motion was made for Leave to file the same, he took occasion to inform the Court, that the Assault and Imprisonment stated in the Bill, relate to a Warrant of Commitment signed by him at the last sitting of the Legislature of this Colony, and by the *express Order* of the *Upper House of Assembly,* for a Breach of Privilege and Contempt committed by the said *T. Powel*; and therefore he submitted it to the Court, whether it was proper to admit such a Bill to be filed; and he likewise reminded their Honours the Judges of the *9th Article* contained in the *Act of Settlement,* I William and Mary, Sess. 2. c.2. of Force in that Colony, "That the Freedom of Speech, and Debates or *Proceedings* in *Parliament,* ought not to be impeached or *questioned* in *any Court* or place out of Parliament."

[78]The Chief Justice[88] declared the Case to be a point of the utmost moment; and as the Bench was thin (only one Assistant Judge being present), the motion for filing the Bill was postponed, and the Attorney accordingly withdrew it for the present.[89]

On the 12th of October (being the first day of Term) the Bill was filed; and on a four-day Rule being served on the Defendant, he made an Affadavit, stating, That the cause of action related

119

solely to matters transacted in the *Upper House of Assembly*, and therefore not cognizable by the Court. On this Affidavit, a Rule was made on the Plaintiff, to shew cause why all Proceedings in this Action should not be stayed; which being Argued on the 16th of October before all the Judges, they were pleased to order the Rule to be made Absolute.

The Chief Justice entered very copiously into the subject, passed some applicable strictures, and in express and direct terms declared the Council *to be an Upper House of Assembly;* in which his Brethren unanimously concurred.[90] Thus was defeated, one of the boldest attempts against the Constitution of this Country, that Faction and Democratical Insolence could possibly devise; and by the virtue and firmness of the superior Judges, the Wound which the King's Government had suffered has been in part healed, and the Authority of the Middle Branch of the Provincial Legislature is now *legally* and *judicially* established.

Few cases ever happened before of so uncommon a nature, in any part of his Majesty's Dominions; and I think the World itself, and every Civilized State in it, may be challenged to produce an instance, where any Public Departments have been more cruelly insulted.—Let every private man judge for himself. His Majesty's Honour-[79]able Council, being the Upper House of Legislature of South Carolina, are first attacked by a publication of their Proceedings without leave of the House; and when the Printer was interrogated, he acknowledged the fact, and refused to give any satisfaction which the Honour even of Private Gentlemen could allow them to accept; and such as he offered, manifested the most daring Disrespect. The House was obliged to Commit Him for a Breach of *Privilege* and *Contempt;* the effect of which Commitment was afterwards *eluded* by Two Justices of the Peace, and Members of the Lower House, who judicially pronounced the Council *to be no Upper House of Assembly*, and thereupon discharged him.—The Council applied to the Assembly for redress; and in lieu thereof, violent Resolutions were made, declaring the Commitment *unprecedented, unconstitutional,* and *oppressive,* and a dangerous violation of the Liberty of the Subject. The Thanks of the House were next given to the Two Justices for their *able, upright,* and *impartial* decision upon the Return of the Habeas

Corpus; their reasons given for the discharge of the said T. Powel were declared to be extremely satisfactory to that House; and this approved Judgment was printed at their desire.

The Assembly, to add further to the Insult, addressed the Governor to Suspend those Members who voted the Commitment, and his Majesty is likewise applied to for their Removal.

The Printer being at large, persisted in publishing the Proceedings of the Upper House; and to aggravate the case, *notes* were added, giving the direct *Lie* to the Council, and stating an unfair apology for the Printer's Conduct when called before them: and to sum up all, the same paper acquaints the Public, that "thus was defeated the most violent attempt that ever had been made in this Province upon the Liberty [80] of the Subject—probably intended to controul the Liberty of the Press."[91] In consequence of these inflamed transactions, the Council found themselves divested of all power, reduced to the most abject state of contempt, their Legislative Authority virtually abolished, and the very persons to whom the King himself had entrusted so large a share in the Administration of Public Affairs, shamefully made the sport and derision of every Order of Men in the Community.

The Upper House, clearly perceiving that fresh Commitments would only produce new insults, as the same or other Justices might be found to discharge the Prisoners upon the like pretences, patiently submitted to this cruel Persecution; and nothing but the most Loyal Affection for the King, a dutiful regard to the Subjects of the Province, and the most sincere attention to his Majesty's Service, could possibly have prevailed upon the Council to have held their Seats a moment longer; but these disinterested motives, and a full confidence that his Majesty will in due time redress these Grievances, powerfully operated upon their minds, and influenced their conduct.

It is remarkable, that notwithstanding the Two Justices (both Members of Assembly) pronounced so pleasing a Decision, which had the honor to be approved by the Commons House, was celebrated, and in fact warmly adopted by them, and admired as the *Apple of their Eye;* out of Six eminent Gentlemen of the Bar,[92] all Members of the House, not one appeared to promote or to aid *poor Powel's Suit.* The Assembly gave their Countenance by *Words,*

Thanks, and *Resolutions;* but here they stopped, and the Lawyers seemingly avoided a Piece of Business, which perhaps they [81] apprehended might be attended with some Risque and Danger; for many will help the *Cry,* who dare not join the *Chace.* It is likewise very strange, that other eminent Gentlemen, not Members of the House, should appear so shy in a case of this pretended moment and importance; and that the conduct of a suit upon the most favourite Idea of the People's Representatives, should be entrusted to the care of a single person; and the rather, as in Popular Cases the Bar have been known to rise like an armed Man, forming a firm *Phalanx* to resist the force of one Crown-Officer in the Law-Department.

The Two Justices have boldly determined that the Council are *no Upper House;* and the superior Judges have judicially resolved *that they are;* it must therefore follow of course, that the *former* have done wrong in discharging a Prisoner committed by the Upper House; and the Assembly can scarce be right in approving an Act in every sense *illegal;* for I have a clear pretence and a just right to call That *illegal,* which is not consonant to the determinations of the King's superior Judges.—The Magistrates seem to me to be in a very aukward situation; for the empty applause given them by one Branch of the Legislature will not so bolster up the *matter,* as either to indemnify them, or to justify their conduct.

Sir William Williams,* being prosecuted for printing and publishing a seditious Libel reflecting upon the Duke of York, the King's Brother, called *Dangerfield's Narrative,* he pleaded to the jurisdiction of the King's Bench, That he being *Speaker of the House of Commons,* caused the same to be printed *by order of the House;* to which the Attorney General Demurred; and judgment was [82] entered for the King, and Sir William was fined 10,000 l. sterling; and on payment of 8000 l. satisfaction was entered on record:[93] Every order, therefore, of a Legislative Body will not always justify indiscriminately the conduct of those who pay obedience to it; and that Body whose order was insufficient to *justify* when obedience was paid to it, would prove a *broken reed*

---

* 2 Show. 471. Tremaine 48.

to rest upon, when approbation only followed an illegal Act, unsupported by any order whatsoever.

I now and then read a little law for my amusement and instruction; and I have a few books which tell me, that a Man may be guilty of a very high offence, by making use of improper pretences to reform Religion, the Laws, or other Grievances, real or *affected;* and that one may commit high Contempts and Misprisions against the King's Person and Government, by doing any thing that has an *immediate* and *direct tendency to weaken his Government,* or *to raise Jealousies between Him and his People.*

Whether the conduct of these Gentlemen exposes them to censure of any kind, I must submit to those Learned in the Laws; for as I know of no Statute which draws a line, or points out precisely the extent of their *Judicial Power,* perhaps they may be allowed to determine (provided a Case leading to it is regularly before them) that an old established plan of Government is worn out, decayed, and prejudicial to the State; that they can give some sound and useful hints for the reparation of certain State Edifices, and substitute something new in the room of old departments. Perhaps it may be perfectly agreeable to their magisterial constitution, to pronounce any branch of Government *useless, unnecessary, or burthensome,* which their own understanding and experience tell them to be so.—The Justices are on *Ground* [83]*too slippery* for me to trace their footsteps farther; I must therefore retire, and indulge myself with a few serious reflections on the Glorious System of our English Constitution; and I beg to recommend a piece of advice well expressed by a learned author,* "Let us keep the balance as even as we can, by forming every estate in the Constitution a controul upon the rest; but it is extravagant to think of leaving the *least strength* or *temptation to individuals to controul Government itself.*"[94]

---

* Law of Forfeitures, p. 126.

FINIS

Answer to
CONSIDERATIONS
on certain
POLITICAL TRANSACTIONS
of the
PROVINCE of
SOUTH CAROLINA

ANSWER to

CONSIDERATIONS

on certain
POLITICAL TRANSACTIONS
of the
PROVINCE of
SOUTH CAROLINA:

Speciosa verbis, re inania aut subdola—quantoque majore libertatis imagine tegebantur, eo eruptura in intensius servitium.   Tacitus.[1]

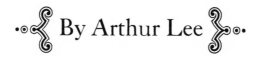

By Arthur Lee

LONDON:
Printed for J. ALMON, opposite Burlington House,
Piccadilly.
MDCCLXXIV.

PREFACE

*The Writer of what is here submitted to the Public, thinks an
Apology necessary for the Freedom and Severity of his Remarks
upon the Author of the "Considerations;" who that Author is, is no
Secret.—His Inconsistency in boasting* of his Attempt to precipi-
tate the Execution of the odious Stamp Act—his triumphing† in the
"local Distresses and Punishment" of the Colony, and his pretended
good wishes‖ for the "Prosperity of South Carolina"—His vain and
frequent Repetitions of his Candor and Love of Truth, and the
glaring Partiality of his State of Facts and illiberal ludicrous Treatment of the House of Assembly, required such Resentment; and it
is justified by his having notoriously incurred the Reproach, Contempt, and universal Detestation of the Inhabitants of that Province
on account of his wicked Practices there, both in his public and
private Characters.*

---

* Consid. P. 5.
† Ibid. P. 30.
‖ Ibid. P. 73.

SOUTH CAROLINA.

It has been the Misfortune of this Country, and was originally the Cause of all our unhappy Disputes with *America,* that Men in Power adopted Opinions, and formed Measures, upon the false and partial Representations of ignorant or interested Individuals. It was to this the Stamp Act owed its Birth. It is from this, that every irritating and offensive Operation has arisen; till the Colonies are almost forced from those Ties of Affection and Respect for this Country, which are the only sure Foundation of their Utility and Attachment.

That the Colonies are discontented and disturbed—that Government is embarrassed, from one End of the Continent to the other—are Facts, which cannot be controverted. In my [2] Opinion, the Cause is equally clear and unquestionable. Since the Dispute unhappily arose between the two Countries, Men of bad Characters, desperate Fortunes, and profligate principles, availing themselves, as such Men ever do, of the Temper of the Times, have recommended themselves, by the basest Means, to Favour in *England.* They have artfully given, not the Intelligence that was true, but that was agreeable; not the Information that was useful to the Minister, but profitable to themselves. It was singularly unfortunate, that they recommended themselves exactly in Proportion to their misleading the Minister. They fostered his Prejudices, perverted his Judgment, and inflamed his Zeal for maintaining the Authority of this Country; which a Moment's true Reflection should have informed him, could never be more dangerously engaged, than in an obstinate Perseverance in Measures, originally wrong and eventually obnoxious.

While Government has been embarrassed, and the People distressed, by the Measures formed on these Misrepresentations, the Authors of them have been rewarded. They have been suddenly advanced to Honors, Dignities, and Places of Responsibility and Emolument, of which they were utterly unworthy. Flattered by their Success, what was experimental at first, became soon a settled Practice; new Methods of invading the [3] Rights of the People were devised, and all Opposition to such Attempts was imputed to the Designs of a factious Few, or to the Contumacy of the Whole. Their Representations still gained Credit; and as bad Men, from being countenanced, grow every Day more daring and flagitious, they are now arrived at such an Extremity of Wickedness as to affirm, that the Constitution and Liberties of the Provinces are merely *ex gratia*,[2] flowing wholly from the Bounty of the Crown,* that they should be abridged or modelled to their Measure; and instead of choosing proper Men to manage the Business of the Crown, the People are to be subdued to the Management of any Man.

There cannot be a stronger Illustration of the Truth of these Reflections, than a Pamphlet which has lately appeared under the Title of *Considerations on certain Political Transactions of the Province of* South Carolina.

The Author of these Considerations introduces himself under the Mask of a Devotee to Truth, which generally covers a premeditated Purpose of Misrepresentation. He tells us, "the great Aim of a worthy Writer ought to be directed to the Search of Truth."[3] Nothing more [4] undeniable; but we shall find his Researches have had a very different Direction, or have failed, most miserably, of their Aim. I trust, that in the Course of these Observations on his extraordinary Performance, he will feel the Force of what he has incautiously quoted from Dr. *Cudworth*—"That Truth is the most unbending and uncompliable, the most necessary, firm, immutable, and adamantine Thing in the World."[4] It is the Want of this adamantine Material, which renders his Work flimsey and unsubstantial; it is the Want of this necessary Ingredient, which must render the Composition contemptible.

Professing not to treat of the Policy of the Stamp Act, he ven-

---

* *Considerations*, p. 37.

tures an Opinion, that the Repeal of it will be an Epoch in the Annals of *British* Story.—And why? Not because it was a memorable Instance of the Wisdom of Parliament in retracting from a Measure impolitic, and unjust; but because, "since that Period the public Affairs of these Countries have been in a State of almost ruinous Distraction; and what was probably meant to inspire Gratitude and Love, has rather kindled Rancour and Disgust— the Affection of the parent State seems to be considered as the Effects of aged Fondness and impotent Attachment: And sorry He is to say, that Concessions have daily [5] produced Usurpation and Resistance; one Claim has been followed by another, which generating more, have multiplied like the increasing Power of Numbers in a Course, as it were, of geometrical Progression."[5]

He ought indeed to be both sorry and ashamed of such Jargon as this. But why would he not favour us with a few Facts in Support of this Rhapsody? Why would he not shew, that Opposition has risen to much greater Violence *since* the Repeal, than *before*— that instead of Congresses of Peace, there have been Councils of War; instead of Riots, there have been Rebellions; and that instead of burning the Stamp Papers, they have burnt the Commissioners of the Customs? Why did he not name some one on this wonderful Series of Concessions? He is mistaken, if he imagines it will please Lord *Hillsborough* and the King's Friends, to say they have made Concessions to *America*. They pride themselves in the Reverse. They pride themselves in maintaining a Right to Tax, when the Exercise of it is useless, and in persevering in Measures which cannot possibly be profitable, and may be highly pernicious. "They have relinquished the Revenue, but judiciously taken Care to preserve the Contention. It is not contended, that the Continuation of the Tea Duty is to produce any direct Benefit what-[6]ever to the Mother Country. What is it then but an odious, unprofitable Exertion of a speculative Right, fixing a Badge of Slavery upon the *Americans*, without Service to their Masters?"*[6]

We have heard of their opposing the Usurpation of this Country over their Property; of their resisting a Claim in Parliament to raise a Revenue upon them without their Consent—but we are yet

---

* Junius.

to be informed, in what this geometrical Progression of Usurpations which they are charged with having made consists. He was too modest to enumerate the many Proofs of "Affection" which *America* has received from the parent State, since the Repeal of the Stamp Act. Such as the Declaratory Act; the Revenue Act; the Suspension of the Legislature of *New York*; the Establishment of a Board of Commissioners; the Appointment of Admiralty Courts; the Troops sent to *Boston*; the violent Resolves of both Houses of Parliament, founded on the Falshoods of Governor *Bernard*;[7] the pensioning of their Judges, and thereby rendering Life, Liberties, and Property insecure; the dangerous, and unconstitutional Commission against *Rhode Island*—and a Multitude of other Measures, all marking the same tender Regard to [7] their Rights, the same parental Attention to their Complaints, manifesting the same *Fondness and Attachment*, and calculated to inspire Gratitude and Love into her redressed and rejoicing Children.

The Gentleman was prudent in waving the Defence of the Policy of the Stamp Act; but on what Ground will he justify the Revival of the odious Principle of that Act, under the Form of Duties imposed on Tea, Paper, Paint, &c. It is from that Act we must date the Renewal of the Disturbances in *America*. The Fire of the Stamp Act was scarce covered by the Ashes of its Repeal, when it was blown up anew, by imposing Duties for the Purposes of a Revenue, and the other oppressive Concomitants of that Imposition. The only Time of Repose was the short Interval between the Repeal of the Stamp Act in 1766, and the passing the Revenue Law in 1767. Since that Time the Colonies have indeed been in a "State of almost ruinous Distraction," not only because it was never totally repealed, but because every Measure has been studiously taken to alarm, and irritate them. They have seen a Revenue raised upon the worst Principles, applied to the worst Purposes. The Business of Spies and Informers has not only been the honourable Employment of those in Office, but the surest Means [8] of Preferment. Hence it is, that more Titles have been conferred, and more sudden and surprizing Elevations have taken Place in *America*, since that Period, than from the First Settlement of the Colonies to that Time. Whoever will enquire into the Cause of those Discontents, which have subsisted in our Provinces, will find it in the Measures I have mentioned; whoever will look a little forward must perceive, that unless these Measures are totally altered, the State of Things will at length arrive at that Point, when the Decision of Heaven alone must direct the Event.

But to put this Writer at once to Shame and to Silence; to shew that the Period from which he dates, and the Causes to which he imputes, the Disturbances in America, are equally false; I will produce Evidence, the decisive Authority of which, I think, no one of his Stamp will controvert—it is that of the Earl of *Hillsborough* and Sir *Francis Bernard.**

Whitehall, *April* 22d, 1768.

To GOVERNOR BERNARD.

"It gives great Concern to his Majesty to find, that the same *Moderation* which ap-[9]peared by your Letter, to have been adopted at the Beginning of the Session, in a full Assembly, had not continued; and that instead of that *Spirit of Prudence and Respect for the Constitution,* which seemed at that Time to influence the Conduct of a large Majority of the Members, a thin House, at the End of the Session, should have presumed to revert to, and resolve upon a Measure of so inflammatory a Nature, as that of writing to the other Colonies on the Subject of their intended Representations against some late Acts of Parliament. His Majesty considers this Step, as evidently tending to *create unwarrantable Combinations,* to *excite* an unjustifiable Opposition to the constitutional Authority of Parliament, and to *revive* those unhappy Divisions and Distractions which have operated so prejudicially to the true Interests of *Great Britain* and her Colonies."[8]

Here we see the fullest Acknowledgement of the Revival of a Revenue Act being the Cause which moved the Assembly of *Massachusetts Bay* from that Moderation in their Measures, and that Respect for the Constitution, which the Repeal of the Stamp Act, ungraciously as it was accompanied by the Declaratory and Mu-

---

* See their Letters.

tiny Acts, had inspired. And this Temper was so very remarkable, that Governor *Bernard*, in his Letter [*10*] of the 30th of *January* 1768, says, "They have acted in all Things, even in their Remonstrance, with Temper and Moderation: They have avoided some Subjects of Dispute, and have laid a Foundation for removing some Causes of former Altercations."⁹

And Lord *Shelburne*¹⁰ to Lord *Charles Montague*, Governor of *South Carolina*, writes—

"My Lord,—I am commanded by the King to acquaint you, that his Majesty has been pleased to receive very graciously the dutiful and affectionate Address of his loyal Province of *South Carolina*. His Majesty sees with great Satisfaction, that his *American* Subjects in general have shewn the sincerest Thankfulness and Gratitude for his paternal Goodness and Condescension, and for the tender Regard and Consideration of his Parliament—and his Majesty rests assured, that his Province of *South Carolina*, as well as his other *American* Provinces, will ever continue to merit his most paternal Regard.—Signed

SHELBURNE"¹¹

The same pacific Disposition, the same Spirit of Accommodation and Reconcilement had manifestly pervaded all the Colonies; since otherwise Lord *Hillsborough* could with no Colour of Propriety have charged the circular Letters with [*11*] a Tendency to *create unwarrantable Combinations, to excite Opposition to parliamentary Authority, and to revive former Distractions*. Indeed their Acquiescence under the Mutiny Act could not have proceeded from any Consideration, but the utmost Reluctance to revive a Dispute with the Mother Country, a Dispute which the *Americans* always felt as most unhappy *Necessity*; and to which nothing but the arbitrary Proceedings, which were soon renewed here, could have compelled them.

So much for the Paragraph which the Author has bestowed upon *America* at large; a Paragraph small indeed, but full of Falshood and Malignity. Let us now attend him through his Observations on the Proceedings in *South Carolina*, which is the particular Object of his Enmity.

Wit is a Weapon not easily wielded nor easily resisted; especially when it is so keen as our Author's, and employed upon so fit a Subject as the Omission of writing Pamphlets upon the Stamp Act. It was indeed highly criminal in the People of *South Carolina* not to employ him upon that Occasion—a small Sum would have engaged him on either Side, and he was probably as capable of Writing then as he is now, unless his new-acquired Dignity should have improved his Faculties.

[*12*] Without attempting to apologize either for their not writing Pamphlets themselves, nor availing their Cause of this Gentleman's Abilities, I shall proceed to shew that the Vote of 1500 l. Sterling, to the Supporters of the Bill of Rights by the Assembly, was *constitutional in its Mode, and laudable in its Intention.*

The Cause of Liberty is common to the whole Empire. The great Foundations of Freedom are the same on both Sides of the *Atlantic*, nor can they be subverted in the one, without being shaken in the other. With how much more Force does my Lord *Chatham*'s Admonition, "that Three Millions of *Americans* reduced to Slavery would be fit Instruments of bringing Subjection upon *Great Britain*,"[12] apply to *America*? The same Lust of absolute Dominion had prompted an Invasion of the Liberties of the People in both Countries; and a corrupt House of Commons was the Instrument of Oppression, as well in *America* as in *England*. To rouse the People, and resist, by all legal Means, those arbitrary Attempts, a Number of Gentlemen, many of them Members of Parliament, and most of them distinguished for Rank and Abilities, associated together under the Title of Supporters of the Bill of Rights. The Principles and Conduct of the Society procured them the Confidence and Respect of the People of [*13*] *England*, and intitled them to the Assistance of those in *America*. The Opposition to an arbitrary Administration, if successful, must have been equally beneficial to the whole Empire, and therefore it was wise Policy in the Assembly of *South Carolina* to promote their patriotic Purposes. A general Redress of Grievances must have followed the Removal or Punishment of those Ministers, from whose evil Counsels all those Grievances arose. Parliaments have been corrupt;

they have betrayed those Rights they were intrusted to preserve, and instead of being the Guardians of public Liberty, have been an Engine of Oppression in the Hand of the Crown. It is our Misfortune to see such a Parliament at present; and in such Circumstances, the most moderate and constitutional Remedy is to persuade the People to be more cautious and select in the Choice of their Representatives—to stipulate the Redress of the principal political Grievances, as the express Condition on which they are chosen—and not to sell their Votes, *lest* their Liberties should be sold in Return. To impress these Principles has been the noble Endeavour of the Society of the Supporters of the Bill of Rights. Nor do they despair of Success. The Foes of Freedom may yet see an *English* Spirit roused, which nothing can resist.

[*14*] But this Writer tells us, his Majesty's Council pronounced this Vote of the Assembly to be neither *honourable, fit, nor decent.**
To relieve us, however, from the Surprize this would occasion, he informs us in another Place.† "That this Council seldom consists of more than Five Persons, and commonly only Three assemble to dispatch the most weighty Concerns." The Consequence of this, continues he, is, that "they fall into Derision and Contempt." There cannot be a better Reason given for their strange Declaration. The Assembly could not feel much Concern about the Opinion of Three or Five ridiculous and contemptible Tools of Government, so far as it touched themselves; but the Consequences to the Public they always lamented.

Not contented with this Invective from the Council, the Author has endeavoured to fix a Charge of great Ingratitude upon the Colony for this Vote. "That the Act, says he, was both idle and wanton, may appear from a Consideration of the *royal Predilection in Favour of this Colony on numberless Occasions.* The King's *Ministers* have ever been *open to Access,* and almost *every Proposition from the Agent* has been attended with *remarkable Suc-*[*15*]*cess:* In War, we have been *peculiarly protected by an early Appointment of Convoys;* and Government has afforded its best Aid to procure *liberal Bounties* on the various *Products of the*

* P. 10.
† P. 72.

Country: In short, the Colony of *South Carolina* may be considered as One of the most favoured Soils in his Majesty's *American* Dominions."[13]

The King, his Ministers, and the Government are much indebted to this Writer, for thus arraigning their Justice and Impartiality. For surely if it were true, that Access has been more easy to the Agent and Petitions of *South Carolina*, than to those of the other Colonies, and that the Trade of the former was more protected by the Appointment of Convoys, than that of the latter; it would be a Proof of Partiality at the Expence of Justice. But they do not deserve the Imputation; because the Facts on which it is founded, are not true. Agents and Petitions are heard of course; and in this therefore it is idle to talk of Predilection. It has however been the Misfortune of the Province to have the Applications of her Agents and the Prayer of her Petitions denied, in repeated Instances, though founded on the clearest Justice. Two or Three Proofs [16] out of Numbers, will be sufficient. The Agent applied in vain against the Repeal of the Paper Money Bill in 1770, which was attended with such infinite Inconveniences to the Province.[14]— The Petition of the House of Assembly, praying that the Offices of Attorney General and Surveyor General, which were united in the Person of *Egerton Leigh*, Esquire, should be separated, as the same Person could not consistently, and without Injury to the Public, hold Two Offices which were intended to check each other, was rejected; the Interest of the Individual outweighing that of the Community[15]—the several Applications and Petitions, which have been made against this grievous Instruction, have totally failed of Success. These Instances are sufficient to shew, that neither the Crown nor its Ministers are justly chargeable with Partiality to the Province, in giving too favourable an Ear to their Complaints. It is true, that the Appointment of Convoys, like every Thing else, during the glorious Administration of Mr. *Pitt*, was regular, and Trade well protected; but this was done equally for all the Colonies, as well as for that of *South Carolina*, and therefore is no Proof of Predilection. Indeed it properly shews the Attention of that great Minister, to the general Interests of his Majesty's Subjects; for every one [17] must know that during a War, *American* Property shipped for *England* is insured in *England*,

Arthur Lee

and therefore, if the Ships are taken the Loss falls, in fact, upon the People of *England*. Safe and regular Convoys are, for this Reason, more beneficial to *England* than to *America*; as the People of the one would suffer an Inconvenience, while they of the other would sustain an actual Loss by the Depradations of the Enemy.

Though it is certain, that Bounties upon the *American* Productions eventually operate to the Advantage of the Colonies; yet it is equally true, that the Benefit of *Great Britain*, and not that of the Colonies, is the sole Motive for granting such Bounties. In Proof of this, I appeal to the Preamble of the Act, which gives a Bounty upon *Indico*, observing only that the Preamble of an Act is an undeniable Record of the Intention of Parliament, in making the Law. The Twenty-first of *George* the Second, Ch. 30, recites, that "whereas the making of *Indico* in the *British* Plantations in *America* would be advantageous to the *Trade of this Nation*, as great Quantities are used in dying the Manufactures of *this Kingdom*; which at present being furnished from *foreign Parts*, the Supply of that *necessary Commodity* is become at all Times *uncertain*, and the *Price fre-*[18]*quently exorbitant*; and whereas the Culture thereof has been found to succeed so well in the Provinces of *South* and *North Carolina*, that there is Reason to hope, by a proper Encouragement, the same may be increased and improved to such a Degree, as not only to answer all the Demands of his Majesty's *British* Subjects, but furnish considerable Quantities to *foreign Markets*.— Be it therefore enacted, etc. etc."[16]

Here we see the Advantage of the Manufactures of this Kingdom, and the Emolument of his Majesty's *British* Subjects, in furnishing this valuable Article of Trade to foreign Markets, were the only Considerations with the Legislature in giving a Bounty on Indico. The Benefit of the Colonies was never in Contemplation; and it is not therefore easy to conceive, how such Acts can claim their Gratitude. The Operation of the Bounty has repaid the Expence a thousand Fold, and fully answered the Expectation of Parliament. For instead of depending on Foreigners for this necessary Article, and being subject to their Extortion, this Country was soon supplied from *America* for her own Consumption, and enabled to supply foreign Markets so as to extend her Commerce, diminishing that of her Rival, and saving herself an immense annual [*19*] Expence. For the accurate Mr. *Anderson* informs us, that till the Operation of this Bounty, "*France* supplied the greatest Part of *Europe* with this Commodity from her *West India* Islands; and *Britain* and *Ireland* were, by common Estimation, reckoned to have paid to *France* about 200,000 1. annually for Indico."*[17]

How much and immediately the Interest of *Great Britain* was concerned in the Object of these Bounties, will clearly appear from the following Passage out of the same Author: "The Necessity which all maritime trading Nations lie under, of being supplied with naval Stores, and more especially *England*'s very Need thereof, as well for the royal Navy, as for her numerous mercantile Shipping, has often put it in the Power of the northern Crowns to distress such Nations as had none of their own. This eminently appeared in the Year 1703, from the Tar Company of *Sweden*, who absolutely refused to let the *English* Nation have any Pitch or Tar (although ready Money was always paid for it) unless *England* would permit it all to be brought in *Swedish* Shipping, and at their own Price, and likewise only in such Quantities as that Company should [*20*] please to permit. This Disappointment (as the late ingenious Mr. *Gee* likewise observes in his Trade and Navigation of *Great Britain* considered, p. 82)[18] put the Government and Parliament on the Method of allowing of Bounties for the Raising of Pitch and Tar, Hemp and Flax, and Ship Timber, in our own *North American* Colonies; as particularly in *Carolina* (the southernmost Parts of which lying near the Latitude of *Lower Egypt*, and the northernmost Part nearly with *Ancona* and *Bologna* in *Italy*, in which the best Hemp and Flax grow.) The First Statute of this Kind, was the Act of the Third and Fourth of Queen *Anne*, ch. x. *For Encouraging the Importation of Naval Stores from her Majesty's Plantations in America*, judiciously setting forth That as, under God, the Wealth, Safety, and Strength of this Kingdom, so much depend on the royal Navy and Navigation thereof, and that the Stores necessary for the same, being hitherto brought in chiefly from foreign *Parts* and by foreign Shipping, at exorbitant and arbitrary Rates—which might be provided in a more certain and beneficial Manner from her Majesty's Plantations in *America*,

---

* On Commerce, V. 2. p. 384, Fol.

where the waste Tracts of Land lying near the Sea and on navigable Rivers, may commodiously afford great Quantities of all Sorts of naval Stores, by due Encouragement, which [21] may likewise tend to the farther Employment and Increase of *English* Shipping and Seamen—and also of the Trade and Vent of the Woollen and other Manufactures and Products, in Exchange for such naval Stores now purchased of foreign Countries for ready Money.—It was therefore enacted, That whoever shall (in Ships and with Sailors, qualified as by the Acts of Navigation) import from the *English* Plantations in *America* the undernamed naval Stores, shall be intitled to the following bounties,* etc."[19]

To free the Manufactures and the Navy of this Country, on which its Wealth, Safety, and Strength depend, from a precarious and expensive Dependence on Foreigners, to extend its Trade, and encourage its very Staple the Woollen Manufacture, were the great and momentous Objects of these Bounties. These Views have been fully accomplished. Surely then if Gratitude be due on either Part, it is from *Great Britain*, which is enabled by the Produce of *America*, to see her Navy ride the Ocean independent of other Nations, while her Expences are diminished, her Trade increased, and the Mart for her Manufactures augmented and secured. And to shew that the Interest of *America* [22] was never considered but that it might be sacrificed, the Commissioners of the Navy are empowered to fix their own Price on the Produce of the *American's* Labour, by the following Provisoe.—"That for the particular Benefit of the royal Navy, the Pre-emption or Refusal of the said naval Stores shall be tendered to the Commissioners of her Majesty's Navy, upon landing the same."[20]—In the same ungenerous and selfish Spirit, Parliament has excluded the *Americans*, by the particular Words of the Act, from the Bounty given in the *Greenland* Whale Fishery.[21]

Such are the Motives from which this Country granted Bounties on the Productions of *America*; Motives which manifestly demand the warmest Returns of Gratitude from the Colonies; We have heard enough of this Nonsense, from much more respectable Persons than this Writer. If he, or any other Man, can produce the

---

* Ibid. p. 238.

Shadow of an Instance, in which this Country did a single Act for the sole or avowed Advantage of *America*, I shall think less contemptibly of that selfish, ungenerous, arbitrary Policy, which pervades all her Laws and Regulations respecting her Colonies. One dwells upon such Subjects with Regret; but it is necessary that such idle Notions and unjust Claims should have an Answer. Should the *Americans* be ever driven to stop all [23] Commerce with this Country for One Year, it will effectually decide the Question. It will then be clearly understood which Country is most dependent on the other, from which the most Aid is received, and from which the greatest Gratitude is due.—But to return—

The Commons House of Assembly, who are the sole Givers of the People's Money, and the sole Judges of the Purposes for which it is given, had exercised their Right in voting the 1500 l. and in the ordinary Course of Proceeding, inserted that Sum in the Estimate of the public Debt annexed to the Tax Bill, as an Article due to *Jacob Motte*, Esquire, for so much advanced by him; the Council, so respectable as our Author describes them, thought proper to return the Bill, or to speak more constitutionally, to refuse giving their Advice to the Lieutenant Governor (the Governor being absent) to pass it.—

If voting this Sum was an unconstitutional Act, or according to the Council, an Act, neither honourable, fit, nor decent—most certainly it was the Duty of the Lieutenant Governor, consulting his Majesty's Honour and Dignity, to have dissolved the Assembly immediately upon passing the Vote on the 8th *December* 1769.— Certainly too it was the Duty of the Council, [24] consistently with that tender Regard which they have since pretended for the Interest of the People, to have advised his Honour to do so.—Such an Exertion of Prerogative, admitting their Representation to be true, would have been equally constitutional, fair, and honourable, and preventive of the Evils which have attended a contrary and insidious Conduct.

But the Lieutenant Governor well knew that such Votes of Credit or Orders to the public Treasurer to advance Money for public Services had been the common Practice, as the Journals of Assembly prove in numerous Instances from the earliest Date, many, in which himself, in the various Characters of a Member of

Assembly—a Member of Council—and Lieutenant Governor, had been particularly concerned.[22]—His Honour therefore did not find it expedient to fly so openly in the Face of Facts.—The Council, ever watchful for Opportunities to advance their own Importance, worked under Ground, transmitted by some secret Emissary a false Representation,—and then in the Author's Language waited for a Breath of Inspiration.—The Meeting of the Assembly was postponed to a distant Day, and the Members kept in Ignorance of the Accusation lodged against them.—At length flattering Assurances arrived, that a Rod was preparing for chastising those who had [25] dared to vote Money, "for supporting the constitutional Rights of his Majesty's Subjects in *Great Britain* and *America*." The Assembly was then suffered to meet, the Council came forth and gave the Alarm by returning the Tax Bill, accompanied by their notable Declaration, that the Grant was neither honourable, fit, nor decent, determined, as appears by their subsequent Behaviour, to maintain their Point, even at the Hazard of ruining the Province —their Plot succeeded—a Contest arose between *them* and the House of Assembly—a Prorogation ensued, and further Time was gained; in which they received the promised Aid from Lord *Hillsborough*, who, upon the Misrepresentation made to him, framed and transmitted the following Instruction signed by the King.

[26]

COPY

GEORGE R
(L.S.)

Additional Instruction to our trusty and well-beloved Charles Greville Montague, *Esq; commonly called* Lord Charles Greville Montague, *our Captain General and Governor in Chief of our Province of* South Carolina *in* America, *or in his Absence to the Lieutenant Governor or Commander in Chief of our said Province for the Time being. Given at our Court at* St. James's, *the 14th Day of April 1770, in the Tenth Year of our Reign.*

Whereas it hath been *represented to us*, that our House of Representatives or Lower House of Assembly of our Province of *South*

Carolina in *America,* have lately* *assumed to themselves* a Power of ordering, without the Concurrence of our Governor and Council, the public Treasurer of our said Province, to issue and advance out of the public Treasury such Sums of Money, and for such Services, as they have thought fit, and in particular, that the said Lower House of Assembly did, on the 8th Day [27] of *December* last past, make an Order upon the said public Treasurer to advance the Sum of Ten thousand and Five hundred Pounds Currency out of any Money in the Treasury, to be paid into the Hands of Mr. Speaker, Mr. *Gadsden,* Mr. *Rutledge,* Mr. *Parsons,* Mr. *Ferguson,* Mr. *Dart,* and Mr. *Lynch,* who were to remit the same to *Great Britain* for the Support of the just and constitutional Rights and Liberties of the People of *Great Britain* and *America:* And whereas it is highly just and necessary, that the most effectual Measures be pursued for putting a Stop to such dangerous and unwarrantable Practices, and for guarding for the future against such *unconstitutional Application of our Treasure,* cheerfully granted to us by our Subjects in our said Province of *South Carolina,* for the publick Uses of the said Province, and for Support of the Government thereof; it is therefore our Will and Pleasure, and you are hereby directed and required, upon pain of our highest Displeasure, and of being forthwith removed from your Government, not to give your Assent to any Bill or Bills that shall be passed by our said Lower House of Assembly, by which Bill or Bills any Sum or Sums of Money whatsoever shall be appropriated to, or Provision made for, defraying any Expence incurred for Services or Purposes not immediately arising within or incident to our said Province of *South* [28] *Carolina,* unless upon special Requisition from us, our Heirs and Successors; nor to any Bill or Bills for granting any Sum or Sums of Money to us, our Heirs and Sucessors, in which Bill or Bills it shall not be provided in express Words, that the Money so to be granted, or any Part thereof, shall not be issued or applied to any other Services than those to which it is by the said Bill or Bills appropriated, unless by Act or Ordinance of the General Assembly of our said Province. And it is our further Will and Pleasure, and you are

---

* That this Representation is false, the Journals of the House of Assembly uniformly prove.

hereby directed and required, upon pain of our highest Displeasure as aforesaid, not to give your Assent to any Bill or Bills that shall be passed by our said Lower House of Assembly as aforesaid, by which any Sum or Sums of Money whatever shall be granted to us, our Heirs and Successors, generally and without Appropriation, unless there be a Clause or Clauses inserted in the said Bill or Bills, declaring and providing that the said Money so to be granted shall remain in the Treasury, subject to such Appropriation as shall thereafter be made by Act or Ordinance of the General Assembly and not otherwise. And it is our further Will and Pleasure, that you take especial Care that in all and every Bill and Bills so to be passed by you as aforesaid for raising and granting public Monies a Clause or Clauses be inserted therein *subjecting the public Treasurer*, or any other Person or Per-[29]sons to whose Custody public Monies may be committed, in case he or they shall issue or pay any such Money otherwise than by express Order contained in some Act or Ordinance of the General Assembly, to a Penalty in Treble the Sum so issued contrary thereto, and declaring him or them to be *ipso facto* incapable of holding the said Office of Treasurer, or any other Office civil or military within our said Province. And it is our further Will and Pleasure, that this our additional Instruction to you be communicated to our Council and Lower House of Assembly of our said Province of *South Carolina*, and entered upon the Council Books.

G. R.[23]

It was in vain the House endeavoured to obtain, from the Governor, Copies of that Correspondence with his Majesty's Ministers on which this singular and unconstitutional Instruction was founded. An Instruction which has been the Cause of constant Contention between the different Branches of the Legislature, and must inevitably continue such, till the Commons House of Assembly shall be disposed to make a formal Surrender of their Privileges and the Rights of the People they represent; or the Crown shall be pleased to retract from an Attempt, prompted by Misrepresentation, arbitrarily to interfere in [30] the Exercise of that which is the peculiar and incommunicable Power of the Commons.

The Author has taken Care to suppress a material Part of this

Instruction, in order to conceal its having originated in Misinformation. He says it recites, "that the *Lower House had lately assumed,*"[24] etc. etc. when in Truth, as the Reader has seen, it recites, "that *it hath been represented to us,* that our House, etc. has *lately assumed,* etc."

That this Representation was false, and the Instruction grounded upon it improper, cannot be more clearly shewn, than by the Report of the Committee upon the additional Instruction, and in Answer to the several Messages, from the Lieutenant Governor, upon this Subject.

Report of the Committee to whom his Majesty's additional Instruction, and his Honour the Lieutenant Governor's Messages, relative thereto, were referred.

"That they have considered the several Matters referred to them, and though they cannot but lament that his Honour should think the *Correspondence between himself and his Majesty's Ministers, in a Matter which concerns* [31] *the Privileges and Proceedings of the House, so secret and confidential, as to refuse a full Compliance* with their just and reasonable Request without the royal Leave. Yet, your Committee are of Opinion that the House should immediately proceed to acquit themselves of the Charge contained in the said Instruction. They have therefore come to the following Resolutions, which they recommend to the House as proper to be adopted upon this Occasion, previously declaring that the Lieutenant Governor's Answers are not so satisfactory as the House had a Right to expect, and that the same be not hereafter drawn into Precedent, as it may be of most dangerous Consequence.

"RESOLVED, That it is the Opinion of this Committee, that this House hath an undoubted Right, which they have at all Times exercised, to give and grant Money to his Majesty with or without a Requisition from the Crown, for any Purposes whatever, whether Local and Provincial or not, whenever they think it necessary or expedient for his Service, of which they are the sole Judges.

"RESOLVED, That it is the Opinion of this Committee, that in order to provide such Money, the House hath a right, upon emergent Occasions, and when the Money is im-[32]mediately wanted, to borrow it upon the public Faith and Credit, solemnly pledged by a Resolution of the House to make good and repay the Money so borrowed; and that the House hath exercised this Right whenever they have thought proper.

"RESOLVED, That it is the Opinion of this Committee, that the House hath, *in such Cases, ordered the public Treasurer to advance the said Money*, who hath accordingly done so upon the Resolution of the House, to make good the same; and the Provision for repaying it to him hath always been made by the Tax Acts; which Measure cannot be unknown to the Lieutenant Governor, whose Sanction, as well as that of his Predecessors, it has often received.

"RESOLVED, That it is the Opinion of this Committee, that the *Order and Regulation of* the House on the *8th Day of December last* (the said Order being never considered by this House but merely as a Vote of Credit) are not unconstitutional, but *agreeable to the Usage and Practice both Ancient and Modern of the Commons House of Assembly of this Province.*

"That the public Treasurer having advanced the Money mentioned in the said Order in [33] pursuance thereof, on the Resolution of the House to repay the same, did in his Account charge it *to the Public*, and not to any *particular Fund*; and that in the Schedule of the Tax Bill, the House inserted the Treasurer's Name, as a Creditor of the Public, for that Sum, intending to repay it in the usual Manner.

"RESOLVED, That it is the Opinion of this Committee, that the House hath never attempted by its single Authority, without the Concurrence of the Governor and Council, to *issue out of the Treasury Money appropriated by Law, and apply the same to other Purposes* than those for which it was *granted*.

"RESOLVED, That it is the Opinion of this Committee, that the Order and Resolution of this House, on the 8th Day of *December* last, cannot be deemed *dangerous or unwarrantable*: That the same would not have been so represented, or the Power of this House, on that Point, drawn into Question, if the Money borrowed had not been applied towards *frustrating the unjust and unconstitutional Measures of an arbitrary and oppressive Ministry.*

"And his Honour the Lieutenant Governor having assured the House, that all his Repre-[34]sentations to his Majesty, by his Ministers, are made with the strictest Regard to Truth.

"RESOLVED THEREFORE, That it is the Opinion of the Committee, that the said Instruction cannot be supported by such Information, but is founded upon a false, partial, and insidious Representation of the Proceedings of this House: *False*, in asserting that the House had lately *assumed* a Power, when in Truth they only *exercised* an *ancient Right, supported* by *constant Usage*; *Partial*, in concealing its Resolution to repay the Money borrowed; and *Insidious*, in artfully insinuating that the House had directed an *unconstitutional Application of the Treasure granted to his Majesty*, in *ordering*, by its *single Vote*, without the Concurrence of Governor or Council, *Money appropriated by Law*, to be applied to *other Purposes*, and that the Censure contained in the said Instruction is altogether unmerited.

"RESOLVED, That it is the Opinion of this Committee, that the Clauses and Provisions in the said Instruction relating to the Appropriation of such Monies as shall be granted by this House, are *unnecessary*; every Law which grants Money sufficiently securing the [35] Appropriation thereof: And as many Evils might arise to the Province, from inserting the Clauses relative to the Treasurer, your Committee think that the House should not submit thereto.

"RESOLVED, That it is the Opinion of this Committee, that a Minister's *dictating how a Money Bill should be framed* is an Infringement of the Privileges of this House, to whom alone it belongs to originate and prepare the same, for the Concurrence and Assent of the Governor and Council, without any Alteration or Amendment whatever.

"RESOLVED, That it is the Opinion of this Committee, that whosoever made the false, partial, and insidious Representation, upon which the said Instruction is founded, and advised such Instruction, are guilty of high Misdemeanours, and are Enemies to his Majesty and the Province.

"And your Committee recommend, that a Copy of these Resolutions be sent to his Honour the Lieutenant Governor, and that the Agent be instructed to represent the Matter to his Majesty in its true and proper Light, undeceive our most Gracious Sovereign, and [36] convince him how much he has been imposed upon by Misinformation—thereby to avert the King's Displeasure from his dutiful and loyal Subjects, the Commons House of Assembly of this Province."[25]

This Report, and the Remarks I shall make upon it, will be a full Answer to that Part of the Pamphlet, which relates to the Proceedings of the Assembly, both in voting the Money and in opposing the Operation of the additional Instruction, transmitted in consequence of the Misrepresen[ta]tions made concerning that Vote. For the Reader will perceive that the Facts and Arguments of the Pamphlet are exactly similar to the Recital and Reasoning of the Instruction; except that in the former they are more exposed and weakened by being drawn out at Length, and rendered ridiculous by an Affectation of Wit.

But I must first do Justice to the Candour and Veracity of this Writer, who has not only recited partially the Instruction itself, but suppressed entirely the Report of the Committee and other Proceedings of the House, in Justification of their Conduct. Did he wish to instruct his Readers in the whole Truth, and nothing but the Truth of these Proceedings? did he expect the Judgment, formed upon a fair [37] and full View of the Facts, would be in his Favour? or did he not rather intend to misinform their Understanding and mislead their Judgment? It is manifest he did; and it is equally true, that such Attempts are invariably prompted by a weak Head and a wicked Heart.

After mistating the Evidence on one Side, and totally supressing it on the other, he has the Confidence to say—"Thus have I most dispassionately and candidly stated every material Circumstance attending this important Subject, nearly in the Words used by the several Parties in the Course of the Transaction; and as far as I can judge, in no Shape contradictory to their genuine Sense and Meaning. I am not conscious that any Thing is omitted that can give Light or Information in the Case; though I have been necessarily obliged to trespass upon my Reader's Patience in order to collect the Substance of every legislative Act, and bring it into a clear Point of View, so far as relates to the Vote and Order of the

Commons House of Assembly; yet I trust that the Matter in Dispute will be now more clearly understood."[26]

It will indeed, Sir, be understood from your stating it just as you would wish, favourably on [38] that Side on which the Perversion of Truth only could obtain Judgment; falsly and injuriously on that, where the true Merits reside. When at the Beginning of your Performance, you professed yourself a downright Placeman, I did not expect any Attempt to impose upon your Reader by an Affectation of Candour and Impartiality. It requires more than puerile Credulity to believe, that a candid and dispassionate Spirit in Politics is compatible with the Principles of a *downright Placeman.*

Quodcunque ostendis mihi sic—incredulus odi.[27]

How poor is the Lieutenant Governor's Pretence, for withholding from the House the Correspondence with his Majesty's Minister, on this public Point. It was *secret and confidential.* The Abuse of these Words, which have been of late Years so frequent with the *American* Governors, makes one almost sick of the Sound. Secrecy will ever be pretended where the Truth is feared; where there is a Consciousness of some unwarrantable Conduct, or evil Design. From the strict Injunctions of Secrecy, which have been mutually interchanged between Lord *Hillsborough* and some of the *American* Governors, a Stranger would be induced to believe, that these were [39] not the official Dispatches between the King's Minister and the King's Governors, upon the public Proceedings of the King's Subjects, in his own Dominions; but the Intelligence of Spies and Informers in an Enemy's Country, or the dangerous Communications of Conspirators plotting some dark and midnight Mischief against the State. No Minister but Lord *Hillsborough* would have endured the Insult of receiving, or have descended to the giving of such Injunctions.

The Vote of the House was not intended, nor did it actually operate to divert the Money of any Fund in the Treasury from the Purposes for which it was appropriated by Law. All the Reasoning therefore against it on that Ground is futile and absurd. Such a Vote of the House never did operate on any Money in the Treasury but what was Surplus; and the very Meaning of this Word excludes the Idea of Appropriation. No Monies can be called Surplus, unless they are unappropriated. When there is no such Surplus in the

Treasury, it operates as a Vote of Credit,§ on the Faith of which the [40] Treasurer advances what the present Exigency requires. This was precisely its Effect in the Case before us. The Treasurer advanced the Sum upon the public Faith, and is himself the Creditor of the Public. The Council were apprised of this, from their Examination of his Assistant. They therefore well knew, that refusing to advise Assent to a Bill for the Payment of it, was only defrauding an Individual of his just Demand. Yet this is the Act which, as this Writer tells us, has procured them his Majesty's Approbation; and which the Governor signified, as he triumphantly declares, with *great Pleasure*, to his insignificant Junto. He has a satirical Turn, and surely means to ridicule Government here, when he represents it as paying Respect and Court to the Council, which he himself has painted in such contemptible Colours.

In Conformity to an Order of the House, and upon a Resolution of the House to make it [41] good, which involves a Pledge of the public Faith, the Treasurer, as has been the constant Practice, advanced the Money required; and when the Assembly made Provision for the Re-payment of it in the Tax Bill, the Council, with a Degree of Wisdom and Justice which, I believe, has no Parallel, rejected the Bill. Is it wise to create continual Confusion in public Affairs, to arrest the Business of the Legislature, to keep up a constant Cause of Contention between the representative and executive Part of Government to the Disquietude of the whole Province, for the sole Purpose of preventing the Payment of a just Debt? For admitting the House had so erred in their discretionary Power of granting Money, that the Sum was granted to Uses ever so improper and unbecoming, or as the Council have it, neither honourable, fit, nor decent; yet it is now irrevocable, nor can any

---

§ The Author of the Considerations elucidates this Point to his Reader, although he will not allow the Explanation to convince himself—he writes P.27—"and since 1754 many Orders occur, some sent [40] for Concurrence and many not—this Difference of Proceeding points out a Distinction, for where they have ordered Monies arising from appropriated Funds which have not been wanted, the Council's Concurrence and Governor's Assent have been applied for—but where the Orders have been general, they have gone upon a Sort of Idea that there were Surplusages and Balances sufficient to satisfy the Order without any intermediate Inconvenience till the same should be replaced by a Tax Bill."

possible Measure of the Council or the Governor recal[1] the
Money, or alter its Destination. The Opposition to the Tax Bill on
this Ground, is therefore evidently useless, and merely vexatious.
But on what Authority is the Use to which it is granted deemed
unfit? We have on one Side, the Opinion of a *full** Assembly, as he
acknow-[42]ledges, which granted it; that of every Assembly since,
and of the People at large, who re-elected those who had passed
the Vote. On the other Side, is the Governor and the Council respectable for the Number, Weight, and Wisdom of Three or Five
Persons? Were this a general Matter of Judgment, who could be in
Doubt which Side was most likely to err? But when we consider,
that it is a Question of giving the Money of the People, and of the
Use to which it is to be applied, in which the Opinion of their
Representatives is the sole Arbiter, and that the Intervention of
the Governor and Council is simply to assent or dissent from the
Law, by which the Mode of levying what is granted by the Commons shall be prescribed; it must appear to be, constitutionally
speaking, presumptuous and unwarrantable in them to decide
upon the Propriety of the Purpose for which the Grant is made;
and much more so, to presume to stile it unfit, dishonourable, and
indecent.

But what was the avowed Purpose for which the Grant was
made, and it is highly indecent to suppose any other,—"was it not
for the Support of the just and constitutional Rights and Liberties
of the People of *Great Britain* and [43] *America?"** Is this a Purpose, as the Council are pleased to say, neither fit, honourable, nor
decent; or, as this foolish Libeller asserts, arbitrary and unjust?
Could the Money of the People be applied to a Purpose more
interesting? could the Power of the House be exercised on a Subject more honourable and becoming? Among the numerous Ex-
ceptions to the Proceedings of Assemblies in *America*, which have
of late Years been taken, by his Majesty's Ministers, not one has
been so entirely futile and splenetic as this. Vain and absurd in its
Object; unjust and injurious in its Consequences; violent and unconstitutional in its Principle. Nor, as the Committee very justly

---

* [41] P. 7.
* [43] See the Order.

observe, could such a Dispute ever have arisen, had not the Support of the just and constitutional Liberties of the People necessarily involved in it an Opposition to the unjust and unconstitutional Measures of an arbitrary and oppressive Administration.

We shall now proceed to shew, that the *Vote of the House was agreeable to the Usage and Practice, both antient and modern, of the Commons House of Assembly in the Province of* South Carolina.

And here we might content ourselves with observing, that this has never been directly or in Argument controverted by the Minister, the [44] Governor, or the Council. They think it sufficient merely to reiterate the vague and indeterminate Assertions, that the Application was unconstitutional, and the Practice dangerous and unwarrantable. We have already proved, that neither of them is constitutionally competent to judge, whether the Application be proper or improper. The Determination of that must, from the Nature of the Thing, and indeed ought to rest solely with those who give the Money. It is plainly inseparable from the Right of giving, to judge of the Use for which the Gift is made; for it is that Judgment which must govern the Resolution to give or refuse. As to the Danger of the Practice, contributing to the Support of the just Rights and Liberties of the People, is certainly dangerous and justly alarming to those Men who mean to subvert them. It is therefore natural enough, that they should endeavour to shield themselves from that Danger by the Exercise of an arbitrary Vote now, and arrogating to themselves the Right of Controul in future.

But our Author admits it to have been the unquestioned Usage till the Year 1737, and since the Year 1752, for the Commons House of Assembly to order Monies to be advanced by the Treasurer, without the Concurrence of [45] Council or Assent of the Governor. One would imagine this Admission must conclude the Question; but to get rid of it by some Means or other, no Matter what, he desires us to reflect what slow Advances infant Societies of Men make towards Regularity or Perfection. How this applies is far beyond my Comprehension, unless it be to prove the Excellence of this Practice, which was not only necessary in the Infancy, but has been adopted in the Perfection of the Society of *South Caro-*

lina. It surely stamps a peculiar Merit upon the Mode that bears the Sanction both of the earliest and the latest Times.

But let us not triumph too soon! This Gentleman has an Argument in petto, which, like Lord *Peter's* brown Loaf,[28] will answer every Purpose. I will not contend with you, says he, about Trifles; I will grant that a particular Mode has been adopted for a Series of Years without Interruption or Controul—what then?—It is but an *Indulgence*, a *mere Tenure at Will*, and the Lord—that is, the Minister, or the Governor, or the Council, or whoever he pleases—may eject you at Pleasure.*

Now under Favour of this dread Lord, I should humbly think that this Argument goes [*46*] rather too far, since if it be valid here, I cannot conceive why it will not be equally conclusive against all our Liberties. But if the good People of *Carolina* should be as dull as myself, and not comprehend how they came to be Tenants at Will, or to hold any of their Privileges on so precarious a Tenure; I am afraid his Premises being instable, his Conclusion, which is certainly very ingenious, will fall to the Ground. There are some old-fashioned People too, who will be constant in thinking, that what has prevailed from the Beginning of the Colony, without Question or Controul, is Part of the Constitution; and that ancient and undoubted Rights are of all others the most sacred and valuable. It is true these must be Men who are not enlightened, as our Author is, by Court Sun-shine, which has the peculiar Faculty of illuminating the Prerogative of the Crown, and obscuring the Privileges of the People. Very willing however to give this Writer Credit wherever he deserves it, I must confess there is one Truth, and that very important too, in his Performance: It is "that Reason has but little Influence in the favourite Schemes of State Intrigues."* I know not any other possible Apology that can be made for this Instruction and its Consequences, even to the Com-[*47*]position of his Pamphlet. Had Reason, Justice, or Wisdom prevailed over those who formed them, they would never have appeared.

Our Author shews an admirable Discernment and Depth in the

---

* [*45*] P. 27, 28.
* [*46*] P. 29.

Principles of Government, when he asks, whether "Chains are more tolerable, because imposed by our own Consent."* Chains is a courtly Synonyme for Laws. And is he yet to learn, that the essential Difference between a free and a despotic Government is, that in the former, Laws are made, or imposed, if that Word will please him better, by the Consent of the People; in the latter, by the Will of the Tyrant? All Laws must, from their Nature, be co-ercive; and we submit to the Resignation of Part of our Liberty, to be secured in the Enjoyment of the Rest.†[29] We may therefore safely answer, that the only Chains which are tolerable, are those imposed by our own Consent.

He thinks he has drawn an Argument of some Weight against the Assembly, from finding that the Instances of granting Orders by their sole Authority are in general for Services within the Colony; though he is obliged to acknowledge, that they have many Times voted Money for external Purposes.‡ But, says he, "their having [48] voted Money to the Sister Colonies, is an Exception to the general Maxim, that they have no Right to dispose of the People's Money and apply it to other Uses than for their own im-mediate Service; and neither this, nor a Grant of Monies upon the royal Requisition, can afford the least Pretence for a Vote grounded upon merely an *ideal* Benefit, such as the Order states."[30] Is then the Preservation of our Liberties, for it is *that* the Order states, an ideal Benefit? To a venal Courtier, to an inveterate Tory, Liberty may appear an ideal Blessing; but to every Man who deserves the Name of *American* or *Englishman*, it is the illustrious Source of every Blessing we enjoy, the most worthy of contributing to and contending for, the sacred Object of our Solicitude and Devotion. But in what Principle, in what Practice of our Constitution did he find this Maxim of the Grants of the People being limited to their own Use? He is not pleased to give any Authority for it. He is to coin Maxims at his Pleasure; if they serve his Purpose, it is suffi-cient. The Delegates of the People stand in the Place, and possess all the Powers of the People. Who is it that can limit the Uses, or

---

* P. 20.
† Locke on Government, ch. 9.
‡ P. 19.

prescribe the Purpose, for which the People, or their Representatives, are to give their own Money? Is it not an Absurdity to suppose [49] his Will limitable, who gives his own, by any Thing but his own Reason and Discretion? Some one must hold the Purse Strings; some one must draw them *ad libitum*.[31] With whom is this Power trusted by the Constitution, with whom can it be so safely trusted, as with those whom the People have chosen from among themselves, whom they may reject or rechuse, who share with them in all the Benefits they procure, in all the Burdens they impose? Could it be reposed, with equal Confidence, in the supreme Power? Mr. *Locke* will answer for me, who lays it down as a fundamental Maxim, "that the Supreme Power must not *raise Taxes* on the Property of the People, without the *Consent* of the People given by themselves, or *their Deputies*."*[32] Much less could this Trust be confided in the Minister or the Governor, or the Council of State, who are not appointed by the People, nor amenable to them, nor necessarily known to them, or connected, or interested with them. The Consent of the People is the sole Requisite to the Gift; and the established Forms of the Constitution make the Consent of their Delegates equivalent to that of the People themselves.

[50] Taking our Author then upon his own Ground, as this Right of the Representative is clearly justified upon the Principles of the Constitution, the People ought not to submit to an unconstitutional Check or Controul from the Minister, or those in Authority under him.

I must not omit to take Notice of what he says, touching the Provisions made by divers Acts; which demonstrably prove, according to him, that Surplus and unapplied Monies in the Treasury cannot be drawn thereout by a Vote or Order of the Commons House alone. He has not vouchsafed to mention those Acts, that we might examine them; chusing, as he generally does, to have us take his Word for the Fact. The single Act which he has condescended to quote, the general Duty Act of 1751,[33] is fallacious and inconclusive to maintain his Position. For in the First Place, it goes only to the Surplus arising from the Duties imposed by that particular Act, nor can the Authority of that or any other such Act

---

* Locke, ibid. ch. 11.

apply to any other Surplus but that from Duties. In the Second Place, it would seem the Legislature was sensible such Surplus was liable to be appropriated by some other Power than that of the General Assembly, unless a Special Provision prevented it, or otherwise there would have been no Ne-[51]cessity for such Precaution. Now I believe the other Branch of the General Assembly, I mean the Governor, never yet pretended to the Right, or presumed to dispose of any Money by its sole Authority; therefore it must have been in the Commons House in which the Right of disposing of the Surplus resided, unless the Appropriation were restrained to the General Assembly, by the special Provision of the Act.

But be this as it will, there is a Distinction between the Surplus accruing from Duties and Taxes. As this Distinction militates against his Side of the Question, he chose to suppress it; or it is not within his Knowledge—*Aut dolo malo, aut ignorantia peccat.*[34] In the Duty Act, the whole Amount of the Duties in certain enumerated Articles is given to the Crown; in the Tax Bill, a specific Sum is granted. Should therefore the Duties produce more than was expected, it is vested in the Crown; but the Surplus of the Taxes remains ungranted, is the absolute Property of the People, and therefore disposable by their Representatives. The Case of the Duty Act is insidiously put, and does not in the least apply to the real Question.

Having thus proved, I hope to the Satisfaction of every candid Enquirer, that the Vote of the House on the 8th of *December* 1769, was [52] laudable in its Purpose and constitutional in its Mode; or to say the least, not Novel—it cannot but move our Indignation, that any Minister should set this up as an Object for public Contention, to the Impediment of all necessary Business, and the infinite Distress and Disquietude of the People. The Measure was obnoxious we know, it was once in the Power of the Lieutenant Governor to have punished the Trespass if there had been any—in a constitutional Way—but it is past and irretrievable, and it is mere childish Peevishness and Spleen to be angry about it now; the House of Assembly which did the Act, no longer exists, therefore cannot be punished; the Treasurer who furnished the Money is no more, and the Vengeance can only fall on his innocent

Posterity. What public Good can this Opposition to an irrevocable Act procure? What private Resentment can it gratify, when the Authors of the Offence are removed from its Reach?

But to do the Contrivers of the additional Instruction Justice, the preventing the Re-payment of the Money advanced on the Faith of the Vote in *December* 1769, is neither the sole nor the principal Intent of the Instruction. That Proceeding was only made a Pretence for abridging the fundamental Rights of the People in their [53] Representatives, by the Minister's usurping the Right of prescribing in what Manner they shall frame Money Bills for the future. The Instruction contains too an arbitrary Injunction (which our Author, with his usual Regard to Truth, softens into a *Provision*) to impose a wanton and rigorous Penalty upon the Treasurer. If the Commons House of Assembly were to send a Money Bill to the Governor, omitting entirely the Provision for the Re-payment of the Money advanced on their Order of 1769, it is plain he would not pass it under this Instruction, unless it were framed precisely according to the Mode which it ordains. It is therefore most clearly an arbitrary Rule of Conduct, prescribed by the executive Power to the Representative, in a Matter, which, by the Constitution, is solely and exclusively in the Arbitration of the Representative; and in which the Crown cannot interfere, without a manifest Infringement of the Constitution, and a dangerous Violation of their Rights.

The Assembly, in their several Answers to the Governor, have made such sensible Observations on the Nature and Import of this arbitrary Instruction, that they cannot be too often repeated, or too well remembered.

[54] "Your Honor," they say, "will excuse our differing totally from your Opinion of the additional Instruction. We cannot but think it as *unnecessary* as it is *unconstitutional*. We did not want to be told, that Monies raised by Law should be limited by express Words, and not by Implication, to the Purposes for which they were raised. Common Sense was sufficient to inform us of that. Such a Clause never is left out of a Money Bill. The last Clause of every Tax Act is added for that very Purpose; and the Instruction is therefore manifestly founded on Mistake or Misinformation—his Majesty's Ministers are fallible as well as other Men, and like them

are subject to Errors, nay, from their high Rank, are, perhaps, of all Men most liable to Misinformation; And we shall undertake to prove that Instructions have been sent to several of the *American* Governors, which were diametrically opposite to Reason, Law, and the Constitution of the Colonies to which they were sent, and consequently were not carried into Execution.* [55] Your Honor

---

* In 1768 Lord *Hillsborough,* Secretary of State for the *American* Department, wrote to Mr. *Penn,* Governor of *Pennsylvania,* to dissolve his Assembly if they would not obey an arbitrary Mandate, which he thought proper to transmit to him.[35]

Happily for that Province, the Wisdom of their Founder has protected them from the Possibility of ever being treated like such in-[55]significant Puppets. On a certain Day in every Year, the Inhabitants assemble, and choose their Representatives, who meet by their own Adjournment. The Governor has it not in his Power to dissolve, prorogue, or adjourn them, by which Means the People can never be deprived of their constitutional Guardians, by the Orders of a weak or arbitrary Minister. Was it not unpardonable in a Secretary of State to disgrace the Crown by discovering such Ignorance in One of its confidential Servants?

In 1764 the Governor of *New York* was ordered by his thirty-second Instruction to "permit and allow Appeals† from any of the Courts of Common Law to him, and the Council and he was required for that Purpose to issue a Writ, returnable before him and the Council, who were to proceed to hear and determine such Appeal. Provided, that in all such Appeals the Sum or Value appealed for do exceed three hundred Pounds Sterling. And if either Party should not rest satisfied with the Judgment of the said Governor and Council, an Appeal was then ordered to be allowed before the King in Council, in *England,* provided the Sum or Value so appealed for exceed five hundred Pounds Sterling."[36] This Instruction was attempted to be carried into Execution. But it was soon perceived, that if it were submitted to, the Use of Juries would be entirely destroyed. Appeals would be perpetually made from their Verdicts, by People who were rich enough to bring their Causes to a Country, where Riches, in the Management of a Law-suit, are known not to be useless.

The Chief Justice[37] and the other Judges of the Supreme Court[38] were unanimously of Opinion, that the Instruction ought not to be submitted to. Their Opinions were given in Writing, very fully, and with great Learning, on the Subject. The Purport was, that Obedience should not be paid to the Instruction, because it *seemed to aim at* [56] *altering the antient and wholesome Laws of the Land.*[39] The farcical Mockery of Justice in the Trial of Sir *Francis Bernard,*[40] the flagrant Attempt to rob Mr. *Penn* of his Property in the River *Delawar,*[41] the Countenance and indecent Applause lately given to a most wicked and impudent Lawyer, who was guilty of a false and malignant Accusation against a worthy and respectable Gentleman,[42] justifies every

---

† Not by Writs of Error, for those were always allowed.

tells us, you shall pay a most strict obedience to your Instruction. We thank [56] you for the Frankness and Candour of this Declaration. Permit us, Sir, following your [57] Honor's Example, with the same Openness to declare, that your Honor cannot be more devoted to the *Will of the Minister* than this House is to their Duty, and their most *gracious Sovereign,* and to the *Interests, Rights, and Privileges of their Constituents.* That they look upon the sole and absolute framing and modelling Money Bills to be One of the most essential and indispensable of those Rights, and that they could not suffer the Interposition of any Person or Power whatsoever, in that Matter, without basely betraying the Trust reposed in them by the People, and consequently injuring the Interest of his Maj-

---

American for shewing the utmost Reluctance in bringing any Cause before the Privy Council.

In 1769, by the Death of Sir *Henry Moore*,[43] at *New York*, the Government of that Province devolved on Lieutenant Governor *Colden*,[44] who received considerable Emoluments by granting Lands. Mr. *Colden* had a very difficult and dangerous Part to act at the Arrival of the Stampt Papers in *New York*, and alone, among all the Officers of Government employed about that disagreeable Business, conducted himself like a Man of Spirit and Honour. Administration, so far from rewarding his long and faithful Services, attempted to plunder him of that Property which Chance had thrown into his Possession. The Earl of *Dunmore*,[45] who is Brother-in-law to Lord *Gower*,[46] was appointed to succeed Sir *Henry Moore* as Governor of *New York*, and arrived there the Year following. He carried with him an Order from Lord *Hillsborough* to possess himself of Half the Salary and Perquisites which Mr. *Colden* had received.[47]

The Lieutenant Governor, with becoming Spirit, refused to pay Obedience to so unjust an Order, and could not conceive upon what Pretence the Demand was made. It appeared that in the Reign of King *William* an Instruction had been given to the Governor, to allow Half the Emoluments of the Government to the Lieutenant Governor, whenever he, the said Governor, should be absent from the Province.[48] This Instruction was intended solely for the Benefit of the Lieutenant Governors; who were often left to support the Expence of maintaining the Dignity of their Office, without having any Allowance for it. The Provision therefore made by the Instruction was [57] extremely proper. In this Instance, likewise, the Judges of the Supreme Court gave their Opinions, in Writing, against the Legality of Lord *Hillsborough*'s Order; and the iniquitous Attempt was dropt. Their Conduct, in these two Instances, must be viewed in the most honourable Light, as they hold their Commissions during Pleasure;—a most improper and precarious Tenure.[49]

If all the illegal, unconstitutional, and absurd Orders sent to the *American* Governors from the Beginning of the Administration of the late Duke of *Newcastle* to the End of that of his Pupil the Earl of *Hillsborough*, were collected, a Folio Volume would not contain them.

esty, who has, in a Manner becoming a Prince of the House of *Brunswick*, declared, *that he has no Interest—he can have none, distinct from that of his People.*

"If the Minister has a Right to interpose and direct us *how Money is to be raised,* he must [58] have an equal Right to dictate *the Sum*; and thus the Power of taxing the People will be in Effect transferred from their Representatives to the Minister; and the Commons House of Assembly, instead of being Guardians of the People's Property, will be made the Instruments of oppressing them, like the *Roman* Senate under the *Caesars*, when the Emperors, by keeping up the Appearance of old Forms, were enabled to carry their Violence to a greater Height than they would have dared to do in their own Names. Should the House submit to the Instruction to which your Honor professes to pay such implicit Obedience, they could not possibly refuse to obey any other. A ministerial Despotism would be thereby established, the most dangerous Degree of Despotism, that, over the Understanding and the Conscience, inasmuch as we are commanded to act diametrically opposite to both, and threatened in case of Refusal. As we cannot be of Opinion that your Honor will in the least advance his Majesty's Interest, by putting a Stop to public Business and injuring the public Credit in order to enforce an Instruction, which you have not attempted to shew is either just, constitutional, or necessary, or more binding than some other Instructions, which your Honor and your Predecessors have laid by as dead [59] Letters and unregarded, so shall we never envy any Glory or Promotion, which you, Sir, may obtain by your zealous Endeavours to deprive the good People of this Country of their most inestimable Rights."[50]

And now upon due Consideration of the Whole of this Business, I presume no Reader can remain unconvinced, that the Pretence on which this Instruction was grounded, namely the Illegality of the Vote of *December* 8th, 1769, is false, frivolous, and unjust—that the Instruction itself is an arbitrary and dangerous Interposition of Prerogative, prescribing that which is not within the Limits of its Controul, the Mode of framing Money Bills, trenching deeply on the dearest Rights of the People, and attempting to convert the Power of the Representative from being a Protection to the Property of their Constituents, into an Instrument of Extortion in the Hands of the Crown. Were it possible, that a House of Assembly should be so lost to every Sense of their Duty to the People, and of their own Dignity, Privileges, and Interests, as to submit to this Usurpation; then indeed would the "Represented be in a State of absolute Vassalage and ruinous Dependence;"—then, indeed, would the People feel the Truth of that received Maxim in Politics, *That no Tyranny is more* [60] *grievous, than a Tyranny under the Form of Law.*

That the Minister should persist in an Attempt so indefensible and so unconstitutional is not surprising in these Times. When the Study of Ministers is to invade the Liberties of the People, especially in *America*, and therefore, that the Governor should be so forward in his Zeal to obey an Instruction, productive of such detrimental Effects, is as little to be wondered at. Nor is it yet more wonderful, that so pernicious an Usurpation should be countenanced by the Council, when we consider that the Business is generally done by a small Junto, under the Direction of a Man desperate in Fortune, abandoned in Principle, and ruined in Reputation. To all the strong Representations which have been made here, to all the irrefutable Facts, and irrefragable Arguments which have been produced on the Part of the Assembly, no Answer has been returned, but that which graces the Edicts of France, *tel est nostre plaisir, such is our Will and Pleasure.* Sic Volo, sic Jubeo-[51]stat pro ratione Voluntas.[52] Yet we are now insulted with being told, that "after the most gracious Condescension on the King's Part, to the ardent Wishes of the Commons House of Assembly, the said Instruction having been ratified and [61] confirmed on a Revision of the Merits, it is the most unpardonable Presumption to look for farther Concessions from the Crown."[53]

The King's Ministers have *"condescended"* to refuse all Relief to the Grievances and Complaints of the People, to persevere in a Measure founded on Misrepresentation, and to subject the whole Province to all the Distress that arises from a Suspension of public Business. The People hardly wish to be distinguished by any more such "Marks of Royal Favor," and it would indeed be unpardonable Presumption in them to look for any farther "gracious Concessions from the Crown." Far from such Exorbitancy, they wish only for the quiet Enjoyment of what are their undoubted Privileges; nor is there any one among them so weak as not to know, that the only remaining Hope of Redress is in a manly and immoveable Assertion of their just Rights, till Time shall have dispelled the thick Cloud, which the Counsels of evil Ministers have spread before the Eyes of their most gracious Sovereign, against his loyal Subjects; and Measures shall be again modelled by Truth and Justice.

Let us now listen to the Logic of our Author in defining what this Instruction is.

[62] "It is," says he, "by Way of *Check*,—must be viewed in the Light of a *timely Correction*, by the executive Power—as a *Call* and *Admonition* to a Third Branch of the Legislature,"—and at last it comes out to be, "no more than the Exercise of that Act of Sovereignty given the Crown by the Constitution, for the Purpose of maintaining the just Balance of the State."* First it is a *Check*, then it rises into *Correction*, then it sinks into an *Admonition*, and at last falls softly down into the *gentle and benign Exercise of constitutional Power*. Thus, like *Poloneus's* Cloud, it is a Camel, a Whale, an Ouzle, or any Thing that may serve his Purpose.[54] But, as it often happens, while he endeavours to entrap others, he entangles himself. He acknowledges that "it was given as a Rule of Conduct to the several Branches of the Legislature;"§ from which it follows inevitably, that it is unconstitutional, because the King confessedly has no Right to direct, instruct, or dictate to either Branch of the Legislature, for if he had, then would the mutual Check and Balance, which he admits, from *Blackstone*, to be the very Essence of the Constitution, cease and be destroyed. This Instruction is therefore upon his own Admission, "a Departure from acknowledged Principles, [63] containing new-fangled Ideas not warranted by, or known to the Constitution."‡ To compel Obedience to this Infringement on the Constitution, it is in Effect said, you must submit to the Rule prescribed for giving and granting your own Money to the Use of those who have robbed you of your

---

* P. 25.
§ P. 26.
‡ P. 26.

Liberty, or you know the Alternative—no Assemblies, no Laws, no Treasure,—public Business interrupted, public Engagements violated, public Faith infringed.—Anarchy and Distress shall attend your Struggles for Rights and Privileges.—The Prerogative given for the Good of the People, shall be employed to insult and abuse their Representatives. Assemblies shall be called (*if at all*) to a Corner of the Country, distant and dangerous—detained in an inclement Season, at the Hazard of Health and Life—insulted with a childish Speech; and, for fear of a Reply, immediately prorogued to the usual Place—and finally to deprive them of the Opportunity of complaining in a constitutional Manner of such insolent and injurious Treatment, they shall be dissolved. The following authentic Papers will at once prove the Possibility of such an injurious Outrage; and the Moderation with which the Assembly resented it. [64] *Lord* Charles Montague *having returned to his Government, called the Assembly to meet him at* Beaufort, *a Village upon an Island 70 Miles distant from the Seat of Government—and after detaining the Members Three Days in Suspense made the following remarkable Speech—*

"Honorable Gentlemen,

Mr. Speaker and Gentlemen of the Commons House of Assembly,

"My constant Attention to preserve the Laws of this Province from Violation was the *only Cause* of my calling the General Assembly at this Time.

"My Knowledge of the Situation of Affairs in this Country, and of her real Interests, and my ardent Wishes to promote them, induced me to summon this General Assembly to meet in this Town.

"I have exercised, and shall continue to exercise the royal Prerogative in such a Manner as in my Opinion may promote his Majesty's Service and the general Advantage of the People over whom I have the Honor to preside: And while I am cautious in the most [65] extreme Degree that I do not violate the Laws. I shall be perfectly satisfied with my Conduct so long as I exercise such Powers only as are constitutional: Such I shall always exercise with the best Intentions, and with a corresponding Firmness.

"A long Space of Time having elapsed since the Inhabitants of this Province have received Benefit from the Deliberations of a Commons House of Assembly, many salutary Laws have expired, and others are near expiring, which ought to be revived and continued; the People have not acquired such new Laws as recent Circumstances have rendered necessary; and the public Creditors, for Years past, are yet unpaid their just Demands.

"I wish the Commons House of Assembly may remember that a Delay of Justice is a Denial of Justice.—Being sensible of the only Cause of the late public Dissentions, and of the Inconveniences and Distress with which this Province is loaded, I cannot but most sincerely lament the distressed Situation of our public Affairs; And as there is not any Instance of a lawful House of Commons having ever appropriated, and caused Money to be issued for public Services, of their sole Au-[66]thority, and against the Consent of the other Branches of the Legislature, or even having at any Time claimed such a Power, so, upon the Principles of our Constitution, of Law, and of Reason, it cannot be allowed that any Commons House of Assembly of this Province can or ought to have any such Power.

"Careful as I am not to invade the constitutional Rights of a Commons House of Assembly, it is my indispensable Duty to endeavour to preserve to each Branch of the Legislature its native Powers of Legislation; and I do earnestly wish that the weighty Affairs of this Province may be deliberated upon and transacted with that truly patriotic Spirit, which can, with Magnanimity, condemn and abandon any Measure that is an Alien to, incompatible with, and destructive of the Rights and Powers of that Mode of Legislation from which our own is modelled, and from which alone the People of this Province derive all their Liberties as *English* Subjects, and all those Rights, Privileges, and Powers of Legislation which can be legally exercised by their Representatives in General Assembly. By as much as you all prize and value the Rights of *English* Subjects, by so much let it be your Care to demonstrate by Acts, which are of much more Consequence than Words, [67] a due Veneration of that Form and Spirit of Government which has granted, and now regulates and preserves those invaluable Privileges to the Inhabitants of the Province.

"As it is your Interest to preserve the *English* Spirit of Government, so it is your Interest to preserve to each Branch of the Legislature such Powers as are peculiar or common to each. In this Case, the safest Means to preserve the Constitution is to maintain each particular Part of it inviolate. Innovations are dangerous, they are, in general, sure to create Contentions, which, unhappily for Mankind, too often make quick Progress to Anarchy.

"Wherefore, let me recommend to you, in the strongest Terms, that you be careful to endeavour to annihilate any Innovation, which, by violating constitutional Privileges of Legislation, thereby evidently tends to destroy that happy Poise of Power which is the peculiar Characteristic and Palladium of Legislature, founded upon and assimilated as nearly as may be to Principles of *British* Legislation; the constitutional Spirit of which is so admirably tempered and compounded, that nothing can endanger or hurt it, but Attempts and Innovations calculated to destroy the Equilibrium [68] of Power between one Branch of the Legislature and the Rest.

"The Commons House of Assembly claiming to issue Moneys for public Services of their sole Authority, has so alarming a Tendency, that it cannot be too anxiously guarded against—such a Measure is evidently capable of destroying and overturning every fundamental Principle of that Constitution of Government, which is the Envy of admiring Nations.—To persist in such an unconstitutional Claim would be in Effect to declare a Design to acquire a Power which is inconsistent with the *English* Constitution; a Measure, which in the natural Consequences of Things is pregnant with the most formidable and certain Dangers to the true Interests of the People of this Province; but to annihilate an unconstitutional Claim is most virtuous and most honorable—such a Proceeding is the most infallible Criterion of a true Patriot and a wise Senator.

"By such a Conduct you will in the most laudable Manner discharge your Duty to your King, to your Country, and to yourselves.

[69] "I am willing to hope for such a distinguishing Proof of true Patriotism from this Commons House of Assembly: Such a Conduct will of course render the Exercise of unusually exercised Prerogatives unnecessary, which, although to a few Persons they may be

displeasing Remedies, to operate against the Disorder of the State, are not therefore the less legal or inadequate to effect their ultimate End, the Good of the People.

"At this my First Meeting with this General Assembly, I chuse to deliver my Sentiments thus fully and candidly, upon a Point of so high Consequence as the Preservation of our Legislative Powers in their native Force. With the best Intentions for the public Service I do recommend this most serious Subject to your most attentive Consideration. I shall at all Times give every Encouragement in my Power to engage you to proceed to the Consideration of public Affairs with that Temper, Candour, and Benevolence which must naturally prevail in public Deliberations when the public Good is truly understood, and is really meant to be promoted: And as I have now Reason to think that the speedy Sitting of the General Assembly in *Charles Town* may induce such Deliberations; and I pledge myself to [70] you, that at all Times I shall exercise my Authority in such Manner as I may think will have a Tendency to induce such Deliberations as may be of public Benefit: I do prorogue this General Assembly to the Twenty-second Day of this instant *October*, to be then held at the usual Place in *Charles Town*, and this General Assembly is accordingly prorogued.—

CHARLES GREVILLE MONTAGUE."

Beaufort, October 10th 1772.[55]

Coupling his Lordship's Declaration in the first and last Paragraph of this Standard of Language, Wisdom and Policy, is all the Comment that I shall make.

"My Knowledge of the Situation of Affairs in this Country, and of her real Interests, and my ardent Wishes to promote them, induced me to summon this General Assembly to meet in *this Town* (*Beaufort*)— and as I have *now* Reason to think that the speedy Sitting of the General Assembly in *Charles Town* may induce such Deliberations as may be of public Benefit, I do prorogue the General Assembly to the 22d *October* instant, to be then held at the usual Place in *Charles Town*."

[71] The Reader is referred to the following Report of the Committee on Grievances, for the Sense of the Assembly upon this extraordinary Occasion.

REPORT.

"That they have considered the several Matters referred to them the 22nd and 24th instant by the House; and though the Committee are of Opinion, that the Governor's calling the Assembly to *Beaufort*, keeping them there Three Days, without permitting them to do any Business, and proroguing them on the very Day, that by Law, was the last that the General Assembly could be discontinued, were such Measures as call for the utmost Resentment of this House, and would well justify their coming immediately to a Resolution to do no Business with his Excellency, until he had given them Satisfaction in the Premises. Yet as the People have been long deprived of the Benefit of Representation, and his Majesty's Service and the Interest of the Colony require the immediate Sitting and Proceeding of the General Assembly on the arduous Affairs of our Country, the Committee therefore recommend, that the House do not carry Matters to that Extremity, but that they enter into the following Resolutions, (*viz.*)

[72] "Resolved, That as this House did not exist when his Excellency formed his Plan of calling the General Assembly to *Beaufort*, his Excellency's Proceeding seems to be founded upon his ill Will to the Body of the Freemen of this Province, inasmuch as he thereby shewed his Purpose of injuring and affronting whomsoever the Freeholders of the Colony should chuse to represent them.

"Resolved, That his Excellency's calling the General Assembly to *Beaufort*, a Place very distant from *Charles Town*, where such Assemblies have always been held (except when malignant and contagious Disorders raged therein) where all the public Offices and Records are kept, at a Time highly dangerous to the Health, and inconvenient to the private Affairs of the Members, was a most unprecedented Oppression, and an unwarrantable Abuse of a

Royal Prerogative, which hath never been questioned by the People of this Colony.

"Resolved, That the Governor's keeping at *Beaufort* the fullest House that ever met at the Beginning of any Session, Three Days before he would receive them with their Speaker, and then immediately proroguing them, was add-[73]ing Insult to Injury, and plainly manifested his Contempt of the People's Representatives.

"Resolved, That his Excellency's proroguing the General Assembly, without suffering them to sit One Moment as a Legislative Body, was at least an Evasion, if not a direct Violation of the Election Law, which enacts, That the Sitting and Holding of the General Assembly shall not be discontinued or intermitted above Six Months, that Time being entirely expired when his Excellency prorogued the House.

"Your Committee recommend, that the Agent be ordered to make the strongest Representations to his Majesty of the arbitrary and oppressive Proceedings of the Governor, and to use his utmost Endeavours to procure the Removal of his Excellency from this Government, or such other Marks of his Majesty's Royal Displeasure as may prevent Governors for the future from thus oppressing the People, by abusing those Prerogatives which were intended for their Benefit.

"And as his Excellency's Speech at *Beaufort* seems wholly calculated to throw the Blame of all the Inconveniences which the Public labours [74] under upon *the Assembly, and charges them with making unconstitutional and unprecedented Claims; your Committee are of Opinion it ought not to pass unnoticed by the House, and therefore recommend the following Message in Answer thereto:*

"*May it please your* Excellency,

"The calling the Assembly at *Beaufort* was such an extraordinary Exertion of the Royal Prerogative, and your Excellency's Conduct there was so unprecedented, that the House could not but suppose your Excellency must have had very cogent Reasons for the Measures you were pleased to pursue on that Occasion. But when we humbly addressed your Excellency to lay your Reasons before us, that we also might see the Benefit which was to arise to the Public from the unusual Exercise of Prerogative, your Excellency, to our great Concern, was pleased to refer us to your Speech, in which no Reason appears, but your Excellency's Will and Pleasure.

"The House therefore cannot avoid taking up the Consideration of those Proceedings of your Excellency, lest they should be drawn into Precedent, and future Governors should attempt to put a Stop to all Freedom of Debate, by harrassing the Representatives of the [75] People from Place to Place, to the Destruction of their Healths and Ruin of their Fortunes, attended with the Inconvenience, Expence, and Danger of removing such Books and Records as are absolutely necessary to the House of Assembly, until the Members be either wearied into Compliance, or the Difficulty of Attendance deter Gentlemen from serving in the Assembly.

"In the Beginning of your Excellency's Speech, you are pleased to inform us, that your constant Attention to preserve the Laws of the Province from Violation, was the only Cause of your calling the General Assembly at that Time; we presume your Excellency means the Election Law, by which the Calling and Sitting of the Assembly cannot be intermitted more than Six Months: It is impossible to say how much we are mortified by this Declaration. Were then neither your Excellency's ardent Wishes to promote the real Interest of this Country and his Majesty's Service—Were not the many Hardships and Injuries which the People of this Colony, and particularly the public Creditors, labour under, for Want of the Deliberations of the General Assembly, and which your Excellency so strongly paints in your Speech, nor even the [76] Consideration that *a Delay of Justice was a Denial of Justice*—Were not all these sufficient to induce your Excellency to call a General Assembly, unless the Law had compelled it?

"Pardon us, Sir, if your Excellency's most extreme Caution, not to violate the Laws, is not so apparent to us, even upon this Occasion, as we could wish; we can by no Means think that a bare Calling of a General Assembly within the utmost Limitation of the Time prescribed by Law, and proroguing them without permitting them to sit even for a Moment, can be such a Calling and Sitting as the Letter, much less the Spirit and Intention of the Law, require.

"Your Excellency declares your entire Satisfaction in your Conduct upon that Occasion. Sir, be pleased to excuse our being of a different Opinion. However, we shall enter into no Altercation on that Subject; but shall appeal to our most gracious Sovereign, not doubting that he will prevent his Governors for the future from misusing his Prerogative to the Injury of his People.

[77] "No Inconveniences to which the good People of this Province have been subjected, can by any Means be imputed to their Representatives, who have ever expressed the utmost Readiness to do their Parts; but to those who rejected their Bills, and denied them Liberty to sit.

"We are at a Loss to understand how your Excellency can with any Propriety apply to this House, what your Excellency mentions about a lawful House of Commons; at any Rate it cannot concern the present House, who had then neither claimed or used any Right or Privilege, other than those usually demanded by the Speaker. And we know of no other Claim made by any late House, nor by former Houses, that has not at least the Sanction of long Usage.

"We heartily join in your Excellency's earnest Wish, and shall do every Thing in our Power, that the weighty Affairs of this Province may be deliberated upon and transacted with that truly patriotic Spirit, which can with Magnanimity condemn and abandon any Measure that is incompatible with, or destructive of, the Rights and Powers of that Mode of Legislation, from [78] which our own is derived. Should your Excellency really join us here, and demonstrate by Acts (which indeed are of much more Consequence than Words) a due Veneration of, and a Compliance with, the true Spirit of the *English* Government, all our Disputes must be at an End; for the only Claim which has prevented the public Business of late, is that most unreasonable and unconstitutional one of the Ministry, to direct and controul the House of Assembly in framing Money Bills; a Claim so glaringly inconsistent with the Rights of the House, that the Ministry themselves do not attempt to support the Propriety of it to our Agent. Yet upon this Matter alone, as does most clearly appear by the Journals, your Excellency was pleased to dissolve the last House of Assembly, and to reduce the Colony to the distressed State it now stands in, and from which we hope your Excellency now means to deliver it by magnanimously supporting the Rights of the People, by preserving inviolate to each

Branch of the Legislature such Rights and Powers as are peculiar to it.

"To annihilate an unconstitutional Claim, as your Excellency observes, is most virtuous and honorable; such a Proceeding is the most in-[79]fallible Criterion, as well of a truly patriotic Governor as a wise Senator.

"Your Excellency condescends to inform the House, that the Conduct above described will of course render the Exercise of unusually exercised Prerogatives unnecessary, which Words the House presume are meant as a Threat, at least against a few Persons among them. The House humbly pray your Excellency to do them more Justice, than to suppose that any Oppressions to which a conscientious Discharge of their Duty may subject them, can or will ever induce them to depart in the minutest Degree from the Rights and Privileges of the People, or betray the Trust reposed in them.

"Your Excellency tells us, that you shall at all Times give every Encouragement in your Power to engage us to proceed to the Consideration of public Matters, with Temper, Candour, and Benevolence. Can your Excellency possibly suppose, that your calling the General Assembly at *Beaufort,* and your Conduct there, were Measures that could by any Means tend to produce Temper and Benevolence? Surely not, unless your Excellency supposes the People to be thereby so intimidated, as to be afraid to support their own Privileges.[80]—Sufficient be it to say, that the House are not so irritated as to put any Stop to public Business, upon which they are ready and willing to proceed with all possible Dispatch."⁵⁶

To reconcile Men's Minds to these outrageous Proceedings, they are told by the Author—"that no Part of the King's Dominions can be injured by this local Difference, nor is the great Machine of Government in the least affected by it; the Punishment is as local as the Dispute itself; the People of the Colony alone suffer in the Cause, which no wise Man can think a good one."*

Such is the unprecedented Manner in which the People have been insulted, their Distresses ridiculed, their Complaints mocked,

* P. 30.

their Liberties invaded. The Machinations of a Governor and a corrupt Council have delivered them up a grateful Victim to the Vengeance of that odious Minister, whose puerile circular Letter they treated with the Contempt it deserved.

I should not condescend to take Notice of the Stuff in this Pamphlet concerning the Bill of Rights, were it not founded on a gross and impudent Falshood. "I have not been able to [81] learn, says the Writer, what the venerable Supporters seriously thought in relation to this Gift. That they laughed at it and enjoyed the Joke, I can easily suppose: That they passed a Sneer upon it and pronounced it an *idle Affair*; that they ridiculed the Credulity of the Donors, and admired their Faith, I can easily believe; but it is not possible to carry our Conjectures any farther.—It is curious to reflect, that the *Silence* is equally as *sullen*, on one Side of the Water, as it is on the other. I cannot learn from Authority, that even the *unavailing Tribute* of Thanks has been returned for all this *legislative Kindness*."* The following excellent Letter from the Society of the Supporters of the Bill of Rights will, if any Thing can, put this Wretch to Shame, and prove at once their grateful Sense of the laudable Attention of the Assembly to the noble Cause they were supporting, and the common Interest of both Countries in the Success of their Endeavours.

[82] *To the Honourable the Commons House of Assembly of* South Carolina.

"Gentlemen,

"We are directed by the Society, Supporters of the Bill of Rights, to transmit to you their Thanks for the very honorable Testimony you have at once given of your own Sentiments, and of your Approbation of their Conduct.

"The same Spirit of Union and mutual Assistance, which dictated your Vote in our Favour, animates this Society. We shall ever consider the Rights of all our Fellow Subjects throughout the *British* Empire, in *England, Scotland, Ireland,* and *America*, as Stones of one Arch on which the Happiness and Security of the Whole are founded. Such would have been our Principle of Action,

---

* P. 31.

if the System of Despotism, which has been adopted, had been more artfully conducted; and we should as readily have associated in the Defence of your Rights, as our own, had they been separately attacked.

"But Providence has mercifully allotted to depraved Hearts weak Understandings: The Attack has been made by the same Men, at the same Time, on both together, and will serve only to draw us closer in one great Band of mutual Friendship and Support.

[83] "Whilst the *Norman* Troops of the First *William* kept the *English* in Subjection, his *English* Soldiers were employed to secure the Obedience of the *Normans*. This Management has been too often repeated now to succeed.

"There was a Time when *Scotland*, though then a separate and divided Nation, could avoid the Snare, and refused, even under their own *Stuarts*, to enslave their antient Enemies. The Chains which *England* and *Scotland* disdain to forge for each other, *England* and *America* will never consent to furnish.

"Property is the natural Right of Mankind; the Connexion between Taxation and Representation is its necessary Consequence. Our Cause is one—our Enemies are the same. We trust our Constancy and Conduct will not differ. Demands which are made without Authority should be heard without Obedience.

"In this, and in every other constitutional Struggle, on either Side of the *Atlantic*, we wish to be united with you; and are as ready to give as to receive Assistance.

"We desire you, Gentlemen, to be persuaded, that under all our domestic Grievances and Ap-[84]prehensions, the Freedom of *America* is our peculiar Attention; and these your public Act and solemn Engagement afford us a pleasing Presage, and confirm our Hopes, that when Luxury, Misrule, and Corruption, shall at length, in Spite of all Resistance, have destroyed this noble Constitution here, our Posterity will not, like your gallant Ancestors, be driven to an inhospitable Shore, but will find a welcome Refuge, where they may still enjoy the Rights of *Englishmen* amongst their Fellow Subjects, the Descendants and Brothers of *Englishmen*.

We are, Gentlemen,

With the greatest Respect,

Your most obedient Servants and
affectionate Fellow Subjects,
John Glynn,   Chairman
Richard Oliver,   ⎫
                ⎬Treasurers
John Trevanion, ⎭
Robert Bernard, ⎫
Joseph Mawbey, ⎪
                ⎬Committee."⁵⁷
James Townsend, ⎪
John Sawbridge, ⎭

    I shall close the Consideration of this pernicious Instruction, and
of the Proceedings of the Governor and Council upon it, with an
excellent Observation from Mr. Justice *Blackstone*. "Whoever will
attentively consider the *English* [85] History, may observe, that
the flagrant Abuse of any Power, by the Crown or its Ministers,
has always been productive of a Struggle, which either discovers
the Exercise of that Power to be contrary to Law, or, if legal, re-
strains it for the future."*⁵⁸

    We come now to the Consideration of a Question, most singular
in its Nature, and important in its Consequence. It was not enough
that his Majesty's Council of State, under the Influence of a factious
and flagitious Leader, should have presumed to controul the Representatives of the People in their antient, essential, and undoubted Right of granting their own Money, and should have
countenanced an arbitrary and unconstitutional Attempt to subject the House of Assembly to the Dictation of a Minister in
framing Money Bills—but this Council, dependent as it is, must
assume the Powers of a Branch of the Legislature, which are competent only to an absolutely independent Body; and, on the Pre-
tense of those Powers, usurp and exercise a dangerous Authority
over the Freedom of the Press, and the personal Liberty of the
Subject. The Origin of this Question was as follows:

    A Member of the Council had protested against some of their
Proceedings, and gave a Copy of [86] that Protest to the Printer,
to be inserted in his Paper. The Protest was printed accordingly.
The Council voted the Printer guilty of a high Breach of Privilege

---

* Comment. Vol. iii, P. 135.

and Contempt of their House, and for this Offence committed him to Gaol. Upon this Commitment, the Printer sued out a Writ of *Habeas Corpus* before Two Justices, the Honorable *Rawlins Lowndes*, Speaker of the Commons House of Assembly, and G. *Gabriel Powel*, Esquire, a Member of that House. Upon full Consideration of the Cause of the Commitment, and the Power by which it was made, the Justices judged it illegal, and discharged the Prisoner. The Law and Reason of that Adjudication are so ably laid down in the Opinion of Mr. *Lowndes* upon the Trial, an Opinion which would do Honour to the most learned Judge in *England*, that it is with Pleasure I present it to the Reader.

The Honorable Mr. Lowndes.

"It appears by the Sheriff's Return of *Habeas Corpus*, that the Prisoner, *Thomas Powell*, stands commited by virtue of a Warrant, dated *August* 31, 1773, from Sir *Egerton Leigh*, President of the Council, said to be by Order of the Upper House of Assembly, for that he had ac-[87]knowledged himself to be the Printer and Publisher of a News-paper called *The South Carolina Gazette*, Numb. 1966, dated *Charles Town, Monday* the 30th Day of *August* 1773, in which Paper is printed Part of the Proceedings of that House on *Thursday* the 26th Day of *August* last, which the House hath resolved to be a high Breach of Privilege, and a Contempt of the House, and ordering that the said *Thomas Powell* should be therefore committed to the Common Gaol of *Charles Town*, during the Pleasure of the House.

"I am sorry that this Matter hath come before me, and that I am obliged to decide upon the Legality of the Commitment. It involves in it a Question of Consequence. If, on the one Hand, the Commitment should be deemed illegal, the Council will so far be deprived of a Power of Commitment for Breach of Privilege. If, on the other Hand, the Commitment should be deemed legal, the Prisoner will be restrained of his Liberty, which is one of the greatest Punishments, next to corporal, that can be inflicted on the Subject. I should be extremely sorry to err either Way. I would gladly have declined the Task, and wish from my Heart some abler Magistrate had been applied to.

[88] "From the Rank and Station I am in, and from my Connec-

tion with the Commons House of Assembly, I may be presumed to be under some Bias and Prepossession in Favour of that House and its Privileges. I confess I am so; but I trust it is no undue Bias or Prepossession; no Propensity to exclude from any other Body of Men, or any other Part of the Community, any Rights, Privileges, or Immunity whatever, which they may, on a fair Inquiry, be found to be intitled to. It was *insisted* however, that I should grant the *Habeas Corpus*, that it was a Writ of Right; and it would very ill have become me, to have been disobedient to so good and salutary a Law, although it had not been enforced with such penal Sanctions as it has to secure its Execution.

"The Laws of the Land provide for the Safety of every Man's Person, his Liberty, and his Estate. By the Great Charter it is provided, that no Freeman shall be taken or imprisoned, but by the lawful Judgment of his Equals, or by the Law of the Land. And many subsequent Statutes expressly direct, that no Man shall be taken or imprisoned by Suggestion or Petition to the King, or his Council, unless it be by legal Indictment, or the Process of the Common Law. By the Pe-[89]tition of Rights it is enacted, That no Freeman shall be imprisoned or detained without Cause shewn, to which he may answer according to Law: And, by the *Habeas Corpus* Act of the 31st *Char.* II. the Methods of obtaining that Writ are pointed out and enforced: All which Statutes, for the Security of the Liberty of the Subject, and expresly made of Force, here, particularly the *Habeas Corpus* Act, which, by an Act of Assembly of this Province passed in 1712, is more particularly accommodated to our local Circumstances, and some Difficulties removed which might otherwise have obstructed the Execution of that wholesome Law.[59] It is in virtue of this Provincial Law, that we were impowered to issue the *Habeas Corpus* which we did in this Case, and are impowered to take Cognizance of the present Matter.

"It appears then, that no Freeman shall be taken or imprisoned, but by the Judgment of his Peers, or by the Law of the Land. No Judgment of his Peers has been given in the present Case against Mr. *Powell*, for Judgment by his Peers means a legal Course of Trial by Jury. It remains then to be inquired into, whether the Law of the Land warrants his Commitment, and consequently Imprison-[90]ment? And whether the Cause shewn is sufficient to authorize his Detention? or whether, if his Commitment is legal, he is bailable or not bailable?

"Either House of Parliament have, from Time immemorial, exercised a Power of Commitment and Imprisonment: And it seems to be a settled Point, confirmed by late Adjudications, that the Courts of Law, or Judges, will not interfere or intermeddle in any Case, so as to discharge a Prisoner committed by either House, during the Sitting of Parliament; that the Houses are the only competent Judges of their own Privileges; and that their Determinations are not to be reviewed or examined by inferior Jurisdictions.

"The Law of Parliament, therefore, being a Part of the Law of the Land, Commitments in consequence thereof, by either House, are not prohibited by *Magna Charta*. And the Judges do now, invariably, so far as has fallen within my Knowledge, remand the Prisoner back to the Place of his Confinement, without affording him any Relief, either by Bail or otherwise.

[91] "The Law of the Land not giving the Council the least Colour of Right to commit for Breach of Privilege, or what they call Contempt of their House, they must found their Claim upon the Usage and Practice of the House of Lords in *England*. It will be necessary, therefore, to enquire what Affinity or Resemblance there is between them, to intitle the Council to a derivative Right to the high Privilege exercised by the Lords.

"The Lords are a permanent Body, inheriting the Right of Legislation independent of the Crown. They are the hereditary Counsellors to the King, and Guardians to the State. The Power of Judicature resides in them, in the dernier Resort. They try their own Members on Life and Death, without being under the Obligation of an Oath. And all these, and many other high Privileges, they inherit from the best of Titles, Prescription, and Usage for Time immemorial. Indeed they are of the very Essence of the Constitution.

"Compare the Constitution of the Council with that of the Lords, and where shall we find Cause to infer, that they possess, or ought to possess, the Powers of the latter?

[92] "The Council are appointed during the Pleasure of the Crown, removeable at Pleasure—and may be suspended by the Governor. They hold their Office, and all the Appendages to it, at Will, and therefore want that most essential Requisite of Inde-

pendency, to constitute them a Branch of the Legislature, or in any Respect to assimilate them to the Lords. Unhappy for the People it is so, much to be wished it were not so; and that while they claim the Power of the Lords House over the Person of the Subject, the Subject had the same Degree of Security for the due Exercise of that Power, which he has in the House of Lords. The People have nothing to fear from the Lords: They are their Guardians, and a Bulwark of Defence against Oppression and Tyranny. They are numerous as well as independent: No private Pique or personal Resentment can influence there.—HERE, the most important Concerns of the Province are often, very often, determined at a Meeting of Three of the Members of the Council; very seldom that they exceed Four; and the Object of their Care is more particularly *the Prerogative.*

"It is true, the Council do in this, as well as some other Provinces, concur in the pass-[93]ing of Provincial Laws. This is in consequence of Instructions from the Crown, restraining the Governor from giving his Assent to any Law that has not that Sanction: And from this single Circumstance it is, I apprehend, that the Council have created themselves an Upper House, and have assumed that Appellation in their Intercourse with the Commons House; although they are invariably stiled, by the King's Instructions, and in their Appointment, *the Council.* From this important Circumstance also, it is, that they would derive to themselves other Powers, incident and indeed indispensably necessary to the House of Lords, but dangerous and unnecessary to be exercised by the Council; as if a Right to advise the Governor to pass or reject a Bill, involved in it, of consequence, all other Privileges belonging to the Upper House of Parliament.

"The Freedom and Liberty of an *English* Subject are of so high Estimation in the Eye of the Law, that, to deprive him of them, it is incumbent on those that would do it, to shew their Right clearly and incontestibly. Loose and vague Reasoning, fallacious Conclusions, specious Inferences, or bold Assertions, will not do: The Judgment of his Peers, or the clear Voice of the Law of the [94] Land, must justify, and nothing else can justify the Commitment or Imprisonment of any free Subject whatever.

"Upon the most mature Consideration, as far as my slender Abilities will enable me to judge, I am of Opinion, That there is no Foundation in Law to warrant the Commitment now under Consideration: That it would be dangerous to countenance such a Usurpation of Power in the Council, would render the Liberty of the Subject precarious, and introduce Novelty and Innovation, destructive of sound Law, and every Principle of Justice.

"The Commitment therefore, in my Opinion, is to be considered merely as a Commitment of the Privy Council; and in that Case, has no other Authority than if done by a private Magistrate. The Subject has his Remedy by *Habeas Corpus* in either Case; and we are to consider, whether the Matter charged is an Offence at Law— and if an Offence, whether bailable or not.

"And I am of Opinion, that it is no Offence at Law—that the Paper referred to in the Commitment, being a Protest from Two Members of the Council, against the Pro-[95]ceedings of that Board, in a certain Matter depending before the Council, and required by One of the Members to be printed by the Prisoner, might lawfully, legally, and warrantably be printed by the Prisoner, acting only in the Way of his Profession; the more especially as it was unaccompanied with any Remarks, Observations, or Additions of his own, but simply and literally as it was received by the Prisoner from One of the Members of the Council. And it is not clear to me, that even the House of Lords would include such a Paper under the general Idea of Proceedings of their House, for which they would punish a Printer who published it. I am therefore for ordering the Prisoner to be released."[60]

This Opinion carries with it irrefutable Argument and Conviction. But our Author, on the contrary, asserts, the Pretensions of the Council to the Powers of an Upper House of Legislature in the Province of *South Carolina*. That the Reader may be enabled to judge, with what Propriety this is asserted, we must take a View of the Constitution of the Colony, from its First Settlement.

[96] The First Charter, granted in the Fifteenth Year of King *Charles* the Second, gives full and absolute Power to *Edward* Earl of *Clarendon*, *George* Duke of *Albemarle*, *William* Lord *Craven*, *John* Lord *Berkeley*, *Anthony* Lord *Ashley*, Sir *George Carterett*, Sir *William Berkeley*, and Sir *John Colleton*, and their Heirs, for

the good and happy Government of the said Province, to ordain, make, enact, and under their Seal to publish any Laws whatsoever, either appertaining to the public State of the said Province, or to the private Utility of particular Persons, according to their best Discretion, by and with the Advice, Assent, and Approbation of the Freemen of the said Province, or of the greater Part of them, or of their Delegates or Deputies.—The same Charter farther declares, that all and singular the Subjects and Liege People of us, our Heirs and Successors, emigrating to the said Province, and the Children of them, and of such as shall descend from them, there born or here-after to be born, be and shall be Denizons and Lieges of us, our Heirs and Successors, and be in all Things held, treated, and re-puted as the liege faithful People of us, our Heirs and Successors, born within this our Kingdom, or any other of our Dominions, to have and enjoy all Liberties, Franchises, and Privileges of this our Kingdom of *England*, and of other our Domi-[97]nions aforesaid; and may freely and quietly have, possess, and enjoy, as our liege People born within the same, without the least Molestation, Vexa-tion, Trouble, or Grievance of us, etc.[61]

The same Privileges and Liberties are re-declared in the Second Charter, granted in the Seventeenth Year of the same Reign.[62]

Conformable to this Charter, the General Assembly consisted of the Lords Proprietors, or their Representative, a Governor, and the Delegates of the People. No Council or middle Branch com-posed the Legislature. This Constitution continued till the Year 1721, when it underwent an Alteration in having the King substi-tuted for the Proprietors; since which a Governor appointed by the Crown, and assisted by a Council of State in the same Nomination, has, with the Delegates of the People, constituted the General Assembly, or legislative Authority of the Colony.

To shew that no Alteration did in Fact take Place as to the Number of Branches constituting the Legislature, it is to be ob-served that the Governor and Council sat together in the same [98] Room, and acted as one Body.* This original Usage is decisive

---

* The following Instances will shew that the original Mode was for the Governor and Council to sit and act as one Body.

Council Chamber, February 10, 1721.—A written Message from the *Gov-ernor and Council* to the Commons House of Assembly, signed by the Gover-nor, and One of the Council.

to shew that the Council were intended to resemble the Privy Council at Home, not the House of Lords, and therefore instead of deliberating as a distinct Branch of the Legislature, they sat with the Governor to advise him in his legislative Capacity.

This is the *"contemporanea Expositio"*[63] of the royal Commission, which is *"fortissima in Lege."*[64] Thus the ambiguous Words of the Commission are, by the contemporaneous Exposition of them, clearly explained to mean, that the Council was intended merely to add Splendour to the royal Governor; and, consisting generally of Gentlemen of the Province, to aid him with their Advice in the Duty of his Office. The King found a Constitution already established upon his own Charter. That Charter suffered no Alteration, but in substituting the Crown in the Place of the Proprietary. By the established [99] Constitution, the People had One-half of the legislative Power. It was not therefore in the Option of the Crown to reduce them to One-third, which would have been the Case had a Council been established as a separate Branch of Legislature.

This Mode of the Governor and Council sitting together as one House of Assembly, continued till Mr. *Lyttleton's*[65] Administration,* when, on some Quarrel with the Governor, the Council removed into another Room. If the Council, therefore, are a distinct Branch or any Branch of the Legislature, they are self-created. Their sitting and acting separately is a late Practice, prompted by a quarrelsome Disposition. It is very lately that they erected a magnificent Bar to their *House*, as they are pleased to term it, and approached (in their own Imagination) a Step nearer to the Dignity of a House of Peers, by choosing a Speaker†—It [100] would be extraordinary indeed if these trifling Acts, proceeding entirely from themselves, should invest them with the high and transcen-

---

Commons House.—Ordered, that Major *Thomas Hepworth* do carry to the *Governor and Council*—the Bill, etc. *June* 13, 1722. The Journals abound with such Proofs.

* Either at the End of Governor *Glen's*,[66] or the Beginning of Governor *Lyttleton's* Administration.

† Such Mimickry has ever been the Harbinger or Attendant of some wanton or violent Attack upon the Privileges of the Representative Body— therefore it is not surprizing, the Council (according to our Author, P. 60,— "are represented as arrogating to themselves *Powers* which never were intended to be bestowed upon them, that the People believe they are mere *Tools* and *Engines* to the Crown, from whom they pretend to derive *Powers*," in order to sanctify their own "Usurpations."

dent Powers of a Branch of the Legislature, and materially alter a Constitution established upon the Practice of so many Years. The very Supposition of it is an absolute Absurdity.

Bearing then these Things in Mind—the original Constitution in which the Legislature consisted of Two Branches only; the Practice of the Governor and Council sitting together as one Branch of Assembly, in which they were only his Privy Counsellors, and the dangerous Impropriety of trusting a dependent Body with Powers which are proper only to an independent Body—the Reader will more easily detect the Fallacy and Weakness of those Arguments, calculated to maintain the Claim of the Council to legislative Privileges, and the Authority grafted upon it.

The Author's Argument drawn particularly from the King's Commission to his First Governor, I have already answered. It is not probable that any such Innovation as he contends for was intended; it is plain, from this Practice immediately ensuing, that no such Intention was [101] understood, and it is certain that such an Innovation would have been violent and illegal.

Our Author, however, is not quite of this Opinion. "Our Constitution, says he, is derivative, and entirely flows from the Crown, is wholly *ex gratia*, and therefore subject to such Modifications upon constitutional Principles, as his Majesty shall from time to time, in his royal Wisdom, see proper and expedient; provided also, that they are not repugnant to any subsisting Laws."‡ A very courtly and convenient Doctrine truly. One would imagine we had got back somewhat more than a Century, into the Days of omnipotent Prerogative. But this Writer has an admirable Knack of contradicting himself. Here he has placed the Inhabitants of *South Carolina* at the Mercy of the Crown, deriving every Thing from its Grace and holding it at Pleasure; yet, in a few Pages, he tells us, the "Colonies are Parts and Parcels of the *British* Empire, and settled by *British* Subjects."‖ Have then *British* Subjects no Rights, but such as flow from and depend upon the Will of the Crown? Is not a *British* King the Creature of the Constitution, and the Subject of the Law? Old *Bracton* tells us, the Law is his [102] Superi-

‡ P. 37.
‖ P. 54.

184

or.§ [67] He is bound, says *Fortescue*, to rule according to Law.* [68] From whence then did he derive this mighty Power of making, modelling, and controuling the Constitution? In Truth, our Author has no Objection to the People's comforting themselves with the empty Name of *British* Subjects, provided they do not presume to claim any of the Privileges essential to that Character.

"I never," says he, "was able to comprehend, how the Commons House of Assembly presumed to liken themselves to the House of Commons of *Great Britain*, and then drop all Sight of that Model from which the other Branches of our subordinate Legislature are manifestly taken."‡

I am glad it is in my Power to assist this "worthy Writer's Comprehension." The Commons of *Carolina* liken themselves to the Commons of *Great Britain*, because they stand in the very same Relation to the People; and the Similitude cannot be extended any farther, because the Council are totally different from the House of Lords. The one is independent, the other dependent; the one permanent, the other precarious; the [*103*] one hereditary, the other at Will. Since then the Council confessedly owes its Institution to the Crown, the People are surely not to blame for its being so utterly dissimilar to that Model on which it was pretendedly framed.

There never was penned a greater Rhapsody of Nonsense and Servility than is contained in the following Paragraph—"The Rights and Privileges of the Commons House are neither created nor recognized by any Statute of *Great Britain*; they arise, as it were, by Grant from the Crown; their Legislature owes its Establishment to the King, and every Claim they set up springs to them from the same Medium through which the Council derive theirs. This being the true State of a plain Fact (*O Impudentiam!*) [69] it follows as a Consequence, that when the Crown gave Permission to call an Assembly, they surely might appoint a Council, and lawfully invest them with the Powers expressed in his Majesty's Commission and Instructions."*

---

§ L. 2. c. 16.
* C. 9.
‡ P. 37, etc.
* P. 37.

The Rights and Privileges of the Commons House spring from the Rights and Privileges of *British* Subjects, and are coeval with the Constitution. They were neither created, nor can they [*104*] be abolished by the Crown. The Charter recognized, but could not create them. The Right of being represented in that Legislature, by whose Acts they are bound, is the unalienable Birthright of *English* Subjects. This Claim is prior and paramount to any royal Grant. The Charter was only a Recognition that emigrating could not work any Forfeiture of the undoubted Rights of the Subject; Rights which are equal, not inferior, to those of the Crown. And shall this antient, undoubted, unalienable Claim, this glorious, this inestimable Birthright, be compared with the Existence of a Council; created and annihilated by the Fiat of the Crown, and removeable at the Pleasure of a Governor, even without assigning a Reason.* The gilded Motes that people the Sunbeams are scarce less permanent or less respectable. The Premises being as opposite to Truth as Light is to Darkness, what becomes of the Conclusion,† "that when the Crown gave Permission to call an Assembly, they surely might appoint a Council, and invest them lawfully with the Powers expressed in his Majesty's Commission and Instruction?" A modest and most logical Conclusion! Because the King has a Right, and of Necessity must vest the Powers of Government, *which he does possess*, in [*105*] his Instrument the Governor; therefore he surely has a Right to alter the Constitution, and invest a Council of his own Creation with Rights and Powers which he *does not possess*. The Powers granted by this Commission and Instruction are far greater than the House of Lords claim or exercise. Not only the Right of Legislation, but that of originating, and framing Money Bills. Yet this Writer talks of the Principles of the Constitution as the Guide of the Crown in these Usurpations, which he modestly stiles Modifications. Such is his Logic; but it would be a public Misfortune, if his Abilities were not as mean, as his Principles are *bad*, and his Purposes pernicious.

We are next presented with an Act of Assembly in 1721, which, because it recites that his Majesty had been pleased to commis-

---

* Witness a Suspension and Removal by Governor *Lyttleton*.[70]
† P. 38.

sionate, under the Great Seal of *Great Britain, Francis Nicholson,* Esquire, Governor, etc. over the Province, with full Powers to call a General Assembly—he stiles a Recognition, expressly shewing that the Powers to call a General Assembly originated with the King himself. One additional Word will render this Assertion perfectly true. It shews that the *Governor's Powers* to call a General Assembly originated with the King himself. Not an Iota more. The Rights of the [106] People to be convened in General Assembly it neither relates to nor mentions. The Power of every Governor most certainly is devolved upon him from the Crown, it originates with the King; but God forbid that the Rights of the People should be held by so precarious a Tenure, or originate with any Being but the King of Kings. The Prerogative of calling Assemblies is a Flower of the Crown, not for the Ornament of the Prince, but for the Use of the People. Prerogative, says Mr. *Locke,* is created for the Benefit of the People, and therefore cannot be exerted to their Prejudice.[71] Not to employ it to the Purposes for which it was given would be injurious and against Law, as that great Lawyer *Finch* will witness, when he declares, "That the King's Prerogative stretcheth not to the doing any Wrong."*[72] The Meeting of Freemen or their Delegates is of Right, not of Grace. When the Bill of Rights declares that for Redress of all Grievances, and for the amending, strengthening, and preserving of the Laws, Parliaments ought to be held frequently, it does not give a new Right, but recognizes an old one, coeval with the Constitution and essential to its Existence. From the Beginning of Record the Participation of *English* Subjects in the Legislature, by whose Acts they were bound, is [107] specifically proved. *The Mirror,* the most antient and authentic Book in Law, tells us, they were assembled Twice a Year under *Alfred.**[73] The Laws of *Edward* the Confessor privilege People coming to Parliament from Arrest.†[74] The following is a Record of Parliament held in the Reign of Canute—*Episcopis,* et *Religiosis, 7 Ducibus, 7 Comitibus,* nonnullis Abbatibus, quamplurimus, gregariis, militibus, ac cum *Populi multitudine copiosa*—

---

* [106] *Finch's* Law, P. 84.
* [107] C. 1.
† C. 3.

ac omnibus adhuc in eodem Parliamento, personaliter existentibus, votis Regis unanimiter consentientibus praeceptum et decretum fuit.‡[75] And shall Subjects, drawing their Rights from so high, so sacred a Source, be told, by a Wretch, whose Vices only have raised him to a Title, that they are *ex gratia*; flowing, like the Powers of the Council, from the Bounty of the Crown? Had the Words of the Act been really a Concession, still they ought to be construed as Words of Civility, not of Subjection, agreeably to the Exposition of the Words, "If it please him" (the King) in the Statute of *Glocester,* which were solemnly adjudged to be Words of Reverence only, not of Resignation.§[76]

[*108*] In the same Strain of Sophistry, he tells us, that the Term Privilege, in the 35th Instruction, "points directly to the Members of the Council, exercising legislative Duties."[77] The Words of the Instruction will prove the Falshood and Fallacy of this Assertion. "It is also our further Pleasure, that the *Council* have the like Power of framing Money Bills as the *Assembly*; and you are expressly enjoined not to allow the *said Assembly,* or any of the Members thereof, any Power or Privilege whatsoever, which is not allowed by us to the *House of Commons.*"[78] Here we see a Discrimination is expressly made between the Council and Assembly, and Privilege is applied to the latter, which is rendered still more explicit by referring to the House of Commons. How poor must this Man's Cause be, when he builds an Argument on Premises, which of itself refutes the Conclusion he draws! Nothing can be more manifest than that neither the Instruction, nor the Act referring to it, has the least Relation to the Council in Point of Privilege, which, as clearly as Words can express, is confined to Members of Assembly alone. As to that Part of the Instruction which does really relate to the Council, and gives them the Power of framing Money Bills, I presume, that even he will not contend that it is legal or of the least Validity. For, after laying it down as an [*109*] "undeniable Position that the King can give no Constitution to the *American* Colonies, but One resembling that of *England,*"[79] it will not be quite consistent in him to suppose or maintain that the King can,

---

‡ Præf. to 9 Co.
§ Hawk. 381.

by his sole Authority, give that Power to his Council in *Carolina* which is not permitted to the House of Peers in *England*.

He very confidently asserts, however, that in consequence of this Instruction, it was the uniform Practice from 1721 to 1735 for the Council to frame, alter, and amend Money Bills, which he appeals to as an irrefragable Argument in Support of the Council's legislative Rights. He has not, however, been pleased to produce a single Instance of this uniform Practice,* and therefore I presume he has none; for he is not [*110*] sparing in Citations, unless they make against his Positions.† But, if in Contradiction to his usual Manner, he should have told a solitary Truth, what would it prove, but that a bad Practice had existed, which, as it ought, has been abolished. If this had been conceived to be a legal Right, why should it have been given up ever since the Year 1735? Surely so long a Disuse of a Practice so doubtful and so short, is the fullest Condemnation either of its Legality or of its Policy. It seems, then, that this irrefragable Argument for the legislative Rights of the Council is founded on nothing more than a dubious Practice, illegal in its Origin, brief in its Existence, and certain in its Abolition.

The few Instances in which Mention is made of Two Houses, Upper House, Legislative Powers, etc. which he has gleaned from obsolete and expired Acts, are ambiguous and inconclusive. In-

---

* It is observable that the Journals, during this Period, abound with Orders, by the Assembly alone, to the Treasurer, to pay Monies out of the Treasury. Governor *Johnson*,[80] the Second Governor under the King's Commission, by a Message to the Assembly, dated the 6th of *May* 1731, which he probably wrote in the Council Chamber, signifies the Expediency or Necessity of paying a Sum of Money for certain public Services, and concludes, without taking the least Notice of the Council, I shall give Orders for the Payment, if *you* approve of it.[81] This, surely, puts as strong a Negative on the Supposition that the Council interfered in framing Money Bills as the Case will admit. It cannot be imagined that the Governor would have offered the Council such an Affront as this Message must have been, had any such Idea been entertained as that they were a legislative Body, to interfere in the Disposal of Money.

† Among other *such* Proofs of this Writer's Modesty and Impartiality, we find *One* in his Recital (P. 39.) of the Eleventh Section of a Provincial Act of Assembly declaratory of the Privileges of the Assembly, in which he has carefully supressed these important Words, "*of Right had, might, could, or ought to have in the said Province.*"—Thus has he mutilated the Clause to suit his own Purpose, and offered it to his Readers as a genuine Quotation of the Law.

deed, they plainly relate to the House formed by the Governor and his Privy Council. But in no Event can doubtful and incautious Words give essential Rights, much less effect so [*111*] important a Work as that of constituting a Branch of the Legislature.

The fulsome Adulation on the *English* Constitution by a Wretch who wishes its Destruction, whose Principles are inimical to the Virtues which support it, is less tolerable than his open Execration. The foulest Breath of Slander, from an avowed Enemy, is Perfume, when compared with that of a treacherous Friend; the Praise of lying Lips and a deceitful Heart.

To review and to refute his Arguments is the same. On whatever Foot he endeavours to fix this legislative Council, it will not stand. Are the King's Commission and Instruction to support it? That cannot be, for they are clearly unconstitutional or irrelative. Will the Term Privilege used in those Instruments and recited in the Act of Assembly avail him? Alas, no! for it manifestly appertains to Members of Assembly in direct Distinction from the Council. Will he then find more Support in the contemporaneous Exposition of the Commission, *etc*? By no Means, for their sitting from the Beginning, with the Governor, is a Demonstration that they neither acted nor were regarded as a separate, distinct, independent Branch of the Legislature. But the framing Money Bills will perhaps [*112*] assist him. Not at all, for not to mention the Doubt whether he can produce a single Instance of it, the Practice, if it ever did exist, has been long since and utterly abolished. Nor will their having originated any Bills whatever relieve him, since he himself owns, that even of this the Examples are not frequent.*
In this Distress can we blame him for imploring the Aid of a few ambiguous, impotent Expressions, forced from the Obscurity of some obsolete Acts? These are Straws, the Catching at which is at once a Symptom of the Weakness and Desperation of the Cause.

The more you consider the Arguments used and the Proofs adduced, the more you are convinced, that they were never intended to act as a distinct Branch of the Legislature; that the Instances of their having done so are doubtful, desultory, and inconclusive; and, upon the Whole, that in the Exercise of their Powers as a Privy

---

* P. 46.

Council they pursued a Mode which so nearly resembled that of a Branch of the Legislature, as to deceive an incautious Observer into a Belief that they really were a separate House of Assembly. There is no Doubt too that under the Cover of their real Character, they have [*113*] sometimes, perhaps artfully, and with a Design of Usurpation, done those Acts which are competent only to legislative Authority. But such Instances, were they more frequent, would not warrant their Claim. The Usage which gives Validity to any Claim must be reasonable,*[82] certain,†[83] and consistent.‡[84] If it can be proved, as I trust this has been, to be unreasonable, dubious, and inconsistent, it cannot be maintained. It is always open to the Enquiry of Reason and the Test of Truth. *Consuetudo nunquam prejudicat veritati*§[85] is a sound Maxim of Law; and no Antiquity can sanctify it if bad.||[86] Upon bringing the Claim of the Council to this Trial, we have found that in fact it *is not*, and upon considering its Constitution we shall perceive that it *ought not* to be a Branch of the Legislature.

That the Council ought not to be a Branch of the Legislature is plain from this Writer's own Admissions. He admits, that the Crown must, in its Modification of the Constitution, be directed by *constitutional Principles.*§—The constitutional Principle he acknowledges to be, that every Branch should be a Check upon the others.* He agrees, that the Council, holding their Places at Will, are dependent on the Crown; † from [*114*] all which the Conclusion is inevitable—that the Council being dependent, cannot act as a Check upon the Crown, and therefore, upon constitutional Principles, ought not to be a Branch of the Legislature. Had this Writer quoted Judge *Blackstone* with any Degree of that Singleness of Heart, which he professes, he would not have deceived others and exposed himself. The express Opinion of that Author is, that the Dependence of any One Branch upon another, is destructive of the Constitution. "For if ever," says he, "it should happen that the Independence of any One of the Three Branches of the Legislature should be lost, or that it should become sub-

---

* Co Lit. 114. || 3 Bur. 1767.
† 1 Rol. 565. § P. 37.
‡ 9 Rep. 58. * P. 24.
§ 6 Rep. 6. † P. 58.

191

servient to the Views of either of the other Two, there would soon be an End of our Constitution."*[87] It is not in the Wit of Man to devise a Method of rendering the Council more completely subservient, than that of its depending for its Existence on the momentary Will and Pleasure of the Crown and of its Governor. Here then, the admitted Fact of Dependence must stand as an insuperable Objection to the vesting any legislative Authority in the Council. There is a Degree of Candour in this Writer, which must strike every one, when he says, "I lay very little Stress upon the Circum-[115]stance of a Governor having it in his Power to suspend; because this is in some Degree provided against in his Instructions; and arbitrary Removals so seldom occur, that they can scarce be supposed to influence the present Subject of Dispute."† It is certainly his Interest to lay as little Stress on this as possible, because it would of itself be fatal to the Pretensions of the Council on constitutional Grounds. I shall not dispute the Infrequency of arbitrary Suspension; but I will venture to affirm, that the Instances of virtuous Opposition to the Will of the Crown, or of the Governor, are precisely as rare; perhaps the Complaisance of the Council, has rendered the Exercise of that Power unnecessary. But it must be remembered that the Power is dangerous, not only which *is*, but which *may be* arbitrarily exercised. If the Boast, the Blessing of *English* Subjects be, that they are governed by Law and not by Will, to give the Will of the Crown such decisive Influence in the Legislature, what is it but to poison the very Fountain of public Security, and endanger every constitutional Blessing we enjoy? Would the Council themselves consider seriously of the fatal Consequences of the Power they contend for, they would relinquish [116] a Claim, which they cannot possess but at the Hazard of destroying the Constitution, and enslaving their Country.

This Author, conscious that his own Character is vulnerable in every Part—faithless and treacherous in the most sacred Trusts under the Crown; in every Respect a bad Member of the Community, very prudently stipulates to "avoid every personal Reflection, and neither to cast a Slur on a single Individual, nor to

---

* Comment. V. 11. P. 51.   † P. 58.

point at the Character, Principles, or Tenets of private Persons."*
But the Character of the Assembly, which ought to be yet more
sacred, he treats with all the indecent Licence of insolent Ridicule
and impudent Invective. Such a Man is a fit Instrument to pander
the lawless Power, which promises to shield the Vices of the Individual under the Privileges of the Body. He charges the contemptible State to which he himself has reduced the Council, to
the malevolent Practices of the Assembly.† Their Declaration—
that a Commitment for Contempt by the Council, in the Character
of an Upper House, is illegal, unconstitutional, and oppressive—he
calls, "a melancholy [*117*] Judgment, big with Danger and subversive of all civil Order; the Bands of our Society," says he, "are
now loosened, the Plan of his Majesty's Government totally disordered, and the Commons are the Vortex which swallows all the
Power."‡

Within a very few Pages we shall find him imputing the Contempt in which the Council are held to themselves, which he just
before so indecently charged upon the Assembly. Let his own
Words bear Witness for him—"And what still adds to the Defect
is, that as several of the Council are frequently and necessarily
absent on their own private Concerns, and it often happens that
others are either absent from the Province, or through Sickness
are unable to attend; the Council seldom consist of more than
Five Persons; and commonly only *Three** assemble to dispatch the
most *weighty Concerns*. This Circumstance lessens the real and
constitutional Dignity which this Body are intended to maintain;
and the *People cannot be taught to reverence or respect* an Institution, the Business whereof is [*118*] transacted, like a Court of
Quarter Sessions, by Three Justices of Peace; *thence it is*, that the
middle Branch is in a Manner overwhelmed by the Force of
Numbers in the Lower House, and that they *fall into Derision and
Contempt* for Want of Members in their own."* If the foolish Dis-

---

* P. 9.
† P. 60.
‡ P. 60.
* [*117*] The Author might with strict Truth have added—Three "downright
Placemen," Monopolists of Offices, and in every Respect dependant.
* [*118*] P. 72.

covery of this Truth were in any Manner meritorious, this Passage might atone for the Falshood of Half his Pamphlet. For it is at once a Recantation of what he had before advanced, and a demonstrative Proof that the Council, as they are now constituted, are utterly unfit to be trusted with such high and important Powers as those of Legislation.

"The Vitals of the civil State," says he, "have received a mortal Wound; but my Hands are not embrued in the cruel Murder."‡

Do you indeed, Sir, wash your Hands of this political Murder? You who were the prime Mover of all the Mischiefs, the Province laments—you who are the sole Author of that daring Attempt upon the Liberty of the Subject, in the Imprisonment of the Printer? The Illegallity of that Commitment [119] has already been irrefragably proved in Mr. *Lowndes*'s Argument; and since you "allow it to be so, if the Council are not a Branch of the Colony Legislature,"* as I have clearly shewn they are not, it must appear to be an arbitrary, unwarrantable Act of Violence and Usurpation. But this Writer affects to apprehend that the Council cannot exist without legislative Powers to protect them. He cannot see any Thing else to "oppose the Sons of Violence and Disorder from intruding into the Council Chamber, over-awing their Proceedings, obstructing the Members in their Deliberations, and committing every Act of Disrespect and Insolence."‡ Is he then ignorant that the Council of *Pennsylvania* are in the same Situation? Did he ever hear of such Consequences attending their Want of this important Privilege? Is there no Civil Power in *Charles Town* to protect any Body of Men legally assembled, from Violence, Intrusion, Insolence, and Riot? But to render this Declamation still more ridiculous and absurd, he has, himself, told us that his Majesty's Privy Council in *England* have no such Privileges.|| Is then the Governor's Privy Council of so much higher Dignity and Importance than [120] the immediate Council of the King, that the former must be vested with Privileges which are denied to the latter, and the one shielded from the Insolence and Disrespect to which the other is exposed?

The Council, he tells us, "are a Sort of Barrier to withstand the

---

‡ P. 61.
* P. 60.

‡ P. 61.
|| P. 41.

Encroachments of the Lower House."* And pray, Sir, who are the Barrier against the Encroachments of the Crown? Does our Constitution know of no Encroachments on the Part of the Crown? Have we heard of no arbitrary Instructions, no dangerous Usurpations? Is the Liberty of the Subject at this Moment unviolated by the unconstitutional Mandate of a Minister, that the Colour of an additional Instruction? O! but it is enough, that this Body was *intended* to maintain a Kind of Balance between the Crown and the People.|| And from whence are we to infer this Intention?— Why, from Dr. *Blackstone's* having said, in speaking of the independent Branches of the *British* Legislature, "that the Two Houses naturally drawing in Two Directions of opposite Interests, and the Prerogative in another still different from them both, they mutually keep each other from exceeding their proper Limits."‡

[*121*] Because an independent House of Lords operates as a Balance between the Prerogative and the People, therefore a dependent, or as he stiles it, an *impotent** Council, is to answer the same End. This is his Logic, this his constitutional Learning. If we may judge of the Intention from the Execution, nothing can be more manifest, than that the Council never was intended to be a Branch of Legislature, because, *from its very Constitution*, it is incapable of answering the Purposes of such a Power. For what Balance can they form between the Crown and the People? what Check, what Controul can they be upon the Prerogative? Would not a School-boy be whipt for proposing to make Two Scales even, by putting all the Weight into One?—did he ever hear of a Servant controlling his Master, a Dependant his Superior?

Is it in the Power of Words to furnish a stronger Argument against the Council's ever having been intended, or being permitted to exercise legislative Powers, than he himself has produced in the following Passage?|| "I think this Body, acting legislatively, ought to be independent, by holding that Station, during the Term of their natural Lives, and [*122*] determinable only on that Event, or on their entire Departure from the Province. But the same

---

* P. 67.
|| Ibid.
‡ Ibid.

* P. 70.
|| P. 69.

Person might, nevertheless, for proper Cause, be displaced from his Seat in Council; which Regulation would, in a great Measure, operate as a Check to an arbitrary Governor, who would be cautious how he raised a powerful Enemy, in the Upper House, by a rash Removal; at the same Time that the Power of Removal would keep the Member within proper Bounds. The like Tenure of his legislative Capacity would likewise sufficiently secure that *Independence* which is so necessary to this Station, and so agreeable to the Constitution of the Parent State." I say nothing of the Importance of every upstart Attorney, commencing Legislator for the Colonies. But if these Alterations be requisite to give the Council *that Independency which is so necessary* to their legislative Station, then they do not now possess that necessary Independence—if *his* Regulation be wanted to make them *operate as a Check to an arbitrary Governor*, then they do not now operate as a Check—it follows, therefore, as a clear and undeniable Conclusion from his own Premises, that the Council being neither independent, nor capable of acting as a Check, it could not, upon constitutional Principles, [*123*] have been intended to represent the House of Lords, and is incompetent and inadmissible to the Powers of Legislation. To complete the Business, he tells us, that, upon his Plan, the Council "*would* possess so much real Independency as to make them superior to Acts of Meanness, Servility, and Oppression,"* which is a plain Acknowledgment that they are not now superior to such Acts; and any Man may judge how utterly incompatible a Situation, subject to Acts of *Meanness, Servility,* and *Oppression* is with the high Trust and Dignity of a Branch of the Legislature.

When this Writer admits with *Milton*, that the true Criterion of civil Liberty is, that of Complaints being freely heard, deeply considered, and speedily reformed, he urges the strongest Condemnation of the Measures of Administration regarding the Colonies. Their Complaints have been received with Reluctance, considered with Ill-temper, and remain totally unredressed. Their Petitions against the Stamp Act were suppressed, their Petitions

---

* P. 70.

since have been received with Resentment, and answered with Asperity, Anger, and Reproach.

[*124*] Sir *Egerton Leigh*, President of the Council, at length comes forward in his own Person. Without the Touch of *Ithuriel's* heavenly tempered Spear, he has started up in his own Shape.* The Account of an Attempt to file a Bill against him, by *T. Powell*, the Printer, for Assault and false Imprisonment, is written so much in the Stile of a wounded Spirit, that there needs not the Use of the first Person to mark the Author. "He reminded their Honors the Judges of the 9th Article contained in the Act of Settlement of Force in that Colony—that the Freedom of Speech, and Debates, or *Proceedings in Parliament*, ought not to be impeached or questioned in any Court of Place out of Parliament."[88] And pray, Sir, did their Honors pay any Regard to this Admonition?—did they not perceive it was impertinently begging the Question? The very Question was, whether the Council were, or were not a House of Parliament. But your Advice was to prejudge that Question, to take it for granted they were a House of Parliament, and to that Assumption apply the Law, and judge their Proceedings not questionable in any Court or Place out of Parliament. This is Law and Logic, fit to be [*125*] recommended by the King's Attorney General to the supreme Judges of the Colony—Logic that would shame a School-boy, and Law that would disgrace a Justice's Clerk.

However, it seems to have had a very different Effect upon their Honors. For the Chief Justice "entered very copiously into the Subject, passed some applicable Strictures, and in express and distinct Terms declared the Council to be an Upper House of Assembly; in which his Brethren unanimously concurred."[89] Thus these reverend Judges, as he states it, seem to have determined upon the Question without hearing it, and began their Function exactly where they should have ended. I wish he had vouchsafed to have favoured us with the copious Argument and applicable Strictures of the Chief Justice, that we might judge, as we may do of Mr. *Lowndes's* Argument, how far they are consonant to Reason and Law. In the mean time, I will venture to affirm, that no Judge

---

* Paradise Lost, B. iv. L. 819.

living can maintain, upon constitutional Principles, that the Council, constituted as it now stands, is, or ought to be an Upper House of Assembly.

The President is determined to be even with the Printer in railing. The Printer had branded [126] the Proceeding of the President's Junto, "as the most violent Attempt that ever had been made in the Province upon the Liberty of the Subject;"[90] and he, to return the Compliment, exclaims against the Printer's Attempt, as one of the "boldest Attacks upon the Constitution that Faction and democratical Insolence could possibly devise."[91] To support his Charge, he appeals to the grossest Misrepresentation of the Fact. "His Majesty's honorable Council, says he, being the Upper House of Legislature of *South Carolina*, are first attacked by a Publication of their Proceedings without Leave of the House; and when the Printer was interrogated, he acknowledged the Fact, and refused to give any Satisfaction which the Honor even of a private Gentleman could allow them to accept;‡ and such as he offered, manifested the most daring Disrespect."[92] The Fact is—that a Printer published the Protest of One of the Members of the Council; that being called upon to answer for it, he declared that Member gave it to him to be printed, which the Member in his Place acknowledged to be true. That not [127] contented with this, the Council, not *being*, but *assuming* to be, an Upper House of Legislature, voted it a Breach of Privilege, and Contempt in the Printer; for which they arbitrarily committed him to Gaol. That this is true, and the Account in the Pamphlet before me utterly false, I appeal to the Warrant of Sir *Egerton Leigh*.

SOUTH CAROLINA
In the UPPER HOUSE *of* ASSEMBLY,
TUESDAY *the 31st Day of* August, 1773.

"Whereas *Thomas Powell* hath this Day, at the Bar of this House, acknowledged himself to be the Printer and Publisher of a

---

‡ The bare-faced Falshood of this Assertion appears by the Protest of *William Henry Drayton*, Esquire, One of the Council, which shall be presently introduced—Hence Administration may determine what Credit ought to be given to the Representation of such an Incendiary under the Mask of *"Truth, Modesty,* and *Friendship."*

News-Paper called *The South Carolina Gazette,* Number 1966, dated *Charles Town, Monday* the 30th Day of *August* 1773, in which Paper is printed Part of the Proceedings of this House on *Thursday* the 26th Day of *August* Instant, which this House hath this Day resolved to be a high Breach of Privilege, and a Contempt of this House, who hath thereupon ordered, That the said *Thomas Powell* should be *therefore* committed to the Common Gaol in *Charles Town,* during the Pleasure of this House.

[*128*] It is therefore hereby ordered, by the House, that you do receive the Body of the said *Thomas Powell,* herewith sent to you, into your Custody, and him safely in the Common Gaol to keep and detain during the Pleasure of this House.

And for so doing this shall be your Warrant.

> *By Order of the House,*
>   EGERTON LEIGH, *President.*

To *Roger Pinckney,* Esq;
Sheriff of *Charles Town*
District, his Deputy and
Deputies, and to the
Keeper of the Common
Gaol in *Charles Town.*[93]

The following Protest is another Proof upon Record of this Author's Veracity:

> A *Protest in the Upper House of Assembly, on Tuesday the 31st of* August, *against the Commitment of* T. Powell, *Printer, etc. upon a Charge of having printed Part of the Proceedings of that House.*

DISSENTIENT.

"*BECAUSE,* until this Day, there has not been any Order, Rule, or Resolution of this House against the Publication of what this [*129*] House may deem its Proceedings. And although in many Instances, Parts of the Proceedings of both Houses of Assembly have been printed, under the Article of News, without any Order from either House; yet hitherto the Printers have not in any Instance been called to Account for such Conduct.

"*Because,* As in the present Instance, the Printer has not made any Misrepresentation of what had been transacted in this House, *and has not even made any Remark;* so I humbly conceive he does not deserve any Punishment whatsoever. For I do not know of any Instance where a Printer has been punished by the House of Lords in *Great Britain*, for having *only published a Protest.*—The only Instance quoted in the Debate, and laid down as a Case in Point, being in my Opinion void of all Foundation. For *Bingley was not committed by the House of Lords, as was erroneously insisted upon, for having printed a Protest; but he was committed by the Court of King's Bench, for refusing to give Bail to answer Interrogatories upon Oath, upon a Charge of printing a Libel against the said Court.*[94]

"*Because,* As the Printer upon his Examination did declare to this House, *that when he printed the Proceedings in Question, he only did,* [130] *as Printers here had been always accustomed to do: That, in doing so, he did not mean any Contempt to this House. That he would not have done the Act which has given Displeasure, had he known it would have violated the Privileges of this House: And that, if such a Proceeding did violate its Privileges, he was very sorry for it, and was willing to ask Pardon of this Honorable House.* Therefore I am of Opinion, that in a free Country, such an Acknowledgment and Contrition, expressed by a Free Man, ought to have been deemed a sufficient Atonement for an Act, which he did not know *was penal,* until declared to be so *post Factum.*

"*Because,* I am of Opinion, that a Printer's publishing the Protests of any Members of this House, especially by their Desire, and without any Remarks whatsoever, *ought not* to be deemed a Violation of the Privileges of this House. For I do conceive a clear Distinction between a Publication of such Proceedings of the House, as are under the Idea of *Votes of the House,* and the Publication of *only the Protests* of some of the Members, and *the Causes of them.* —I apprehend, that *a Protest is a Witness,* the very Meaning of the Word, of the Propriety of the Conduct of the protesting Member; and as it is the public Justification [131] of his Conduct, so in common Justice to the Party, it cannot be too publicly made known. Therefore, as it is the very Nature of a Protest, that the Dissent and Reasons should be known, so they cannot be more generally made known, than by printing them in a Gazette. And as the very Protest in Question says it was made, *'lest we should be thought to have meditated, or even to have countenanced a Measure so fatal to the*

Freedom of our Country,' so unless the Protest was published, it is evident, the main and express Purpose of it could not be accomplished. Therefore, as the Protest was entered with Leave, and remained upon the Journals approved by this House, so, in my Opinion, an Implication must necessarily follow, that the Purpose of it ought by a natural Consequence, *and as a Matter of Course, to be published.* Thus, in my Opinion, there was a *clearly implied Leave from the House* for the Publication of the Protest and the Cause of it.

WILLIAM-HENRY DRAYTON."[95]

Whatever there was uncommon, heinous, or cruel in this Proceeding, was unquestionably on the Part of the Council, which never would have been capable of such an Act, but for the Counsels of One of the worst and most abandoned of [*132*] men. At the Beginning of his Pamphlet, we heard this Author cry out in Triumph, "I fly to the great Bulwark of our Liberties—the Press—and as it is the peculiar Privilege of a free-born Subject of *Great Britain* to consider the Legality, Justice, and Propriety of public Measures, no Man, with any Face of Reason, can blame my Conduct in this Respect."*—Where was this Bulwark of Liberty, where this Privilege of a free-born Subject, when a Printer was deprived of his Liberty in this arbitrary Manner? Is it the Baronet's Idea, that the Press is to be only a Vehicle for Falshood and Abuse against the Assembly and the People?—But when the Proceedings of the Council are in Question, then must the Seal of Silence under the Terror of Imprisonment be fixed upon it.

The Attack he has made upon the Bar, I shall leave the Gentlemen of it to repel, as they shall please, either in or out of the *Phalanx,* in which he has marshalled them.

The new Baronet informs us, he has read a *little* Law for his Amusement and Instruction. Very little, God knows, and to less Purpose. How far that little may have contributed to his Amusement, I will not venture to pronounce; but of this I am sure, that it has failed of instructing him. He [*133*] has learnt however, that

---

* P. 9.

ARTHUR LEE

one may commit high Contempt and Misprisions against the King's
Person and Government, by doing any Thing that has an immediate
and direct Tendency to weaken his Government, or to raise Jealousies between him and his People. Why has he not conformed
his Practice to this Precept? Why did he furnish or contribute to
furnish those Misrepresentations which produced an Instruction
that has weakened and disturbed his Majesty's Government. Why
has he by continual Contention, by inciting the Crown to Enmity
against the Province, and an Infringement of their constitutional
Rights, endeavoured to raise Jealousies between the King and his
good People?

To imbitter the Life of an Individual, to poison one Man's
Peace, or take his Life by Violence or Fraud, is highly flagitious.
But to subject the whole Community to the Bitterness of Bondage,
to poison the Fountain from which all our Blessings flow, to stab at
once, through our sacred Constitution, the common Life of all—is
the utmost Extremity of human Wickedness. It surpasses far the
Flagitiousness of him, who fired the *Ephesian* Dome; it realizes the
execrable Wish of that greatest of all the Monsters which *Roman*
Despotism nourished. Be this then our Author's Recommendation,
be this his [134] Fame—that he has exceeded the worst Character
of Antiquity in atrocious Wickedness.

I have thus pursued this Writer through all his Paths of Sophistry
and Deception. He has fenced with the Question through Four-
score desperate Pages. Evasions, hardy Assertions, and daring
Falshoods have emboldened him to put the real Merits at Defiance.
But, I trust, in vain. It has been my Endeavour to bring them fully
before the Public. I hope the Execution has not entirely disappointed the Intention. I hope it has appeared to every candid
Reader—That the Vote of Money to the Supporters of the Bill of
Rights was wise in its Policy, and constitutional in its Mode; calculated to conciliate a general Union in Opposition to a general
Attempt upon the Liberty of the Subject, and executed agreeably
to the undoubted Right and Practice of the Commons House of
Assembly—That the additional Instruction, impeaching this Vote,
and directing the future Mode of framing Money Bills, was unnecessary and unconstitutional, founded on wilful Misrepresentation, and arbitrarily executed to the Interruption of public Business
and the general Distress of the Province; unnecessary, because the

202

Act was irrevocable; unconstitutional, be-[*135*]cause the Right
of framing Money Bills is the absolute and incommunicable Privilege of the Representatives of the People—That the Council are not
a distinct Branch of the Legislature, because from their First Appointment, they sat with the Governor as his Privy Council, and
from thence only acquired the Appearance and Appellation of an
Upper House,—because the Crown, to whom they owe their Existence, *could not legally*, nor *has expressly*, constituted them a legislative Body; and finally, because, from their entire Dependence
upon the Crown and the Governor, they must operate directly the
Reverse of a constitutional Check upon the Prerogative; and, upon
constitutional Principles, cannot be trusted with that high Power
which they must inevitably abuse—that therefore their Commitment of the Printer for Contempt, as a Breach of the Legislature,
was a dangerous Usurpation, and utterly illegal.

These Positions are so clear and indubitable, that contrary Conclusions, with whatever Subtlety and Speciousness they may be
urged, must be fallacious. The Web may be wove with such
Cunning, that we cannot trace each Thread, and point out the
particular Defect, though the whole Piece is evidently bad. That
is not indeed the Case in the "Considerations;" for [*136*] not only
are the Conclusions manifestly false, but the Errors which lead to
them palpable and gross.

The Commons House of Assembly may say in this Question, as
wise Men have said before them,* that no People ever trusted
more in the Goodness of their King, so far as regarded themselves
only; but that the true Liberty of the Subject consists not so much
in the *gracious Behaviour*, as in the *limited Power* of the Sovereign,
and that seeing there has been a *public Violation* of the Laws by
his *Ministers*, nothing can satisfy them but a *public Amends*.

[*137*]   POSTSCRIPT

Since the preceding Sheets were sent to the Press, it was discovered that the Protest said to be made by *W. H. Drayton*, Es-

---

* Sir *Thomas Wentworth* and Judge *Blackstone*.[96]

quire, is a Copy of one which he had entered the 31st *August* 1773 and which had remained on the Journals of the Council until the 2d *September*, when it was altered by the Council after it had been printed and published in the *South Carolina Gazette*.—This Fact appears in Mr. *Drayton's* subsequent Protest against a Resolution of Council, that the former was, *"false, scandalous, and malicious,"* in which he avers, that except a few very trifling Errors of the Press, "All the other Parts of the Protest published in the said Paper, were *literally* as were expressed upon the Journals the 31st *August*, and remained so till the 2d Day of *September, when* they were altered after Eleven o'Clock, before which Time the Protest was published."[97]

Amidst this jarring between the Members of the Council, it is not difficult to form a Judgment on which Side the Truth lies—for we do not find, even in the amended Protest as it now stands upon the Council Book, any Thing like "the most daring Disrespect" in the Conduct of the [*138*] Printer; but on the contrary that he declared, "when he printed the Proceedings in Question he only did as other Printers had *always* been accustomed to do; that in doing so, he did not mean any Harm to the Council." And from the Printer's own Account, which is supported by Mr. *Drayton's* Protest both in its original and mutilated State, we have the following Evidence—"that when he was informed by the Council that his Publication was adjudged a high Breach of Privilege and a Contempt, and that *therefore* he must ask Pardon, he answered, that he had no Intention by the Publication to offend the Honourable Board, that had he known it to be a Breach of Privilege he certainly should not have done it, that if he had erred it was owing to his Inexperience, and that he was very sorry for it.—He was then ordered into the Custody of the Serjeant at Arms (an Officer created by the Council) and being brought in again, he was told that he must ask Pardon without any *Ands* or *Ifs*, otherwise he should be committed to Gaol.—To which he replied, that as he did not know he had committed any Fault, it was hard to confess himself guilty and be obliged to beg Pardon, but if he could be convinced that he had been guilty of a Breach of Privilege he should be very willing to ask Pardon."[98]—[*139*] This is a true State of the Case, which stands uncontradicted, except by a violent Resolution of a

Board of Council consisting of Three or Four Members in general
Terms, in which it does not appear that even that small Number
were unanimous.

The Reader will judge whether the innocent Printer's Answers
"manifested the most daring Disrespect," and whether it is necessary to enlarge the Powers of the Council, who now flatter themselves with the Hope of Protection from the Ministry against a just
Complaint for this violent Attack upon the Freedom of the Press
and the Liberty of the Subject.—Possibly they may expect not only
Protection, but *"Approbation for this fresh Mark of their Zeal
and Duty."

The Council of *South Carolina* have often and especially of late
been so far misled, as to assume to themselves the Dignity and
Powers of the House of Lords; but in the present Case, they have
exercised a Degree of Tyranny in Vindication of their "ideal"
Privileges, for which it seems they could find no Precedent|| in
the Trans-[*140*]actions of the Peers, and manifested the Truth of
Mr. *Drayton's* Charge in his Second Protest, that their Proceedings
were "arbitrary and unjust."

---

* Consid. P. 15.

|| "The only Instance quoted in Debate and laid down as a Case in Point,
being in my Opinion void of all Foundation, for *Bingley* was not committed
by the House of Lords for having printed a Protest, etc."—*Drayton's* Protest.

FINIS.

NOTES

1. *Ars Poetica*, 282–83. A free translation is: when liberty is carried to excess, it must be restrained by law.
2. Furthest limit.
3. The argument was made by the South Carolina Commons in trying to force the opening of the port of Charleston during the Stamp Act crisis. See Commons Journals, XXXVII, pt. I, pp. 46, 47–48, 48–50. (January 22–24, 1766).
4. William Bull, Jr. (1710–1791), was lieutenant governor. Appointed to that post in 1759, he served as interim governor five times, in 1760–1761, 1764–1766, 1769–1771, and 1773–1775.
5. Egerton Leigh had brought the Stamp Act to South Carolina the previous June. Commons Journals, XXXVII, pt. I, pp. 47–48 (January 23, 1766).
6. Sir Edward Coke, *The Second Part of the Institutes of the Lawes of England* (London, 1642). All three references refer to the proclamation of statutes by sheriffs acting under the king's writ. The quotation, which is substantially correct, is from p. 526.
7. This order and resolution are quoted substantially correctly and may be found in Commons Journals, XXXVIII, 215 (December 8, 1769).
8. The mercantile firm of Messrs. Hankey and Partners, "Bankers in Fenchurch Street" in London, conveyed the gift. See Committee of Correspondence to Messrs. Hankey and Partners, December 9, 1769, in John Almon, ed., *The Correspondence of the Late John Wilkes with His Friends* . . . (5 vols.; London, 1805), V, 42–43.
9. Jacob Motte (1701–1770) was public treasurer from 1743 to 1770.
10. The Society of the Gentlemen Supporters of the Bill of Rights. For the most extensive recent discussion of the composition and goals of this group see Rudé, *Wilkes & Liberty*.
11. A liberal paraphrasing of the letter of the committee of correspondence not to the agent, as Leigh puts it in his footnote, but to Robert Morris, secretary to the Bill of Rights Society, December 9, 1769. This letter is published in "Correspondence of Charles Garth," *South Carolina Historical and Genealogical Magazine*, XXXI (April, 1930), 132–33.
12. Robert Morris.
13. The Tax Bill was sent to the Council on March 30, 1770. See Commons Journals, XXXVIII, 366 (March 30, 1770).
14. The Council's message paraphrased here by Leigh may be found in the *South Carolina Gazette*, April 12, 1770. It was expunged from the Commons Journals on April 7, 1770. See Commons Journals, XXXVIII, 382.

15. These proceedings may be followed in Commons Journals, XXXVIII, 387–92 (April 7–10, 1770).
16. The General Assembly was prorogued on April 11. See *ibid.*, 392–93.
17. The General Assembly met on August 14, 1770, and Bull communicated the instruction to the Commons on August 16. See *ibid.*, 397, 402–405 (August 14, 16, 1770).
18. The instruction, quoted by Leigh substantially correctly, may be found in *ibid.*, 403–405, and in Labaree (ed.), *Royal Instructions*, I, 208–209.
19. These proceedings may be followed in Commons Journals, XXXVIII, 410, 412–14, 418, 420, 422–23, 430, 434–41, 443–46, 449–50, 453 (August 21–23, 29–31, September 4, 6–7, 1770). Bull's letters to Hillsborough on August 23 and September 8, 1770, describing this session are in Transcripts of Records Relating to South Carolina, XXXII, 316–30.
20. Bull prorogued the General Assembly on September 8, 1770. See Commons Journals, XXXVIII, 456.
21. The quotation is correct and was in Hillsborough's letter to Bull, December 11, 1771; it may be found in Transcripts of Records Relating to South Carolina, XXXII, 432–33.
22. The two treasurers appointed by ordinance of the General Assembly in 1770 upon the death of the old treasurer, Jacob Motte, were Benjamin Dart (1729–1782), a prominent member of the Commons House, and Henry Perronneau (d. 1786), the candidate of Lieutenant Governor Bull and the Council.
23. These proceedings may be followed in Commons Journals, XXXVIII, 577–84 (November 4–5, 1771).
24. Lord Charles Greville Montagu (1741–1784) was governor of South Carolina from 1766 to 1773. He had been in England during the early stages of the Wilkes Fund Controversy and did not return until September, 1771.
25. Montagu's speech, quoted by Leigh substantially correctly, is reprinted in the *South Carolina Gazette*, April 9, 1772.
26. The agent was Charles Garth (c. 1734–1784), M.P. for Devizes, 1765–1780.
27. The instructions from the South Carolina committee of correspondence and the petition from Garth to the Crown here referred to were dated April 10, 1772, and [June 2, 1772], respectively, and may be found in "Correspondence of Charles Garth," *South Carolina Historical and Genealogical Magazine*, XXXIII (April, 1932), 136–38 (July, 1932), 238–44.
28. The letter, quoted substantially correctly by Leigh, was dated June 13, 1773, and may be found in Transcripts of Records Relating to South Carolina, XXXIII, 270–71.
29. Sacred Trust.
30. Leigh refers to section 1 of "An Act for Appointing a Publick

Treasurer, and other Publick Officers," September 20, 1721. This act is published in Cooper and McCord (eds.), *Statutes*, III, 148–49.

31. Leigh here refers to section 36 of "An Act for . . . Granting to His Majesty Certain Taxes and Impositions . . . ," June 14, 1751. It is published in *ibid.*, III, 739–51.

32. This instruction, quoted substantially correctly by Leigh, is printed in Labaree (ed.), *Royal Instructions*, I, 203–204.

33. The quotation is correct and is from Sir William Blackstone, *Commentaries on the Laws of England* (4 vols.; Oxford, 1765–1769), I, 154–55.

34. The session began on August 9, 1773, and Bull's message to the Commons House was placed before it on August 11. See Commons Journals, XXXIX, pt. 2, pp. 30, 35–36.

35. The Council's address and Bull's answer are printed in *South Carolina Gazette*, August 16, 1773.

36. These proceedings may be traced in *ibid.*, August 16, 25, 1773, and in Commons Journals, XXXIX, pt. 2, pp. 48–49, 51–53 (August 18, 20, 1773). Bull's account of them may be found in his letter to Dartmouth, August 26, 1773, Transcripts of Records Relating to South Carolina, XXXIII, 292–300.

37. This word was printed "disapproved" in the original but was corrected in the Erratum on p. 83 of the original pamphlet.

38. The two councillors were John Drayton (d. 1779), planter and member of the Council, 1761–1775, and his son William Henry Drayton (1742–1779), member of the Council, 1771–1775. Their protest of August 26, 1773, is printed in *South Carolina Gazette*, August 30, 1773.

39. Thomas Powell, former librarian of the Charleston Library Society, was publisher of the *South-Carolina Gazette* in partnership with Peter Timothy and Edward Hughes in 1772 and then after Hughes's death in August with Timothy alone. He left Charleston immediately following this dispute. A brief sketch is in Hennig Cohen, *The South-Carolina Gazette 1732–1775* (Columbia, 1953), 248–49.

40. These proceedings may be followed in detail in *South Carolina Gazette*, September 2, 1770, published by Peter Timothy while Powell was in custody.

41. Roger Pinckney, former provost marshall, was sheriff of Charleston District.

42. Rawlins Lowndes (1721–1800), member of the Commons House for much of the period from his first election in 1749 until his death, was speaker from 1763 to 1765 and again from 1772 to 1775.

43. George Gabriel Powell (d. 1779) had been a member of assembly for much of the time since his first election in 1751.

44. One of the designated quorum of justices of the peace, a majority of whom were required to transact business.

45. The reference is to section 1 of "An Act to Impower . . . the Gov-

ernour . . . to Execute . . . the Habeas Corpus Act," December 12, 1712. It is published in Cooper and McCord (eds.), *Statutes*, II, 399–401.

46. The opinions of Lowndes and Powell are in *South Carolina Gazette*, September 15, 1773, Postscript. They were based upon the defense of Thomas Powell by Edward Rutledge (1749–1800), a young patriot lawyer, which was published in *ibid.*, September 13, 1773.

47. These proceedings may be followed in Commons Journals, XXXIX, pt. 2, pp. 77–96 (September 8–11, 13, 1773).

48. The Council's address, transmitted by Bull with his letter to Dartmouth of September 18, 1773, may be found in Transcripts of Records Relating to South Carolina, XXXIII, 311–16. Bull's letter is in *ibid.*, 303–310.

49. This was a standard clause in commissions to royal governors. See the commission of June 15, 1739, to one of Montagu's predecessors, James Glen, in Labaree (ed.), *Royal Instructions*, II, 819.

50. By grace.

51. Francis Nicholson (1655–1728), earlier governor or lieutenant governor of New York, Virginia, Maryland, and Nova Scotia, was the first royal governor of South Carolina, 1721–1725.

52. The act referred to is "An Act for a most joyful and just Recognition of the immediate, lawful and undoubted Succession of His Most Sacred Majesty King GEORGE, To the Crown of Great Britain, France, and Ireland, of the Province of South Carolina, and all His Majesty's Dominions, etc.," August 18, 1721, in Cooper and McCord (eds.), *Statutes*, III, 125. The quotation, which is an example of very liberal paraphrasing that does no violence to the meaning of the act, is from the preamble and section one.

53. The act referred to is "An Act to ascertain the manner and form of electing members to represent the inhabitants of this Province in the Commons House of Assembly . . . ," [September] 19, 1721, in Cooper and McCord (eds.), *Statutes*, III, 135–40. Section 11 is on p. 128, and the quotation is a liberal paraphrase.

54. From day to day.

55. The instruction, which Leigh quotes substantially correctly, is in Labaree (ed.), *Royal Instructions*, I, 112–13.

56. An account of this contest may be found in Greene, *Quest for Power*, 52–67.

57. Contemporary explanations have great weight in law. This phrase is used in some variant by Coke on each of the pages cited from *The Second part of the Institutes*.

58. The quotation is correct from Nicholas Trott (comp.), *The Laws of the Province of South Carolina* (Charleston, 1736), 405. Trott prints the title only; the full text of the act is in Cooper and McCord (eds.), *Statutes*, III, 186–88.

59. The act referred to is "An Act to empower the Honourable Thomas

Broughton . . . with the advice and consent of His Majesty's Honourable Council . . . to lay an Embargo . . . ," February 5, 1737, in Cooper and McCord (eds.), *Statutes*, III, 455–56. The quotation, which is accurate, is on p. 455.

60. The quotation is correct from Trott (comp.), *Laws of the Province of South Carolina*, 397. The law repealed by the Privy Council on June 27, 1723, was "An Act for the good Government of Charles-Town," June 23, 1721.

61. The act referred to is "An Act for ascertaining Publick Officer's Fees," May 29, 1736, in Cooper & McCord (eds.), *Statutes*, III, 414–23. The clauses quoted, correctly, are on p. 421.

62. The history of this law is discussed in Greene, *Quest for Power*, 157–58.

63. The passage referred to is in the Commons Journals, XXIX, 421 (May 11, 1754).

64. By the sense of the term.

65. The quotation is substantially correct from Blackstone, *Commentaries on the Laws of England*, I.

66. The statute cited is "An Act to Prevent the Planting of Tobacco in *England*, and for Regulating the Plantation Trade," 1670, in Thomas Ellyne Tomline, *et al.* (comps.), *The Statutes at Large* (20 vols.; London, 1811), V, 410–14. The quotation is a liberal paraphrase of paragraph ten on p. 412.

67. The act referred to is "An Act for the Encouragement of Trade," 1663, in *ibid.*, V, 194–201. Section five is on p. 195.

68. The act referred to is "An Act for prohibiting the Planting, Setting or Sowing of Tobacco in *England* and *Ireland*," 1664, in *ibid.*, V, 46–48. The reference is to the phrase in the preamble, "the Colonies and Plantations of this Kingdom in America."

69. *The Reports and Arguments of that Learned Judge Sir John Vaughan* (London, 1677). The page citation—350—is clearly wrong; the discussion on that page has to do with a suit between Edward Thomas and Thomas Sorrell over Sorrell's selling wine by retail without a license, and the point at issue was the King's power to dispense with corporations. Rather, Leigh was almost certainly referring to page 400, which is part of a long opinion (pp. 395–420) by Vaughan "Concerning Process out of the Courts at Westminster into Wales of late times and how anciently." The question considered on page 400 was whether any process could issue into Wales from the courts of England. Contrasting the previous state, when Wales was solely "the Empire of the *King of England*," with the present state, when, after its entire submission to England, Wales became "the Dominion of the *Kingdom of England*," Vaughan argued that processes could in the second state issue from English courts into Wales because "*Wales* [had come] . . . to be of the Dominion of the *Crown of England*, and was obliged of such

Laws as the *Parliament of England* would enact purposely to bind it." He went on to point out, however, that the English courts still had nothing directly to do with the administration of justice in Wales any more "than now they have with the *Western Islands, Barbadoes, St. Christophers, Mevis, New England,* which are the *Dominions of England,* and so is *Ireland,* the *Isles of Garnsey and Jersey* at present, all which may be bound by Laws, made respectively for them by an *English Parliament.*" The inference is, as Leigh indicated, that the laws of England follow Englishmen into dominions of the realm of England that lie outside the territorial realm.

70. *Ibid.,* 401–402. Here Vaughan, continuing the discussion referred to in the note above, cites Coke's declaration in Calvin's Case (7 Rep. 20) that "Writs of *non remedatia,*" which involve not the "particular Rights or Properties of the *Subjects,* but the *Government* and *Superintendency* of the King," could issue out of English courts "into *Dominions* belonging to *England,*" a relevant example being a writ to prevent people "withdrawing to avoid the Law into other of *his Dominions.*" Further to prove "the [English] *Law* to be so to other subordinate Dominions," Vaughan cited reversals of decisions by the Court of King's Bench in Ireland by the Court of King's Bench in England.

71. One extends to the other.

72. Here Leigh refers to the first clause of Article IX, "That he introduced an arbitrary government in his majesty's foreign plantations . . . ," which Leigh misquotes, significantly, in view of the above citations to Vaughan, omitting the word *foreign.* The articles of impeachment against Clarendon in 1667 are conveniently reprinted in W. C. Costin and J. Steven Watson (eds.), *The Law and Working of the Constitution: Documents 1660–1914* (2 vols.; London, 1952), I, 155–57.

73. By authority of the Crown.

74. This act may be found in Cooper and McCord (eds.), *Statutes,* II, 401–16. The several clauses referred to and paraphrased by Leigh are on pp. 401–402, 413–15.

75. The verse cited reads: "And Sampson took hold of the two middle pillars upon which the house stood, and on which it was borne up, of the one with his right hand, and of the other with his left."

76. The quotation is correct. The Bill of Rights is conveniently reprinted in Costin and Watson (eds.), *Law and Working of the Constitution,* I, 67–74. The article here cited is on p. 70.

77. This case, which involved Mr. Thomas Sheridan, an Irish Protestant in the service of James, Duke of York, occurred during the Exclusion Crisis of 1680–1681, It may be followed in *Journals of the House of Commons,* IX, 675–77, 681, 687, 702 (December 9–11, 13, 15–16, 23, 1680; January 7, 1681). Sir William Jones (1631–1682) was a whig lawyer and M.P.

78. The decision in the Case of the Aylesbury Men is reprinted in Costin and Watson (eds.), *Law and Working of Constitution*, I, 279–84. The proceedings relevant to Leigh's point occurred in the wake of the decision, however, and involved the refusal of the judges to honor the application for a writ of habeas corpus by the Aylesbury men, who had been committed to Newgate by the House of Commons, on the grounds that the Commons was exclusive judge of its own privileges. These proceedings are briefly described in Thomas Pitt Taswell-Langmead, *English Constitutional History* (10th ed.; Boston, 1946), 651.

79. Leigh's father, Peter Leigh (1712–1759), then high bailiff of the City of Westminster and later chief justice of South Carolina, 1753–1759, was intimately involved in this case. It was he who first brought the charges against Murray for obstructing him in holding the Westminster election that led to Murray's refusal to kneel before the speaker, his subsequent commitment, and the refusal of the judges of the Court of King's Bench to grant his suit for a writ of habeas corpus. This affair is briefly described in Taswell-Langmead, *English Constitutional History*, 656–57. It may be followed in *Journals of the House of Commons*, XXVI, 21, 27–28, 31–33, 36–37, 40, 42, 48, 62, 164, 166 (January 28, February 1, 4, 6, 8, 13–14, 18, 22, 25, April 2–3, 1751).

80. The quotation from Blackstone, *Commentaries on the Laws of England*, I, is correct.

81. The greatest power.

82. Public Law.

83. Private Law.

84. The quotation, which is correct, is from Dr. Ralph Cudworth, *A Treatise Concerning Eternal and Immutable Morality* (London, 1731), 270. Cudworth (1617–1688) was master of Christ's College Cambridge, and one of the Cambridge platonists. This work was published posthumously.

85. The quotation is a very free rendering of John Milton's *Paradise Lost*, Book IV, lines 305–311:

> Her unadorned golden tresses were
> Dishevell'd, but in wanton ringlets wav'd
> As the Vine curls her tendrils, which impli'd
> Subjection, but requir'd with gentle sway,
> And by her yielded, by him best receiv'd,
> Yielded with coy submission, modest pride,
> And sweet reluctant amorous delay.

86. The quotation, which is correct, is from the second paragraph of Milton's *Areopagitica: A Speech for the Liberty of Unlicensed Printing*, first published in 1644.

87. Edward Rutledge.
88. Thomas Knox Gordon was chief justice of South Carolina, 1771–1775.
89. These proceedings are described, in places in almost identical language, by Leigh in a letter to Lieutenant Governor Bull, September 18, 1773, Transcripts of Records Relating to South Carolina, XXXIII, 325–26.
90. These proceedings are described, again in almost identical language, by Leigh in a letter to Bull, October 16, 1773, and by Bull in a letter to Dartmouth, October 20, 1773, Transcripts of Records Relating to South Carolina, XXXIII, 327–33.
91. This comment, quoted accurately by Leigh, was made in the *South Carolina Gazette*, September 13, 1773.
92. The "Six eminent Gentlemen of the Bar" who were also members of the Commons were James Parsons (1724–1779), Charles Pinckney (1731–1782), John Rutledge, Jr. (1739–1800), Thomas Bee (c. 1730–1812), Charles Cotesworth Pinckney (1746–1825), and Thomas Heyward, Jr. (1746–1809).
93. The case cited, which is reported correctly by Leigh, is that of The King *against* Williams (1634–1700). The two reports cited by Leigh are 2 [Sir Bartholomew] Showers' King's Bench Reports, 471, and Sir John Tremaine, *Placita Coronae: of Pleas of the Crown in Matters Criminal and Civil* (London, 1723), 48–55.
94. The quotation, which is correct, is from Charles Yorke, *Some Considerations on the Law of Forfeiture, for High Treason* . . . (2d ed.; London, 1746), 126.

NOTES TO THE *Answer*

1. The question is from the *Annals*, Book I, ch. 81, 1. 10: A plausible profession this in words, but really unmeaning and delusive, and the greater the disguise of freedom which marked it, the more cruel the enslavement into which it was soon to plunge us. The last clause should read *tanto eruptura ad infensius servitium.*
2. By grace.
3. *Considerations*, 1.
4. *Considerations*, 75, as quoted from Dr. Ralph Cudworth, *A Treatise Concerning Eternal and Immutable Morality* (London, 1731), 270.
5. *Considerations*, 2–3.
6. The quotation, which is substantially correct, is from *Letter* XXXIX, May 28, 1770, *Letters of Junius* (London, 1772), 102.
7. Francis Bernard (1712–1779), governor of Massachusetts Bay.
8. This letter, quoted essentially correctly and written the day following Hillsborough's famous circular letter requiring American governors to dissolve any legislature that considered the Massachusetts

Circular Letter of February 11, 1768, may be found in John Almon (ed.), *A Collection of Interesting Papers* . . . *1764–1775* (London, 1777), 203–205.

9. Except for the omission of a parenthetical phrase that does not alter its meaning, the quotation is correct. It is from a letter from Bernard to Shelburne, January 30, 1768, and was printed in *Letters to the Ministry from Governor Bernard, General Gage, and Commodore Hood* . . . (Boston, 1769), 5. Lee probably was quoting from the London edition, published by J. Wilkie in 1769 or 1770.

10. William Petty, second Earl of Shelburne (1737–1805), was secretary of state for the Southern Department in charge of colonial affairs, 1766–1768.

11. The date of this letter, which is quoted substantially correctly, was October 25, 1766. It may be found in Transcripts of Records Relating to South Carolina, XXXI, 270–72. The section quoted is on p. 270.

12. A liberal paraphrase of Chatham's statement, in his speech against the Stamp Act in the House of Commons on January 14, 1766, that "I rejoice that America has resisted. Three millions of people, so dead to all the feelings of liberty, as voluntarily to submit to be slaves, would have been fit instruments to make slaves of the rest." The speech may be found in William Cobbett (ed.), *The Parliamentary History of England* (36 vols.; 1806–1820), XVI (1765–1771), 97–108. The statement paraphrased is on p. 104.

13. *Considerations,* 17–18. The quotation is essentially correct, though the italics were added by Lee.

14. This incident, which involved the disallowance of a paper money bill passed in South Carolina in 1769, is described in Greene, *Quest for Power,* 392–93. The agent, Charles Garth, described his unsuccessful attempt to prevent the disallowance in a letter to the Committee of Correspondence, November 24, 1770, "Correspondence of Charles Garth," *South Carolina Historical and Genealogical Magazine,* XXXIII (1932), 118–19.

15. The South Carolina Commons first complained of "the incompatibility of some of the Offices held by Mr. Leigh and Mr. [Thomas] Skottowe Members of His Majesty's Council" in a report on the state of the colony, June 24, 1766 (Commons Journals, XXXVII, 175–76). Garth's unsuccessful efforts to persuade colonial officials in London to deprive Leigh and Skottowe of all but one of their offices may be followed in his letters to the Committee of Correspondence, September 26, November 24, 1766, January 31, March 12, 1767, Garth Letter Book, pp. 2, 14, 19, 25, 28.

16. The quotation, which is accurate with the exception of the italics added by Lee, is from the preamble to "An Act for encouraging the making of Indico in the British Plantations in America," 1748. It may be found in Tomlins *et al.* (comps.), *Statutes at Large,* X, 419.

17. The quotation, which is actually only a paraphrase, is from Adam Anderson, *An Historical and Chronological Deduction of the Origin of Commerce, from the Earliest Accounts to the present Time . . .* (2 vols.; London, 1764), II, 384.
18. Anderson is here quoting from Joshua Gee, *The Trade and Navigation of Great-Britain Considered . . .* (London, 1729), Ch. 29, "The Danger of Depending on the Czar of Muscevy for Hemp and Flax . . . ."
19. The quotation is substantially correct from Anderson, *Historical and Chronological Deduction*, II, 238. The statute, liberally paraphrased by Anderson, may be found in Tomlins *et. al.* (comps.), *Statutes at Large*, VI, 492–95.
20. The quotation, which is a liberal paraphrase, is from Section V of "An Act for encouraging the Importation of Naval Stores . . . ," *ibid.*
21. The statute referred to is "An Act for the Encouragement of the *Greenland* and *Eastland* Trades, and for the better Securing the Plantation-Trade," 1672, in *ibid.*, V, 422–25. The exclusion referred to is made in Sections I and II, pp. 422–23.
22. Twenty-two such instances between May 13, 1752, and February 2, 1770, from the Commons Journals were listed by the committee of correspondence in its letter to Garth, September 6, 1770, "Correspondence of Charles Garth," *South Carolina Historical and Genealogical Magazine*, XXXI (July, 1930), 244–53.
23. This instruction, quoted substantially correctly, may be found in Labaree (ed.), *Royal Instructions*, I, 208–209.
24. *Considerations*, 11.
25. The report, which is here quoted essentially correctly, with italics added by Lee, may be found in Commons Journals, XXXVIII, 430–33 (August 29, 1770).
26. *Considerations*, 16.
27. Horace, *Ars Poetica*, 188: If scenes like these before my eyes be thrust/They shock belief and generate disgust.
28. Lord Peter was a character in Jonathan Swift's *Tale of a Tub* (1704). The allusion is to Section IV.
29. John Locke, *The Second Treatise of Government*, ix, 123, 131. In the most recent and best scholarly edition of the *Two Treatises on Government* (Cambridge, Eng., 1960), by Peter Laslett, the relevant sections are on pp. 395 and 398–99.
30. A liberal paraphrase of *Considerations*, 19.
31. At pleasure.
32. A liberal paraphrase of Locke's statement "The *Supream Power cannot take* from any Man any part of his *Property* without his own consent," *Second Treatise*, ix, 138 (p. 406 in the Laslett edition of *Two Treatises on Government*).
33. "An Act for . . . Granting to His Majesty Certain Taxes and Impositions . . . ," June 14, 1751, in Cooper and McCord (eds.), *Statutes,*

III, 739–51. Leigh's discussion of this act is on p. 23 of *Considerations.*

34. An error of either bad faith or ignorance.

35. The letter referred to is Hillsborough's famous circular letter of April 21, 1768, which was sent to governors of twelve colonies requiring them to prorogue or dissolve their assemblies if those bodies took any notice of the Massachusetts Circular Letter. Hillsborough's letter is conveniently reprinted in Jack P. Greene (ed.), *Colonies to Nation: 1763–1789* (New York, 1967), 143. The effect of the letter in Pennsylvania is described by Theodore Thayer, *Pennsylvania Politics and the Growth of Democracy 1740–1776* (Harrisburg, 1953), 143–44. John Penn was governor.

36. This instruction, which was first issued to a New York governor in 1753 rather than in 1764, may be found in Labaree (ed.), *Royal Instructions*, I, 325–27. The quotation is actually a very loose and condensed paraphrase.

37. Daniel Horsmanden (1694–1778) was appointed chief justice in 1763.

38. William Smith, Sr. (1697–1769) and Robert R. Livingston (1718–1775) were the associate justices.

39. This episode is described at length by Milton M. Klein, "Prelude to Revolution in New York: Jury Trials and Judicial Tenure," *William and Mary Quarterly*, 3d ser., XVII (October, 1960), 439–62. For a brilliant analysis of the judicial proceedings in the case that grew out of this affair—*Cunningham* v. *Forsey*—see Joseph H. Smith, *Appeals to the Privy Council from the American Plantations* (New York, 1950), 390–416. A contemporary history of the case, which includes the judicial decision is *The Report of an Action of Assault, Battery, and Wounding, Tried in the Supreme Court of Judicature for the Province of New York, in the Term of October 1764, between Thomas Forsey, Plaintiff, and Waddell Cunningham, Defendant* (New York, 1764). The point, made by Judge Horsmanden, that an instruction could not alter the ancient laws of the land, may be found in this *Report*, 9–10.

40. Lee here refers to the hearing before the Privy Council on February 28, 1770, upon a complaint by the Massachusetts House of Representatives against Governor Francis Bernard. On March 14 the Privy Council formally dismissed the charges as "groundless, vexatious and scandalous." These proceedings may be followed in W. L. Grant and James Munro (eds.), *Acts of the Privy Council of England, Colonial Series* (6 vols.; London, 1908–1912), V, 211–14.

41. Lee refers to an incident which followed a petition by William Henry, Earl of Rochford, on March 17, 1773, for a grant "of several islands, grounds and shoals in Delaware Bay." These pieces of land were claimed by Thomas Penn, proprietor of Pennsylvania. Although the Board of Trade reported that the lands had never been

granted by the King to anyone and might therefore be granted to Rochford, the Privy Council Committee on Plantation Affairs persuaded Rochford on April 22, 1773, to abandon his petition after it was discovered that much of the area was occupied and had been improved. This case may be followed in *ibid.*, V, 332–35.

42. A reference to the recent (January 29, 1774) attack by Attorney General Alexander Wedderburn (1735–1805) upon Benjamin Franklin before the Privy Council for his part in relaying the Hutchinson Letters to Massachusetts patriots. The affair is described in some detail by Carl Van Doren, *Benjamin Franklin* (New York, 1938), 469–73.

43. Sir Henry Moore (1713–1769), governor of New York, 1765–1769.

44. Cadwallader Colden (1688–1776), holder of several Crown offices in New York and lieutenant governor, 1761–1776.

45. John Murray, fourth Earl of Dunmore (1732–1809), governor of New York, 1770–1771, and then of Virginia, 1771–1776.

46. Granville Leveson-Gower, second Earl of Gower (1721–1803).

47. Hillsborough's order, dated July 16, 1770, may be found in Edmund B. O'Callaghan *et al.* (eds.), *Documents Relative to the Colonial History of the State of New York* (15 vols.; Albany, 1853–1887), VIII, 223.

48. This instruction may be found in Labaree (ed.), *Royal Instructions*, I, 281–82. In several variant forms it had been given to New York governors between 1687 and 1709.

49. This whole affair is treated from a pro-Colden point of view in Alice M. Keys, *Cadwallader Colden: A Representative Eighteenth Century Official* (New York, 1906), 348–53. The beginnings of the dispute may be seen in Colden to Hillsborough, November 10, 1770, December 6, 1770, and Dunmore to Hillsborough, December 5, 1770, in O'Callaghan *et al.* (eds.), *Documents Relative to the Colonial History of the State of New York*, VIII, 249–52, 256–58. The opinions of the judges are described in Colden to Earl of Dartmouth [April, 1774?], *Collections of the New-York Historical Society*, LVI (New York, 1923), 220–21, and Colden to Dr. William Samuel Johnson, May 8, 1771, *ibid.*, X (New York, 1878), 322–23. Other papers in this case may be found scattered through *ibid.*, 231–328.

50. This address is drawn from two separate messages of the Commons House to Lieutenant Governor Bull. The first paragraph is from a message of January 24, 1771 (Commons House Journals, XXXVIII, 465), and the second, which contains a few embellishments by Lee, from a message of February 9, 1771 (*ibid.*, 481–82).

51. So I wish, so I command.

52. Will stands for reason.

53. *Considerations*, 14–15.

54. A reference to the exchange between Hamlet and Polonius near the end of Scene II, Act III, *Hamlet*.

55. The speech, which is quoted substantially correctly, may be found in Commons Journals, XXXIX, pt. 1, 4–6 (October 10, 1772).

56. The report of the committee on grievances and the Commons' address to Montagu, both quoted essentially correctly, are in Commons Journals, XXXIX pt. 1, 20–24 (October 29, 1772).

57. This letter had in fact been published in Charleston, first in the *South Carolina Gazette*, August 23, 1770, and then in the *South Carolina Gazette and Country Journal*, August 28, 1770.

58. The quotation and citation are correct from Blackstone, *Commentaries, Book the Third*, "Of Private Wrongs."

59. This law is in Cooper and McCord (eds.), *Statutes*, II, 399–401. The English act is from 31 Car. II, ch. 2, in Tomlins *et al.*, *Statutes at Large*, V, 458–65.

60. Lowndes's opinion, which is here quoted substantially correctly, is in Commons Journals, XXXIX, pt. 1, 82–86 (September 8, 1773).

61. This charter, dated March 24, 1663, is printed in Mattie Erma Edwards Parker (ed.), *North Carolina Charters and Constitutions 1578–1698* (Raleigh, 1963), 76–89. The clauses cited, which are virtually verbatim quotes, are on pp. 78–79, 81.

62. This charter, dated June 30, 1665, is in *ibid.*, 91–104.

63. Contemporary explanations.

64. Have great weight in law.

65. William Henry Lyttelton (1724–1808) was governor of South Carolina, 1756–1760.

66. James Glen was governor of South Carolina, 1738–1756, though he did not come to the colony until 1743.

67. Henry Bracton, *Legibus et Consuetudinibus Angliae*, Book II, Chapter 16, Section 3. In discussing the question of whether private individuals ought to dispute royal charters, Bracton declares: "But the king has a superior, for instance, God. Likewise the Law, through which he has been made King" (in the English edition by Sir Travers Twiss, published in 6 volumes in London, 1878, I, 269).

68. Sir John Fortescue, *De Laudibus Legum Anglie*, Chapter 9, entitled "A King ruling politically is not able to change the laws of his kingdom." An excellent modern edition is by S. B. Chrimes (Cambridge, Eng., 1942). Written in 1468–1471, this work was first published in 1545–1546.

69. Oh! Shamelessness.

70. A reference to the suspension and removal of William Wragg by Lyttelton in 1756–1757. For an excellent brief discussion of the history and significance of this incident see M. Eugene Sirmans, "The South Carolina Royal Council, 1720–1762," *William and Mary Quarterly*, 3d ser., XVIII (July, 1961), 373–92, esp. 388–91.

71. Locke discusses the prerogative in these terms in the *Second Treatise*, xiii–xiv, 156–68 (in the Laslett edition of *Two Treatises on Government*, 417–27).

72. Sir Henry Finch, *Law: Or, A Discourse Thereof in foure Books* (London, 1636). The quotation, which is correct, is actually on p. 85. The proposition being discussed by Finch is whether the King "also . . . hath a prerogative in all things that are not injurious to the subject."

73. *The Book called the Mirrour of Justices*, a highly inventive work, perhaps by Andrew Horne (d. 1328), Chapter III: "Of the original Constitutions," paragraph 1 (in the modern edition by William Joseph Wheeler in the *Publications of the Selden Society*, VII [London, 1895], 8).

74. Chapter 3 of the almost certainly apocryphal "Leges Edovardi Regis," published, among other places, in William Lambarde, *Apxaionomia* (Canterbury, 1654), 138, does not refer to exemptions from arrest for members of Parliament. Lee obviously borrowed this citation directly from the section on "Privilege of Parliaments" in Sir Edward Coke, *The Fourth Part of the Institutes of the Lawes of England*. In the 5th edition (London, 1671), this section and the citation are on pp. 24–25.

75. By the bishops, by the monks, seven dukes, seven counts, several abbots, very many common soldiers, with a great multitude of people—as well as all sorts hitherto in the same Parliament, personally appearing, having unanimously consented to the prayers of the King, it was ordered and decreed. This passage is a drastically condensed version of a statement on the seventh unnumbered page of the preface to *La Neufme Part des Reports de Sr. Edw. Coke . . .* (London, 1615).

76. William Hawkins, *A Treatise of the Pleas of the Crown: Or, A System of the Principal Matters Relating to that Subject, digested under their Proper Heads* (1st ed.; London, 1716), 381. Hawkins's argument is that the King's power to pardon "if it pleases him" is not really discretionary. That phrase, according to Hawkins, was "spoken only out of Reverence to him, and not as intended to make the Right of the Subject to such a Pardon precarious."

77. *Considerations*, 41.

78. *Ibid.*, 40.

79. *Ibid.*, 54.

80. Robert Johnson (1676–1735) was governor of South Carolina under the proprietors, 1717–1719, and for the Crown, 1730–1735.

81. Commons Journals, May 6, 1731, [no volume number], 676.

82. The citation is to Section 170 of Sir Edward Coke, *The First Part of the Institutes of the Lawes of England: or, A Commentary upon Littleton . . .* (London, 1633), 114. The point under discussion is the force of custom in establishing security of tenure in burgage, and Coke argues that "no custome is to bee allowed, but such custome as hath bin used by title of prescription, that is to say, from time out of minde."

83. The citation is to the section on "Custome" in Henry Rolle, *Un Abridgement de Plusiers Cases et Resolutions del Common Ley . . .* (London, 1668), 565, where Rolle declares that "*Un Custome voit estre certein*" and that "*Tiel Custom serra void pur defalt de certaintie.*"

84. The case cited is William Aldred's Case from Coke's 9th Reports, 58, in which Aldred brought suit against Thomas Benton "for erecting a hogstye so near the house of the plaintiff that the air was corrupted." The point at issue was whether the defendant's use of his freehold was limited by the custom attached to the plaintiff's property, of good light, air, and a prospect over the defendant's property, and Sir Christopher Wray, the chief justice, with the rest of the Court of King's Bench concurring, argued that "When a man has a lawful easement or profit, by prescription from time whereof, &c. another custom, which is also from time whereof, &c. cannot take it away, for the one custom is as ancient as the other." The relationship between the two "customs" must in other words remain "consistent."

85. Custom at no time prejudices truth: a dictum laid down in Sir John Molyn's Case, Coke's 6th Reports, 6.

86. The citation is to the case of *Money et al.* v. *Leach*, which involved the validity of the use of general warrants in the Wilkes case. Dryden Leach, the printer, brought action in the Court of Common Pleas against John Money, James Watson, and Robert Blackmore, the King's messengers, for breaking and entering his house. During the hearings Justice Yates and Justice Aston gave it as their opinion that the warrants, though often used in the past, were illegal because "no degree of antiquity can give sanction to a usage bad in itself."

87. The quotation, though not exact, is generally accurate, but the citation should be to pp. 51–52 of Blackstone's *Commentaries*, II.

88. *Considerations*, 77.

89. *Ibid.*, 78.

90. *Ibid.*, 79–80.

91. *Ibid.*, 77.

92. *Ibid.*, 79.

93. This order is quoted correctly and may be found in *South Carolina Gazette*, September 2, 1773.

94. William Bingley (c. 1736–1799), bookseller and publisher in London, published issue no. 47 of *The North Briton* on May 10, 1768, for which he was committed by the Court of King's Bench to Newgate, where he remained for 72 days for refusing to answer questions upon oath; afterwards he was transferred to King's Bench Prison for debt. See H. R. Plomer, *A Dictionary of the Printers and Booksellers who were at Work in England . . . from 1726 to 1775* (Oxford, 1932), 25, 143–44.

95. Drayton's dissent is quoted substantially correctly and may be found in *South Carolina Gazette*, September 2, 1773.

96. A faithful rendering of the general sentiments in the letter of Thomas Wentworth, first Earl of Strafford (1593–1641) to Charles I, May 1, 1641, a few days prior to his execution. This letter was published as *The Earle of Straffords Letter to His Majestie . . . 4 May, 1641* ([London], 1641). The citation to Blackstone is, presumably, to *Commentaries*, I, Ch. 7: "Of the King's Prerogative," 230–70, esp. 237–38, where Blackstone discusses the right of the people to examine and punish wicked ministers guilty of "public oppression."

97. Drayton's "second" dissent is in *South Carolina Gazette*, September 13, 1773.

98. Powell's remarks and the Council's response are in *ibid.*

INDEX